Pikto·Louvre

Catherine Rager

Pikto-Louvre

The stories behind
the pictures

The author and publisher would like to thank Isabelle Jullien for her editorial assistance and Germaine Lucas and Charles Ehlinger for their technical advice for the French edition.
The editor is especially grateful to Susan Ashcroft and Lisa Davidson for their collaboration on the English edition.

Cover :
Rogier van der Weyden : *Annunciation* (detail)
Eugène Delacroix : *Liberty Guiding the People* (detail)
Louvre, Paris.
Photographs Réunion des musées nationaux

© 1991, Éditions Adam Biro,
28, rue de Sévigné, 75004 Paris

ISBN : 2-87660-119-2
Dépôt légal : août 1991
N° d'édition : 0121

Introduction

Over the centuries artists have drawn inspiration from the scriptures, Greco-Roman mythology, legends, tales, literature and history. The scenes represented by paintings and sculptures would have been familiar to the artist and his contemporaries, but their meaning is all too often lost on us. How many of today's museum visitors can recount with certainty the dramatic events which took place at the wedding of Thetis and Peleus, or explain why Laban was desperately searching for his idols in Jacob's baggage?

Although the subject is not the most important element in a painting, it is nevertheless vital: an understanding of the subject is an essential element in the appreciation of the work and inevitably increases our enjoyment. A lack of knowledge is frustrating and can even be misleading. It is regrettable to visit museum galleries, as we frequently do, resigned to not understanding the events which unfurl before our eyes.

The aim of this unique book is to tell the stories behind the paintings, thus refreshing fading memories. All the paintings in the Louvre that depict real or legendary scenes are classified in alphabetical order according to their French titles. Each painting is followed by an explanation of the figures, the setting and the action.

All the paintings that depict a story are included. Portraits, still lifes, genre paintings and landscapes, unless they merely serve as a backdrop for scenes with figures, have been omitted. Paintings of saints, heroes and gods have been included only if they form part of a story, but not if they are merely portraits. In theory, allegories are not covered by this book, but those which are famous or of particular interest have been described.

Titles of paintings, unlike those of books, are neither fixed nor unique. A single painting may have different titles according to whether you refer to the museum catalogue, an exhibition catalogue, a caption in an art book or simply oral tradition.

This difficulty had to be resolved for PIKTO-LOUVRE. **The titles given in French are those indicated on the frames of the paintings in the Louvre**, i.e., those most accessible to the museum visitor. Other French titles, which feature in the museum's general catalogue, appear in alphabetical order, but the reader is referred back to the main title. When paintings by several artists depict the same subject but have different titles, these titles are cross-referenced to the main explanation.

The English titles have been taken from *Paintings in the Louvre* by Gowing or from publications available in the Louvre. Other titles not included in these works have been translated for the English version of Pikto-Louvre. Where necessary, English variants have been included.

Example:

La Madeleine aux pieds du Christ by Pierre Subleyras is also known as **Le Repas chez Simon**. The explanation is given under the title **Madeleine aux pieds du Christ**. **Le Repas chez Simon** is listed under R and refers the reader to **Madeleine aux pieds du**

Christ. Dirck Barendsz' painting of the same subject entitled **Onction de Béthanie** is listed under O, but also refers back to **Madeleine aux pieds du Christ**.

This is designed to make the book simple to use. The reader may, however, be confronted with an unexpected title (e.g., if a painting traditionally housed in the museum is moved for an exhibition or referred to in an art book). For this reason an index of the names of figures and places depicted in the paintings is provided. If, for instance, instead of **Psyché et l'Amour** or **Histoire de Psyché**, which both refer back to **Amour et Psyché**, the visitor encounters a fourth title, **Psyché and Cupidon**[1], by looking up "Psyche", he will have no difficulty finding the various paintings portraying this figure.

1. In painting, the gods of antiquity are referred to by their Roman, not Greek, names. This tradition has been respected to simplify the book's reference system. The Greek equivalents of Roman gods are given in the glossary.

List of abbreviations

O.T. : Old Testament.
Hist. : History.
Imag. : Scenes imagined by the artist.
Leg. : Legend.
Lit. : Main literary sources.
Myth. : Classical mythology, mainly Greco-Roman.
N.T. : New Testament.
Christ. Trad. : Christian tradition, apocryphal texts (not included in the Hebrew or Protestant canons of the Old Testament), popular tradition, combination of history and legend.

The index includes a short explanation of figures which recur in several paintings or the writers who inspired the painters (with the corresponding page numbers if their names are included in painting titles).

Abraham et les trois anges *(Abraham and the Three Angels)*

Gérard de Lairesse
André Lèbre

(O.T.) Abraham, the eldest Hebrew patriarch, was resting at the entrance of his tent when he caught sight of three travelers. He hurried to bring water to wash their feet, gave them milk and curds, had a calf prepared and asked his wife, Sarah, to prepare cakes for them. The three men were in fact angels who had come to announce the birth of a child to the couple. Sarah, laughed when she heard the news as her husband was ninety, and she was eighty and barren. The angels asked her, "Is anything too wonderful for the Lord?" She later gave birth to a son, Isaac.

Abraham et Melchisédech *(Abraham and Melchizadek)*

Giovanni Castiglione

(O.T.) Melchizadek was king of Jerusalem 1,800 years before Christ and, although he appears to be a mythical figure, he was considered a Messiah by the Christians. Abraham returned victorious from a battle with four kings who had abducted his nephew Lot. Melchizadek welcomed him and blessed him, serving bread and wine. In return, Abraham gave him a tenth of the booty.

Abraham renvoyant Agar et Ismaël *(Abraham Banishing Hagar and Ishmael)*

Philip van Dyck

See **Agar dans le désert.**

Abraham s'apprête à sacrifier Isaac *(Abraham Preparing to Sacrifice Isaac)*

Antonio Burrini

See **Sacrifice d'Abraham.**

Abraham, Sarah et l'ange *(Abraham, Sarah and the Angel)*

Jan Provost

See **Abraham et les trois anges.**

Absalon percé d'une lance par Joab or Paysage avec Absalon percé d'une lance par Joab (Absalom Pierced by Joab's Lance)

Giovanni Battista Viola

(O.T.) Absalom was David's third son who rivaled his father for possession of Jerusalem. When he entered the city, David fled with all of his household. Absalom wanted to pursue his father, but ill-advised, did not and thus gave David time to regroup his army. Absalom was defeated and fled on a mule. As he passed under a tree, his hair caught in the branches. The mule continued and he was left suspended in midair. The pursuing soldier spared him as David had requested that his son should not be hurt. However, Joab, commander of the army, learned of Absalom's predicament and rushed to kill him. David grieved when he heard the news.

Accouchement et la mort de Rachel (L') (The Death of Rachel)

After Francesco Furini

ab
___
12

(O.T.) Rachel was the wife of Jacob. After many years without a child, she gave birth to a son, Joseph, while she was still living with her husband in her father's house (See **Jacob venant trouver les filles de Laban** and **Jacob reprochant à Laban de lui avoir donné pour femme Lia au lieu de Rachel**). Jacob took Rachel back to Canaan where she gave birth to her second son whom she named Benoni, "son of my sorrow," for she died after giving birth. Jacob called this son Benjamin, "son of the right hand," fortunate son.

Achille combattant (Achilles in Combat)

Augustin Franquelin

(Myth., Lit.) Achilles, son of the goddess Thetis and a mortal, was a demigod. Protected by Minerva, he was by far the greatest Greek warrior. He sulked in his tent after a quarrel with Agamemnon, king of Kings (see **Ulysse remettant Chryséis à son père**) and did not come out until his friend Patroclus was killed by Hector.

Then, clad with new armor forged by the god Vulcan, he proceeded to terrorize the Trojans. Homer described him in the *Iliad*: "Thus Achilles ran amuck with his spear, like a driving wind that whirls the flames this way and that when a conflagration rages in the gullies on a sun-baked mountainside and the high forest is consumed. He chased his victims with the fury of a fiend, and the earth was dark with blood."

Achille dépose le cadavre d'Hector aux pieds du corps de Patrocle *(Achilles Laying Hector's Body at Patroclus' Feet)* Joseph Benoît Suvée

(Myth., Lit.) By killing Hector, Achilles eliminated the main defender of Troy, but above all he avenged the death of his friend Patroclus, killed by Hector (see **Achille traînant le corps d'Hector devant les murs de Troie...**).

Achille jouant de la lyre avec Patrocle, sous sa tente, surpris par Ulysse et Nestor *(Achilles Playing His Lyre)* Giuseppe Cades

(Myth., Lit.) Following a dispute with Agamemnon (see **Ulysse remettant Chryséis à son père**), Achilles, hero of the *Iliad*, withdrew to his tent and refused to fight. The Trojans, who feared him more than any other warrior, took advantage of his absence and massacred many Greek soldiers. The Greeks held council and the wise old Nestor suggested they send ambassadors to Achilles to weaken his resolve. He chose several men, including Ulysses, and himself led the group. They found Achilles "singing of famous men and accompanying himself on a tuneful lyre" and his friend Patroclus listening to him in silence. The two men received the ambassadors courteously, but Achilles said he would not change his mind unless Hector, son of King Priam, and captain of the Trojan army, challenged him personally.

Achille traînant le corps d'Hector devant les murs de Troie sous les yeux de Priam et d'Hécube qui implorent le vainqueur *(Achilles Dragging the Body of Hector Around the Walls of Troy)*

Antoine François Callet

(Myth., Lit.) This is an episode from Homer's *Iliad*. While Achilles sulked in his tent, refusing to fight (see **Ulysse remettant Chryséis à son père**), the Trojan hero Hector killed his friend Patroclus. Achilles then killed Hector, but was not satisfied with this revenge. He tied the body by the feet to his chariot and then spurred on his horses, so that Hector's head dragged in the dust, while Hector's parents, Priam and Hecuba, looked on horrified from the ramparts. Achilles later gave in to Priam's pleading and returned Hector's body, which had been miraculously preserved by Apollo.

Acis et Galatée se dérobant aux regards de Polyphème *(Acis and Galatea)*

François Perrier

(Myth.) Galatea, daughter of the sea god, Nereus, was herself a goddess. She was courted by the monstrous Cyclops Polyphemus, who serenaded her with panpipes, but was herself in love with the handsome Acis, son of the god Pan. One day Polyphemus discovered them entwined on the seashore. Acis attempted to flee, but Polyphemus threw an enormous rock and crushed him. Galatea then changed Acis into a stream, an allusion to her own ancestors, the sea gods.

Actéon métamorphosé en cerf *(Acteon Changed into a Stag)*
See **Diane et Actéon**.

Francesco Albani

Adam et Ève *(Adam and Eve)*

Adriaen van der Werff
Joos van Cleve

(O.T.) According to Genesis, God created the heavens and the earth. He first created light, and then heaven, the land and the waters, vegetation, the sun and the moon, animals and lastly the first couple. On the seventh day, the Sabbath, he rested. In an older version, God created Adam from clay, planted a garden of delights, called the Garden of Eden or Paradise, and then formed the first woman, Eve, from his rib, as a companion for him.

Adam et Ève chassés du paradis terrestre *(Adam and Eve Expelled from Paradise)*

Giuseppe Cesari

(O.T.) Adam and Eve, the first man and woman, lived in the garden of Eden (see **Printemps** or **Paradis terrestre**). The devil, disguised as a snake, tempted Eve into picking the only forbidden fruit in the garden and offering it to Adam. This was the fruit of the tree of knowledge of good and evil. After eating the fruit, Adam and Eve lost their innocence and discovered their nakedness. Their attempts to hide

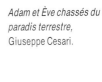

Adam et Ève chassés du paradis terrestre, Giuseppe Cesari.

ad

15

themselves attracted God's attention. He discovered their disobedience and had them chased from Paradise. (They are traditionally said to have been banished by archangel Michael). At the same time curses were placed on the first parents. Woman was condemned to suffer during childbirth and to be ruled over by man; man was condemned to toil the thorny land to find sustenance.

Adieux de Coriolan à sa femme *(Coriolanus Bids His Wife Farewell)*

attributed to Étienne Aubry

(Hist.) Coriolanus, a Roman general (5th century B.C.) who had conquered the Voluscians at the battle of Corioli (hence his name), angered the tribunes by proposing the abolition of their functions to the Senate. He was accused of having illegally distributed booty to the army and was banished from Rome. When he was led home by his grieving friends, he showed no sign of weakness at the sight of his wife and mother in tears. He urged them to be patient, entrusted the children to them and went into exile with the Voluscians, Rome's worst enemies. He then led the Voluscians in their siege of Rome (see **Volumnie et Véturie devant Coriolan**).

Adieux d'Hector et d'Andromaque *(The Farewells of Hector and Andromache)*

Antoine Coypel
Joseph-Marie Vien

(Myth., Lit.) This is an episode from Homer's *Iliad*. While the battle raged between the Greeks and the Trojans, Hector retreated for a moment's rest to search for his wife, Andromache. She had left the palace to observe the fighting from the top of the wall and he went to meet her there. He found her with a handmaid who was holding their son, Astyanax, in her arms. Strictly speaking, this was not a farewell scene as they met again. It was a moving and tender meeting during which Andromache voiced her fears. The dramatic tension was relieved for a moment as Hector bent to kiss his

son. Astyanax shrank back at the sight of his father's plumed helmet and his fear made his parents smile.

Adonis conduit près de Vénus par les Amours *(Adonis Being Led to Venus)*, also known as **L'Eau**
See **Mort d'Adonis**.

Francesco Albani

Adoration de l'Enfant (L') *(The Adoration of the Holy Child)*
(Christ. Trad.) Jesus has just been born in a stable in Bethlehem (see **Nativité**). His mother Mary and his foster father Joseph kneel before him, worshiping the Christ Child.

Francesco Francia
Josse Lieferinxe
Lorenzo Lotto

Adoration des bergers (L') *(The Adoration of the Shepherds)*
(N.T.) Just after Jesus was born in Bethlehem (see **Nativité**), the angels announced the birth of the Savior to shepherds who were watching their flocks in the neighboring fields, saying, "And this will be a sign for you: you will find a babe wrapped in swaddling cloths and lying in a manger." The shepherds left their flocks with the angels and went to find the Child. They came

Follower of Bassano
Abraham Bloemaert
Bourdon
Giovanni Castiglione
Scipone Compagno
Luca Giordano
Jean de Gourmont
Georges de La Tour
Charles Le Brun
Le Nain

bearing humble gifts: a lamb with its feet bound, foretelling the sacrifice of Jesus; a staff, symbol of the shepherd guiding his flock; and the pipes whose harmonious sounds attract the crowds.

Same subject: **Adoration des bergers avec donatrice**, Palma Vecchio. **Adoration des bergers avec Saint Benoît**, Girolamo Mazzola Bedoli. **Nativité avec adoration des bergers**, Charles de La Fosse. **Adoration des bergers entre Saint Jean évangéliste et Saint Longin**, Giulio Romano.

Jean Michelin
Cornelis van Poelenburgh
José de Ribera

Adoration des mages (L') *(The Adoration of the Magi)*

(N.T.) Just after Jesus was born in Bethlehem (see **Nativité**), the Three Wise Men of the East, Gaspar, Melchior (the old man) and Balthazar (the black king), saw a star which outshone all the others. The star began to move and led them to the cradle where they knelt before the newborn Child with their precious gifts: Gaspar brought frankincense, a symbol of divinity; Melchior gold, a sign of royalty; and Balthazar myrrh, a sweet-smelling resin used to embalm the dead and a symbol of the sacrifice. On their way, the Magi had made inquiries and when Herod the Great, king of the Jews, learned of their questions, he became suspicious (Who was this child whom they so revered?) and ordered the killing of all the newborn males in Judea (see **Massacre des Innocents**).

Cologne, 14th century
Italian, 16th century
Apt the Elder
Studio of Luca Signorelli
Simon Bening
Giannicola di Paolo
Jacob Jordaens
Charles de La Fosse
Pietro Lorenzetti
Bernardino Luini
Jean-Baptiste Mallet
Bernardo Parentino
Peter Paul Rubens
Pierre Subleyras
Jean Tassel
Victor Wolfvoet

Agar dans le désert *(Hagar in the Desert)*

(O.T.) Hagar was the Egyptian handmaid of Abraham's wife Sarah. As she was old and barren, Sarah suggested that Abraham beget a child with Hagar (a custom not uncommon at the time). Hagar conceived and taunted Sarah for her sterility. Sarah banished Hagar, who fled to the desert. On the advice of an angel, she returned to give birth to her son Ishmael. When Ishmael was thirteen, Isaac, the miraculous son of Sarah and Abraham, was born (see **Abraham**

Charles-Joseph Natoire

L'Adoration des mages, Studio of Luca Signorelli.

Abraham renvoyant Agar et Ismaël, Philip van Dyck.

et les trois anges). Sarah's hatred of Hagar increased and she asked Abraham to banish Hagar so that Isaac would be the sole heir. Abraham agreed and sent them away after supplying them with bread and water. He asked the Lord to assure him that no ill would befall them. When her supplies were exhausted and she had withdrawn to avoid witnessing her son's death, an angel called Hagar and showed her a nearby well. They were both saved and Ishmael later became the founder of a great people.

Same subject: **L'ange apparaissant à Agar dans le désert**, Pier Francesco Mola. **Abraham renvoyant Agar et Ismaël**, Philip van Dyck. **Agar et l'Ange**, Jean François Pierre Peyron.

Agar et l'Ange *(Hagar and the Angel)*　　Pierre Peyron
See **Agar dans le désert**.

Age d'argent (L') *(The Silver Age)*　　Lucas Cranach
(Myth.) The Silver Age, the second Age of Mankind, followed the magnificent Golden Age (see **Plaisirs de l'Age d'or**). Jupiter had usurped his father, Saturn, innocence and happiness were already diminishing, and suffering had begun. However, the appearance of Bronze Age men seriously endangered happiness on Earth. According to Hesiod, they emerged from the bark of the ash tree, whose wood served for their lances. They were extremely strong and conquered the men of the Silver Age, bringing with them the notions of property, inequality, injustice, plundering and war. In the following period, in which we are now said to be living, the Iron Age, Nature had become sparing with her gifts and vice and crime had invaded the world. The goddess of justice, Astraea fled to heaven in horror.

Agonie de Saint Augustin (L') *(The Agony of Saint Augustine)*　　Carle van Loo
(Christ. Trad.) This Doctor of the Church, who

left behind impressive works, including *The City of God*, died in 430 at the age of seventy-six. He was a bishop in Africa when the Vandals destroyed the country. According to tradition, he prayed for death so that he would be spared the sight of the destruction and his wish was granted. Saint Augustine is shown, just before dying, blessing a sick man. He had asked his disciples to transcribe on the wall opposite him the seven penitential psalms which he read repeatedly.

Alceste se dévouant à la mort pour sauver son époux Admète *(Alcestis Sacrificing Herself to Save Her Husband)*, also known as **Mort d'Alceste (La)** *(Death of Alcestis)* or **Héroïsme de l'amour conjugal (L')** *(Heroism of Marital Love)* — Pierre Peyron
(Myth., Lit.) Alcestis was a beautiful and virtuous princess. She was courted by King Admetus of Thessaly who, with Apollo's help, met challenges to win her hand. However, on their wedding day Admetus forgot to make a sacrifice to Diana, and the goddess filled the nuptial suite with snakes. This was a grave

Alceste se dévouant à la mort pour sauver son époux Admète, Pierre Peyron.

omen: Admetus was to die. Apollo promised to appeal to his sister Diana and obtained a concession from Fate. Admetus would not die on the appointed day if someone was willing to die in his place. Only Alcestis volunteered. Hercules, passing by the palace where she lay unconscious, was told the story and, touched by such love, sought Alcestis in Hades and brought her back to life, younger and more beautiful than ever.

Alexandre au tombeau d'Achille
(Alexander at Achilles' Tomb)

Thomas Blanchet

(Hist., Lit.) Before his expedition to Persia, Alexander the Great stopped in Ilium (Troy) and paid tribute to the heroes of the war. He went to Achilles' tomb and anointed one of its columns with oil. He and his companions ran naked around the tomb; he then laid a crown on it and addressed Achilles, congratulating him on having had a faithful friend (Patroclus) during his lifetime and a great chronicler of his exploits after his death (Homer).
Same subject: **Alexandre le Grand devant le tombeau d'Achille,** Hubert Robert.

Alexandre et Campaspe chez le peintre Apelle *(Alexander and Campaspe with the Painter Apelles)*

Giovanni Battista Tiepolo

(Hist., Lit.) Alexander the Great asked Apelles to paint his mistress, Campaspe, a courtesan reputed to be the most beautiful woman of her time. While painting her, Apelles fell in love with his model. Alexander relinquished her with his characteristic noble detachment.
Same subject: **Apelle peignant Campaspe**, Nicholas Vleughels.

Alexandre et le médecin Philippe
(Alexander and his Doctor Philip)

After Eustache Le Sueur

(Hist., Lit.) Alexander the Great fell ill during his campaign and was cared for by his doctor, Philip

of Acarnania. He received a letter accusing
Philip of being bribed by the enemy, Darius, king
of Persia. Darius had promised his daughter's
hand to Philip if he poisoned Alexander. When
Philip entered his room with a number of other
doctors, Alexander held out the letter of denunciation. At the same time, to demonstrate his
confidence, he took a drink from the cup Philip
brought. Plutarch describes this dramatic scene
and the expressions of the two men: Philip indignant on reading the letter and Alexander serene,
the incarnation of nobility.

Alexandre et Porus *(Alexander and*
Porus)

Charles Le Brun

(Hist., Lit.) Porus, was king of part of India. Despite his 30,000 men and 100 elephants, he was
defeated by Alexander in the battle of Hydaspes
(326) and taken prisoner. When Alexander
inquired how he wished to be treated, he replied,
" Treat me as a king ought. " Impressed by such
dignity, Alexander not only left Porus his
kingdom but also presented him with territories
he had conquered.

Alexandre et Timoclée or **Timoclée**
captive amenée devant Alexandre
(Alexander and Timoclea)

Domenichino

(Hist., Lit.) Thebes was conquered by Alexander
and sacked by his soldiers. The house of Timoclea, a noble and virtuous Theban woman, was
pillaged and razed. After raping her, the captain
asked if she had any gold or silver hidden. She
pretended that her treasure was hidden in a
well, and as the captain bent over the well, she
pushed him in and then threw stones to knock
him out. She was brought before Alexander in
chains. He was so impressed by her courage and
dignity that he had her released.

Alexandre le Grand devant le tom-
beau d'Achille *(Alexander the Great at*
the Tomb of Achilles)

Hubert Robert

See **Alexandre au tombeau d'Achille**.

Alexandre Sévère faisant distribuer du blé au peuple de Rome dans un temps de disette *(Alexander Severus Distributing Wheat)*

Noël Coypel

(Hist.) This painting is a tribute to the Roman emperor Alexander Severus (208-235) who reigned by virtue and not by luxury. He eliminated taxes and improved conditions for both the people and the soldiers.

Alliance de Jacob et de Laban *(The Alliance Between Jacob and Laban)*

Pietro da Cortona

See **Laban cherchant ses idoles**.

Aman irrité de ce que Mardochée ne se lève pas pour l'adorer *(Haman Angered by Mordecai's Refusal to Kneel Before Him)*

Jean Restout

(O.T.) Mordecai, Esther's cousin, was unknown until Esther was chosen as queen by King Ahasuerus (see **Toilette d'Esther**), but then obtained an official position in the court. He angered Haman, the chief minister, by refusing to kneel before him, since Jews kneel only before God. Haman's hatred of Mordecai led him to plot the massacre of the Jews. His plan backfired: Ahasuerus was indebted to Mordecai for saving his life and he also learned that his beloved wife, Esther, was herself Jewish (see **Evanouissement d'Esther**).

Amour dérobe la foudre à Jupiter (L') *(Amor Stealing Lightning from Jupiter)*

Eustache Le Sueur

(Myth., Imag.) Amor, a primitive and powerful god, evolved over the centuries into the chubby, jesting child known as Cupid. However, the former traits are still evident in this prank imagined by the painter. The mischievous child is not afraid of stealing Jupiter's supreme attribute — lightning.

Amour et Psyché *(Amor and Psyche, also known as Cupid and Psyche or Psyche Receiving the First Kiss of Love)*

François Gérard
François-Edouard Picot

(Myth.) Psyche was the youngest and most beautiful of three sisters. She was so beautiful that even Venus was jealous of her, but Psyche could not find a husband as men were afraid of her beauty. Troubled, her parents consulted an oracle who advised that she be abandoned on a rock where a monster would come to take her away. Cupid caught sight of her and was charmed. She was lifted off the rock by the wind Zephyrus and deposited in a valley. There she fell asleep and awoke to find herself in an enchanted palace where all her wishes miraculously came true. At night she was joined by a mysterious lover who forbade her to look at his face. If she did, she would lose him. She was happy, but missed her homeland and her family. Although her sisters were allowed to visit her, they were envious of her palace and treasures. They began to sow doubt: was this unknown lover the monster the oracle had spoken of? One night, Psyche lit a lamp and observed the sleeping Cupid. She marveled at his beauty, but a drop of oil fell on his face, waking him, and he fled. Venus devised expiatory tasks for Psyche. Later, unable to live without her, Cupid persuaded Jupiter to pardon Psyche and make her a goddess so that they might marry.

Same subject: **Histoire de Psyché**, Hendrick de Clerck. **Psyché et l'Amour**, French, 19th century.

Amour ordonne à Mercure d'annoncer son pouvoir à l'univers (L') *(Cupid Commands Mercury to Announce His Power to the Universe)*

Eustache Le Sueur

(Myth., Imag.) Mercury and Cupid are mythological figures, but the episode is sheer fantasy. Mercury was the messenger god who traveled rapidly in his winged sandals. He may have been Cupid's father.

Amour reçoit l'hommage de Diane, d'Apollon et de Mercure (L') *(Diana, Apollo and Mercury Paying Tribute to Cupid)*
Eustache Le Sueur

(Myth., Imag.) In this painting Cupid appears as the powerful figure described in archaic myths (more recent legends transformed him into a chubby, mischievous child) with Diana, Apollo and Mercury paying tribute to him. Although his relationship with Diana, virgin goddess, or with Apollo is not clear, Mercury is sometimes considered to have been his father (see **Naissance de l'Amour**).

Amour, réprimandé par sa mère, se réfugie dans les bras de Cérès (L') *(Cupid Seeking Refuge in the Arms of Ceres)*
Eustache Le Sueur

(Myth., Imag.) Here Cupid is depicted in the attitude of a sulking, mischievous child. His mother, Venus, scolds him while he seeks refuge in the arms of the goddess Ceres.

Amours de Pâris et d'Hélène (Les) *(The Love of Paris and Helen)*
Jacques-Louis David
See **Pâris et Hélène**.

Ananie imposant les mains à Saint Paul *(Ananias Healing Saint Paul)*
Jean Restout

(N.T.) Paul had just been converted (see **Conversion de Saint Paul**) and was still called Saul, the name associated with his severe persecution of the Christians. Jesus appeared to Ananias and told him where he could find Saul. Ananias hesitated because he had heard of Saul's deeds. Jesus replied, " Go, for he is a chosen instrument of mine to carry my name before the Gentiles and kings and the sons of Israel." So Ananias went to Saul and placed his hands over his eyes, thus restoring his sight, lost when he fell from his horse. He then baptized him Paul. This Ananias should not be confused with Ananias, husband of Sapphira (see **Mort de Saphire**).

Anaxagore et Périclès *(Anaxagoras and Pericles)*

Augustin-Louis Belle

(Hist., Lit.) Anaxagoras went to Athens to study philosophy, leaving behind his homeland and possessions (5th century B.C.). He became friend, tutor and adviser to Pericles. Busy with the government, Pericles appeared to have forgotten Anaxagoras. Reduced to poverty and feeling abandoned, Anaxagoras retired to his bed, covered himself with a cloak and prepared to die of hunger. When Pericles learned of this, he rushed to Anaxagoras'bedside, implored him and at the same time reproached him for wanting to die when he was most in need of his advice. Anaxagoras replied "Pericles, even a lamp has oil put into it by those who need it."

Andromaque et Pyrrhus *(Andromache and Pyrrhus)*

Pierre-Narcisse Guérin

(Myth., Lit.) Pyrrhus, Achilles'son, abducted Hector's wife Andromache after the sack of Troy. In Racine's play *Andromache* she was courted by Pyrrhus and initially refused, but relented in order to save her son Astyanax whom the Greeks wanted to murder. The other two figures in the painting are Hermione, daughter of Helen, who loved Pyrrhus (she had been engaged to him previously), and Orestes, who loved Hermione, but whose love was unrequited.

Andromaque et Pyrrhus,
Pierre-Narcisse Guérin.

Andromède *(Andromeda)*, also known as **Andromède attachée au rocher par les Néréides**
See **Persée délivrant Andromède**.

Théodore Chassériau

Ange annonce aux bergers la naissance du Christ (Un) *(An Angel Announces Christ's Birth to the Shepherds)*
See **Annonce aux bergers**.

Govaert Flinck

Ange apparaissant à Agar dans le désert (L') *(Hagar and the Angel)*
See **Agar dans le désert**.

Pier Francesco Mola

Ange apparaît à Joachim *(The Angel Appearing to Joachim)*
See **Rencontre d'Anne et de Joachim à la Porte Dorée**.

Master of the Life of the Virgin

Ange de l'Annonciation *(The Angel of the Annunciation)*
See **Annonciation**.

Simone dei Crocifissi

Ange et Tobie (L') *(Tobias and the Angel)*
See **Tobie et l'Ange**.

Alfred Moullion

Angélique *(Angelica)*
See **Roger délivrant Angélique**.

Jean Auguste Ingres

Angélique et Médor *(Angelica and Medoro)*
(Lit.) Angelica, heroine of Ariosto's *Orlando Furioso*, was rescued from a sea monster by Ruggerio (Roger) (see **Roger délivrant Angélique**). She was not interested in Ruggerio or any of her other suitors, including Orlando, and took

French, 16th century
Toussaint Dubreuil

refuge in a forest. One day in a clearing, she discovered the charming young Saracen Medoro, who was injured and tended his wounds. She fell in love with and eventually married him, so infuriating Orlando that he turned into a savage beast and pursued her. However, she had a magic ring, which made her invisible.

Anna Selbdritt
Alsace, 15th century
See **Sainte Anne trinitaire.**

Anne de Boleyn condamnée à mort
(Anne Boleyn Condemned to Death)
Pierre-Nolasque Bergeret
(Hist.) Anne Boleyn was the second wife of the King Henry VIII of England, who had six wives. He repudiated two of his wives and had two others, including Anne, executed. A fifth wife died during childbirth and the last, Catherine Parr, survived him.
Anne was raised in the French Court and was beautiful and charming. After meeting her, Henry thought only of divorcing his first wife, Catherine of Aragon. A combination of political and personal circumstances led him to break with the Pope who opposed the divorce and to establish the independent Church of England. He then married Anne, who was already expecting Elizabeth I, future queen of England. Three years later he fell desperately in love with one of Anne's maids of honor, Jane Seymour. In 1536 he called together a special court, which convicted Anne of adultery and condemned her to death. During the trial she was hysterical, but at the time of the execution she was extremely calm. Anne was thus admired for her nobility and courage.

Anne et Tobie *(Anne and Tobias)*
Gérard Dou
See **Lecture de la Bible** or **Anne et Tobie.**

Anne présentant à Éli son fils Samuel   Gerbrand van den Eeckhout
(Hannah Presenting Her Son Samuel to Eli)
(O.T.) Eli (not to be confused with the prophet Elijah) was a great Hebrew priest in the 11th century B.C. In the temple he caught sight of a woman murmuring as if she were drunk and called to her. She replied that she had come to pray because she was barren. He said, "Go in peace, and the God of Israel grant your petition which you have made to him." Shortly after, the woman, Hannah, gave birth to Samuel. She presented him to Eli and offered him as a servant in the temple.

Annonce à Sainte Anne (L') *(The Annunciation to Saint Anne)*   Wilhelm Ziegler
See **Rencontre d'Anne et de Joachim à la Porte Dorée.**

Annonce aux bergers (L') *(The Annunciation to the Shepherds)*   Govaert Flinck
Bernardino Luini
(N.T.) When Jesus was born, angels appeared to the shepherds who were watching their flocks that night in the surrounding fields. The angels announced the divine birth and said, "Glory be to God in the highest and on earth peace to all men with whom he is pleased" (see **Adoration des bergers**).
Same subject: **Annonce faite aux bergers,** Rhine, 15th century, Rome, 17th century. **Ange annonce aux bergers la naissance du Christ,** Govaert Flinck.

Annonciation (L') *(The Annunciation)*   Cologne, 14th century
Naples, 17th century
Giovanni Balducci
Studio of Bicci di Lorenzo
ascribed to Bon Boullongne
Carlo di Braccesco
Agostino Carracci
Jacopo del Casentino
(N.T.) The angel Gabriel appeared to Mary, who was betrothed to Joseph, announcing that she would give birth to a child who would be the Son of God. "How can this be?" asked Mary. "I have no husband." "The Holy Spirit will come upon you," replied the angel, "and the power of the Most High will overshadow you." Mary sub-

mitted saying, "I am here to serve the Lord. Let it be as you have said."

Same subject: **Salutation angélique,** Eustache Le Sueur, Rogier van der Weyden.

Lorenzo di Credi
Bernardo Daddi
Claude-Guy Hallé
Charles de La Fosse
Guido Reni
Sassoferrato
Andrea Solario
Giorgio Vasari
Bartholomaüs Zeitblom

L'Annonciation, attributed to Bon Boullongne.

Apelle peignant Campaspe *(Apelles Paints Campaspe)*
See **Alexandre et Campaspe.**

Nicolas Vleughels

Apollon amoureux de Daphné *(Apollo and Daphne)*
See **Apollon et Daphné.**

Nicolas Poussin

Apollon et Daphné *(Apollo and Daphne)*
(Myth.) Apollo pursued Daphne, daughter of a river god and one of Diana's favorite nymphs. The young girl fled, but as Apollo drew near she invoked her father Peneus who transformed her

Francesco Albani
Théodore Chassériau
Giovanni Battista Tiepolo

into a laurel tree. Apollo observed her transformation with dismay, but then adopted the laurel as his emblem and crowned heroes, artists and poets with its leaves.

Same subject: **Apollon amoureux de Daphné**, Nicolas Poussin.

Apollon et Daphné, Giovanni Battista Tiepolo.

Apollon et Marsyas *(Apollo and Marsyas)*

(Myth.) The satyr Marsyas picked up the flute that Minerva had thrown down in anger, after being mocked for her puffed cheeks. Once Marsyas had become an expert, he challenged Apollo and his lyre to a musical contest. The Muses were to chose the best musician and the loser would be at the mercy of the winner. Not surprisingly, Marsyas lost. Apollo tied him to a pine tree and flayed him. Then, stricken with remorse, he broke his lyre and transformed poor Marsyas into a river.

Same subject: **Supplice de Marsyas**, Filippo Lauri.

French, 17th century
Perugino

Apothéose des héros français morts pour la patrie pendant la guerre de la Liberté *(The Apotheosis of French Heroes)*, also known as **Ombres des héros français reçus par Ossian dans l'Elysée aérien (Les)**

Anne-Louis Girodet

(Imag.) This is an homage to the Napoleonic Wars. In the foreground we see Marshal Desaix, Kléber, Marceau, Hoche and others. Ossian was a legendary Scottish warrior, hero of conflicts between two clans: the brave Morvens and the cowardly and treacherous Loclins. This paradise is a sort of Valhalla where the Morven heroes greet the French, while beautiful maidens bring them flowers.

Apothéose d'Homère, also known as **Homère déifié** *(The Apotheosis of Homer)*

Jean Auguste Ingres

(Imag.) Homer, crowned by Victory, is shown on the steps of his temple, receiving the tribute of grateful famous men. At his feet are the *Iliad* and the *Odyssey*, depicted as his daughters. In the lower right corner are La Fontaine, Tasso, Mozart, Poussin and Corneille; in the left corner are Racine, Molière, Boileau, Longinus (Greek philosopher), Fénelon, Gluck and Camoëns (Portuguese poet). Behind them, from left to right, are the poet Horace, Pisistratus (the governor of Athens who had the first edition of Homer published), Lycurgus (Spartan legislator), Virgil in white who is introducing Dante, Raphael, Sappho, Alcibiades, the painter Apelles holding Raphael's hand, Euripides, Menander (Greek satirist), Demosthenes, Sophocles with his rolled manuscript, Aeschylus, Herodotus and Orpheus. On the other side of Homer is Pindar raising his lyre, followed by Hesiod, Plato, Phidias, Michelangelo, Aristotle and the Greek astronomer Aristarchus, Alexander the Great. Between the figure personifying the *Odyssey* and Pindar is the fabulist Aesop.

Apôtres découvrant le tombeau de la Vierge (Les) *(The Apostles at the Tomb of the Virgin)*

Giannicola di Paolo

(Christ. Trad.) It is not known whether the Virgin Mary remained in Jerusalem after the death of Jesus or whether she went to Ephesus with the apostle Saint John, to whom her son had entrusted her. The city of Ephesus claims her tomb and an ancient church, half hidden in the rocks, said to have been her sepulchre. Here, the apostles find the tomb empty because Mary has been borne to heaven by angels (see **Assomption**). Most texts say that her assumption was witnessed by the apostles.

Apparition de Jésus aux trois Marie *(Jesus Appearing to the Three Maries)*

Laurent de la Hyre

(Christ. Trad.) In the Gospels, Jesus did not appear to the three Maries after his resurrection. Matthew mentioned an angel who appeared to Mary Magdalene and to another Mary; according to Luke, the holy women saw two angels. According to Mark and John, Jesus appeared in person only to Mary Magdalene. The figures vary, but the message of the resurrection remains the same.

Apparition de l'Immaculée Conception à six personnages *(The Immaculate Conception)*

Bartolomé Esteban Murillo

See **Immaculée Conception**.

Apparition de la Vierge et de l'Enfant Jésus à Saint Hyacinthe *(The Virgin and Child Appearing to Saint Hyacinth)*

Ludovico Carracci

(Christ. Trad.) Saint Hyacinth was a Polish Dominican friar who completed his novitiate in Bologna, Italy, where his cult is celebrated. He was zealous in his worship of the Virgin (see **Saint Hyacinthe sauvant la statue de la Vierge...**) and was granted special favors. One day she appeared to him, holding Jesus in her arms and said, "Rejoice, my son Hyacinth, for your prayers have found favor with my Son and all that you ask him will be granted."

Apparition de la Vierge à Saint Jacques le Majeur *(The Virgin of the Pillar Appearing to Saint James the Greater)*
(Christ. Trad.) This scene took place on the banks of the Ebro in Spain where five of the disciples, one of them James the Greater, were resting in the cool evening air. Surrounded by angels, the Virgin appeared in a cloud atop a jade pillar, and commanded the disciples to build a church on the very spot where they are seated.

Nicolas Poussin

Apparition de la Vierge à Saint Simon Stock *(The Virgin Appearing to Saint Simon Stock)*
See **Vierge du Carmel apparaissant à Saint Simon Stock**.

Giovanni Battista Tiepolo

Apparition de la Vierge, accompagnée de Sainte Agnès et de Sainte Thècle, à Saint Martin *(The Virgin Appearing to Saint Martin)*
(Christ. Trad.) Saint Martin is France's most popular saint. His biographer Sulpice Severus describes him as being full of goodness and quiet resolution, qualities which enabled him to overcome dangers and, most often, to convert his enemies. One day when he was alone, his disciples were troubled to overhear him in animated conversation. He told them that the Virgin Mary and Saints Thecla and Agnes had visited him, and that this was not the first time. He advised them not to speak of the visitations.

Eustache Le Sueur

Apparition de l'ombre de Samuel à Saül chez la pythonisse d'Endor *(The Spirit of Samuel Called up before Saul by the Witch of Endor)*

Salvator Rosa

See **Ombre de Samuel apparaissant à Saül chez la pythonisse d'Endor.**

Apparition de Saint Gervais et de Saint Protais à Saint Ambroise
Philippe de Champaigne

(Saints Gervase and Protase Appearing to Saint Ambrose)

(Christ. Trad.) These two saints, twin brothers, were martyred under the reign of Nero, a Roman emperor in the 1st century (see **Saint Gervais et Saint Protais, amenés devant Astasius, refusent de sacrifier à Jupiter**). A Christian hid their bodies in a stone casket along with a written account of their lives and martyrdom. According to legend, toward the end of the 4th century, Saint Ambrose, a theologian and bishop of Milan, was praying in church when two strikingly handsome young men appeared to him. For three nights running, they visited him during his prayers. On the third night they revealed where the saints had been buried. Excavations began immediately and the miraculously preserved bodies of Saints Gervase and Protase were uncovered before the assembled bishops.

Apparitions de Saint Jerôme *(The Apparitions of Saint Jerome)*
Sano di Pietro

See **Mort et apparitions de Saint Jerôme.**

Archange Raphaël quittant la famille de Tobie (L') *(The Archangel Leaving the Family of Tobias)*
Rembrandt

(O.T.) Tobit, the aged, blind father of Tobias, sent his son to collect a debt of ten silver talents from one of his debtors. Tobias departed and was guided by a stranger who called himself Azarias. Tobias stayed briefly with a couple and married their daughter Sarah. Meanwhile, Azarias found the debtor and brought the ten talents to Tobias. Tobias returned home with his wife and, following Azarias'instructions, cured his father's blindness. When Tobit wished to reward his son's mysterious companion, Azarias refused and it was discovered that he was, in fact, the archangel Raphael. (Sarah, Tobias'wife, should not be confused with Sarah, wife of Abraham and mother of Isaac.)

Same subject: **Tobie et l'ange,** Salvatore Rosa.

Ariane abandonnée *(Ariadne Abandoned)*

Théodore Chassériau

(Myth.) Ariadne saved Theseus from the Minotaur by giving him a ball of thread which he used to find his way out of the Labyrinth of Knossos, Crete, guarded by the monster with the body of a man and head of a bull. When Theseus set off triumphant for Athens, Ariadne accompanied him out of love. But when they stopped at the island of Naxos, he deserted her while she lay sleeping on a riverbank. She was soon comforted by the arrival of Bacchus who married her and made her a goddess.

Same subject: **Bacchus et Ariane,** Italian, 17th century, Giovanni Antonio Pellegrini, Johann Georg Platzer. **Festin de Bacchus et d'Ariane,** Daniel Vertangen.

Arion jouant de la lyre *(Arion Playing His Lyre)*

After Louis de Silvestre

(Hist., Lit.) The poet Arion most certainly existed, but none of his works have survived. Herodotus recounts that during a voyage he was robbed and thrown into the sea by sailors, but was rescued by a dolphin who was charmed by his lyre.

Arrestation de Jésus (Parement de Narbonne) *(The Narbonne Altar-Frontal)*

French, 14th century

(N.T.) After the Last Supper and Jesus'prayers in Gethsemane (near the foot of the Mount of Olives), while it was still night, a crowd arrived bearing swords and clubs, accompanied by soldiers of the Roman consort and Jewish tax collectors. Judas, the betrayer, received thirty pieces of silver for delivering Jesus whom he identified with a kiss (the kiss of Judas). In the Gospel according to John, however, Jesus identified himself to the soldiers. Both versions agree that he offered no resistance. Nevertheless his wrists were bound and he was led away. One of the disciples, probably Peter, struck the slave of the high priest in a rage and cut off his ear. Jesus immediately calmed his friends who were prepared to fight. (Also see **Cène** and **Christ au jardin des Oliviers**.)

Arrivée à Bethléem *(The Arrival in Bethlehem)*
See **Nativité**.

Francisco Collantes

Arrivée de Louis XIV au camp devant Maëstricht (juin 1673) *(King Louis XIV Arriving at the Camp Near Maastricht)*
(Hist.) This is an episode from the war between France and Flanders. Louis XIV had an army of 40,000 men and the siege (in which d'Artagnan died) was organized by Vauban. The city, strategically located on the Meuse, was attacked often and capitulated in June 1673.

Adam Frans van der Meulen

L'Ascension *(The Ascension)*
(N.T.) This is Jesus'final appearance on earth. The eleven disciples were gathered (Judas, who had betrayed Jesus, was absent). When they saw Jesus they were afraid. He reproached their faithlessness and broke bread with them to prove that he was truly resurrected. He then took them to Bethany, blessed them and ascended to heaven, leaving them filled with great joy.

Italian, 16th century
Padua, 14th century
Hans Memling

Assassinat de l'évêque de Liège (L') *(The Assassination of the Bishop of Liège)*, also known as **Guillaume de la Marck, surnommé le Sanglier des Ardennes** *(William de la Marck, the Wild Boar of the Ardennes)*

Eugène Delacroix

(Lit.) This episode is taken from Walter Scott's novel *Quentin Durward*. The odious William de la Marck, surnamed the Wild Boar of the Ardennes, led a revolt in Liège and invaded the archbishop's palace where he feasted with his allies and soldiers. In the middle of the feast, he had the bishop, whose power he wished to usurp, dragged into the room. The bishop had been ill treated and was disheveled, but demonstrated his courage and dignity. He reproached the Wild Boar for his conduct. William gave the signal and the bishop was struck dead by the waiting executioner. The hero, Quentin Durward, took advantage of the tumult to kidnap the Wild Boar's son and thus further his cause.

Assomption de la Vierge *(The Assumption of the Virgin)*
(Christ. Trad.) Three days after she was buried, Mary, mother of Jesus, was borne to heaven by angels in the presence of the apostles and the holy women. Same subject: **Assomption**, Matteo Bonecchi, Pierre Subleyras.

Philippe de Champaigne
Martin Knöller
Laurent de la Hyre
Giambattista Piazzetta
Nicolas Poussin
Pierre-Paul Prud'hon
François-André Vincent

Atala portée au tombeau, Anne-Louis Girodet

Atala portée au tombeau, also known as **Funérailles d'Atala (Les)** or **Mort d'Atala** *(The Burial of Atala)*
(Lit.) Atala, heroine of Chateaubriand's (French romantic author) book by the same name, lived

Anne-Louis Girodet

with a tribe of North American Indians. Her father, chief of the tribe, condemned one of his prisoners, Chactas, to be burned alive. Atala fell in love with the prisoner, released him and fled with him. They took refuge with a priest, Father Aubry, who pronounced their wedding vows. Alas, Atala was of Christian origin and before her birth her mother had vowed her to chastity. Atala did not consummate her marriage but took her life in despair. Father Aubry had just enough time to hear her confession before she died. Her beloved, Chactas, helped the priest bury her.

Athalie chassée du temple *(Athaliah Led From the Temple)*

Antoine Coypel

(O.T., Lit.) After the death of Joram, king of Judah (9th century B.C.), his son and successor was assassinated in a plot. Athaliah, wife of Joram, wishing both to avenge her son's death and retain power for herself, had forty-two of her descendants killed. She seized the crown but one child escaped the massacre, young Joash. The priest Jehoiada received him in the temple where he grew up. Athaliah learned of the existence of the child whom Jehoiada was going to crown under the protection of the royal guard. She heard the trumpets announcing the event and hurried to the temple where she was seized by the guards, taken outside and slain.

Auguste devant le tombeau d'Alexandre *(Augustus at Alexander's Tomb)*

Sébastien Bourdon

(Lit.) This scene is described by the Roman biographer, Suetonius. Alexander died in Babylon which Augustus in fact visited. If Augustus saw a tomb of Alexander in Egypt, it could only have been a cenotaph (empty tomb). Nevertheless, in his *Lives of the Caesars*, Suetonius recounts that Augustus had the tomb opened and the body removed. He then placed a crown on Alexander's head and paid homage to him.

Aurore et Céphale (L') *(Aurora and Cephalus)* Pierre-Narcisse Guérin
See **Céphale et l'Aurore.**

Automne (L') *(Autumn)*, also known as **Grappe de raisin rapportée de la Terre promise (La)** *(The Grapes from the Promised Land)* Nicolas Poussin
See **Grappe de raisin rapportée de la Terre promise.**

Aveugles de Jéricho (Les), also known as **Christ guérissant les aveugles (Le)** *(Christ Healing the Blind)* Nicolas Poussin
(N.T.) As Jesus passed, the invalids and the sick rushed toward him as they had heard of the miraculous healings. In Jericho, two blind men called out to attract his attention and their neighbors attempted to hush them. Jesus told them to approach, asked them what they wanted and cured them. Having recovered their sight, they became devout followers.

Bacchus et Ariane   Giovanni Antonio Pellegrini
See **Ariane abandonnée.**

Bal à la cour de Henri III *(Ball Held at*   French, 16th century
the Court of Henry III)
(Hist.) This painting depicts a ball held at the
Louvre to celebrate the marriage of Anne, duke
of Joyeuse and Marguerite de Vaudémont, on
September 24, 1581.

Bal du duc de Joyeuse *(The Ball of the*   French, 16th century
Duke of Joyeuse)
See **Bal à la cour de Henri III**.

Banquet d'Hérode (Le) *(The Banquet*   Fra Angelico
of Herod)   Lorenzo Monaco
(N.T.) This is not Herod the Great, but his son,
Herod Antipas. Herod Antipas abducted Herodias, his brother's wife, and repudiated his own
wife to marry her. The prophet John the Baptist
condemned his behavior, but because of his

popularity, Herod was afraid to have him put to
death. He devised a plan with Herodias, whose
daughter, Salome, danced magnificently. He
invited his neighbors to a banquet and asked
Salome to dance for all; delighted by her dance,
he promised to grant her all that she desired.
Duly indoctrinated by her mother, she asked for
the head of John the Baptist. Herod had only to
grant her wish, feigning great embarrassment.
Thus John the Baptist was beheaded (see **Décollation de Saint Jean-Baptiste**).

Baptême de l'eunuque éthiopien   Herman Nauwincx
par le diacre Philippe *(Saint Philip*   Lambert Sustris and studio
Baptizing the Ethiopian Eunuch)
See **Saint Philippe baptisant l'eunuque de la
reine Candace.**

Baptême de Saint Daniel par Saint   Giuseppe Diziani
Prosdocime de Padoue *(Saint Prosdo-
cimus of Padua Baptizing Saint Daniel)*

(Christ. Trad.) Saint Prosdocimus, a saint from the East, was the first bishop of Padua. He converted Daniel, a Jew, who was martyred in 168 A.d.

Baptême du Christ (Le) *(The Baptism of Christ)*

Cornelis van Haarlem
Giannicola di Paolo
Jean Restout

(N.T.) Jesus was thirty when he went to John the Baptist who was living in the desert preaching penitence and saying, " the kingdom of Heaven is at hand " (see **Saint Jean baptisant le peuple**). Jesus asked to be baptized, but had to insist, for John had recognized him as the Messiah and wanted to be baptized by him. When Jesus was baptized, the Spirit of God descended like a dove, alighting on him, and a heavenly voice declared him to be the Son of God.

Barque de Dante (La) *(The Barque of Dante)*

Eugène Delacroix

See **Dante et Virgile, conduits par Phlégias...**

Barricade (La), 1848, *(The Barricade, Rue de la Mortellerie, June 1848)*, also known as **Souvenirs de guerre civile** *(Memory of Civil War)*

Ernest Meissonier

(Hist.) In France in February, 1848, after days of revolution King Louis Philippe abdicated and the the Second Republic was declared. But in June, workers, whose living conditions had remained equally poor, rose up against the government. They put up barricades in the east of Paris, but the insurrection was defeated. The painter Meissonier, who was at the time captain of the artillery in the National Guard, was charged with defending the Hôtel de Ville. He led the attack against the barricade in the nearby rue de la Mortellerie. He left a written account of his horror at the spectacle, and the drawing he made from memory when he returned home has been conserved.

Barrière de Clichy (La) *(The Gate at Clichy)*   Horace Vernet

(Hist.) After the disastrous retreat from Russia, Napoleon I suffered several defeats. The Prussian and Russian armies threatened Paris. They attacked on March 30, 1814, and the gate at Clichy was forced. On March 31, despite determined resistance, Paris capitulated. Napoleon was dethroned on April 1.

Bataille d'Arbelles (La) *(The Battle of Arbela)*   Charles Le Brun

(Hist.) It was in Arbela, Assyria, in 333 B.C., that Alexander the Great won the brilliant victory over King Darius of Persia that allowed him to proclaim himself king of Asia.

La Bataille d'Arbelles by Jan Brueghel has now been identified as the battle of Issus (see **Bataille d'Issus**).

Bataille de Constantin contre Maxence (La) *(The Battle of Constantine and Maxentius)*   Studio of Charles Le Brun

See **Vision de Constantin**.

Bataille de Lens par le prince de Condé *(The Battle of Lens)*   Franz Josef Cassanova

(Hist.) During the reign of Louis XIV, the north of France was constantly attacked by the Flemish, the Burgundians and the Spaniards. Condé defeated the Spaniards on August 20, 1648, at the Battle of Lens in Picardy.

Bataille de Poitiers *(The Battle of Poitiers)*, also known as **Roi Jean à la bataille de Poitiers (Le)**   Eugène Delacroix

(Hist.) This battle took place in 1356 during the Hundred Years' War. John the Good, king of France, lost and was taken prisoner by Edward, the Black Prince (son of King Edward III of England). The city was recaptured from the English by Du Guesclin in 1372.

Bataille de San Romano (La) *(The Battle of San Romano)*
Paolo Uccello

(Hist.) This battle took place in 1432 between the Florentines and the Sienese. There are three panels: one in the National Gallery in London, the second in the Uffizi Gallery in Florence and the third in the Louvre. Each panel represents a different scene from this memorable battle. Here, Florentine commander Nicolò de Tolentino, surprised by the Sienese, managed to resist for eight hours, then counter-attacked with reinforcements led by Micheletto da Cotignola. The Florentines were victorious.

Bataille de Taillebourg *(The Battle of Taillebourg)*
Eugène Delacroix
Gustave Lassalle-Bordes

(Hist.) This battle was initiated and won by Saint Louis in Saintonge, against Henry III of England.

Bataille d'Issus (La) *(The Battle of Issus)*
Jan Brueghel

(Hist.) Previously called **La Bataille d'Arbelles**, this painting in fact represents the battle which Alexander launched and won in 333 B.C. in Issus against King Darius of Persia and his immense army. Alexander entered Persia and found great riches. Darius fled, but his wife and daughter fell into Alexander's hands. He treated them with absolute generosity (see **Famille de Darius aux pieds d'Alexandre**).

Bataille entre les Romains et les Carthaginois *(The Battle between the Romans and the Carthaginians)*
Antoine Dieu

(Hist.) The wars between Rome and Carthage (Punic Wars) spanned more than a century and led to the ruin of Carthage, which was burned and razed in 146 B.C. (This battle has not been identified with certitude.)

Bélisaire demandant l'aumône *(Belisorius Begging)*

Jacques-Louis David

(Hist.) Belisorius was a brilliant Byzantine general in the period when the center of the Roman empire was in Byzantium (6th century). He was known for his exploits against the Goths who attempted to invade Rome. He was, however, unable to save the city and was implicated in conspiracies. He lost favor and had both his functions and possessions removed. Toward the end of his life, he returned to favor, but is traditionally represented as a blind old beggar accompanied by a young guide. Here he is recognized by one of his former comrades-in-arms.

Bergers d'Arcadie (Les) *(The Shepherds of Arcadia),* also known as **Et in Arcadia ego**

Nicolas Poussin

(Myth.) Arcadia was ruled by Arcas, son of Jupiter, and the nymph Callisto. This mountainous country in the central Peloponnesus, which maintained pastoral traditions for a long period, is described by the poets as a land of delights. However, this paradise was only temporary as proves the inscription that the shepherds are reading on the tomb. The inscription, *Et in Arcadia ego,* is often translated as "I too (lived) in Arcadia," but may be more correctly translated as "I too (am found) in Arcadia," referring to death.

Bethsabée au bain *(Bathsheba at Her Bath)*

Jacob van Loo
Rembrandt

(O.T.) David killed Goliath (see **David tenant la tête de Goliath**) and became king of Israel by succeeding Saul. One evening as he was walking on the roof of his palace, he saw an extremely beautiful woman bathing in the courtyard of her home. He inquired about her and discovered that she was Bathsheba, wife of an officer named Uriah. David seduced her (taking advantage of his position as king, whom she could hardly refuse) and she conceived. David hoped that Uriah would believe that he was the father of the child, but it was wartime and abstinence was the rule for soldiers. Uriah would not visit his wife. David then made a decision he would regret all his life. He sent Uriah on a mission to Rabbah where he was sure to perish. As planned, Uriah was killed and David married Bathsheba. The child died seven days after its birth. Bathsheba's second son was King Solomon. The letter from David which Bathsheba is holding is not mentioned in the Bible; it was invented by the painters.

Les Bergers d'Arcadie,
Nicolas Poussin.

Bethsabée au bain,
Rembrandt.

Bethsabée recevant la lettre de David
(Bathsheba Receiving David's Letter)
(O.T., Imag.) Bathsheba learns that her husband
Uriah has been killed. David, who announces the
news, was responsible for his death. (See **Beth-
sabée au bain**.)

Wilhelm Drost

**Bienheureux Ranieri Rasini délivre
les pauvres de la prison de Florence
(Le)** *(The Blessed Ranieri Rasini Freeing
the Poor from a Prison in Florence)*
(Christ. Trad.) The poor, imprisoned in the dun-
geons of Florence, wrote to Ranieri (Saint
Ranieri was a Franciscan monk in the 12th century) who immediately appeared and helped the
prisoners pass through the wall.

Sassetta

**Bienheureux Ranieri Rasini montre
aux frères réunis en prière l'âme de
l'avare de Citerna emportée par les
démons (Le)** *(Saint Ranieri Rasini and
Citerna's Soul)*
(Christ. Trad.) Ranieri, a monk from Borgo San
Sepolcro in Italy in the 12th century, was
blessed with the gift of prophecy. He told a rich
and greedy man in the neighboring village of
Citerna that he would soon die and be damned.
Ranieri also predicted that everyone would witness his soul being taken to Hell. Shortly after,
while Ranieri was in the church choir with his
brethren, they saw demons in the form of animals carrying off the wicked man's soul.

Sassetta

**Boissy d'Anglas saluant la tête du
député Féraud** *(Boissy d'Anglas Greeting the Head of Deputy Féraud)*
(Hist.) Boissy d'Anglas was the deputy of the
States-General in 1789. Being a moderate, he
voted against the execution of Louis XVI. On
May 20, 1795, the Convention was invaded by the
masses who demanded bread and protested
against the Assembly's policy. They brought
with them the head of one of the murdered depu-

Alexandre-Évariste Fragonard

ties, Féraud, impaled on a pike. Boissy d'Anglas'
sang froid has been described by chroniclers.

Bon Samaritain (Le) *(The Good Samaritan)*

(N.T.) On the road from Jerusalem to Jericho, a
man was beaten and stripped by robbers, and
left half dead on the roadside. A priest and a
Levite, assistants to the priests of the Temple of
Jerusalem, saw him but passed on the other
side. A Samaritan (a people scorned by the Jews)
stopped and helped him. Jesus told this story to
illustrate that a "neighbor" is anyone in need,
whether a stranger or a friend.

Théodore Chassériau
Jean Gigoux
Jacob Pynas
School of Rembrandt

Bonaparte au pont d'Arcole *(Bonaparte on the Bridge at Arcola on November 17, 1796)*

See **Général Bonaparte au pont d'Arcole**.

Antoine-Jean Gros

Bonaparte franchissant
les Alpes, Paul
Delaroche.

Bonaparte franchissant les Alpes Paul Delaroche
(Bonaparte Crossing the Alps)
(Hist.) On May 21, 1800, as Provence was threatened by the Austrian general Melas, Bonaparte
crossed the Great Saint Bernard Pass with his
army; he entered Milan victorious on June 2.

Bonaparte visitant les pestiférés de Antoine-Jean Gros
Jaffa *(Napoleon Bonaparte Visiting the
Plague-stricken at Jaffa)*
(Hist.) During the Eastern campaign, Bonaparte
conquered the city of Jaffa in Palestine, but the
plague decimated his troops.

Borée enlevant Orithyie *(Boreas* Sebastiano Conca
Abducting Orithyia) Giovanni Antoni Pellegrini
(Myth.) Boreas, the north wind, portrayed as a
winged demon, was one of the Titans, primitive
forces of nature. He carried off Orithyia,
daughter of King Erechtheus of Athens, while
she was playing with her friends. He took her to
Thrace, a kingdom of the northwest said to be
home of the wind, where she bore him two children.

Brutus condamnant ses fils à mort Guillaume Guillon
(Brutus Condemning His Sons to Death) called Lethière
(Hist.) In 509 B.C. Lucius Junius Brutus was the
first Roman consul. He learned that his two sons
were plotting the restoration of the Tarquins,
enemies of the Republic. He himself had to condemn them to death and fulfilled the duty sto-
ically. This Brutus, who lived in the 6th century
B.C., should not be confused with Marcus Junius
Brutus, nephew of Cato, Julius Caesar's adopted
son and assassin.

Buisson Ardent (Le) *(The Burning* Francisco Collantes
*Bush; God Orders Moses to Lead the
Israelites Out of Egypt)*
(O.T.) Moses had fled from the Pharaoh and was
leading his flocks in search of pastures when he

saw a bush that burned without being consumed. He had not yet recovered from his surprise when he heard the voice of God calling to
him from the bush. God revealed His name and
ordered Moses to lead the Israelites out of Egypt
where they were oppressed and to take them to
the Promised Land of Canaan, "a land flowing
with milk and honey." This was the Exodus. But
first Moses had to convince the Pharaoh to
release the Israelites. God advised him to go
with his brother Aaron, who spoke well, and He
also granted him magical powers, including the
ability to turn a rod into a serpent (see **Moïse
changeant en serpent la verge d'Aaron**).

Le Calvaire, Giovanni Bellini.

Calvaire (Le) *(Calvary)*

(N.T.) The word *calvary*, in Latin *calvaria*, meaning "skull," comes from the Armenian *gulgota*, which became *golgotha* in Hebrew. The hill in Jerusalem on which Jesus was crucified can be called either Calvary or Golgotha. It is "the place of a skull," the supposed burial place of Adam. Paintings entitled Calvary show Christ on the cross, either alone or between the two thieves who were crucified with him. At the foot of the cross, there may be a group of soldiers sharing Jesus'clothes or casting lots for his tunic and a group of followers in tears: Mary, the mother of Jesus, swooning, the holy women and John the Evangelist, to whom he entrusted his mother. A curious crowd often surrounds the main figures.

Other paintings depict Calvary after the crowd has departed: Jesus has been completely abandoned or is accompanied by only several praying followers.

Same subject: **Calvaire avec un moine chartreux**, Jean de Beaumetz. **Calvaire avec saint Dominique**, Fra Angelico. **Calvaire avec saint Job au pied de la croix**, Francesco Francia. **Cal-**

Giovanni Bellini
Karel Dujardin
Josse Lieferinxe
Master of the Death of
Saint Nicholas of Münster
Master of Saint Clare
Andrea Mantegna
French, mid-15th century
David Teniers the Elder
Veronese

vaire avec saint Denis, Henri Bellechose. **Christ en croix**, French, 19th century, Philippe de Champaigne, Michel Dorigny, Nicolas Tournier, Simon Vouet. **Christ en croix adoré par deux donateurs**, El Greco. **Christ en croix avec la Vierge, saint Jean et le bienheureux Gilles**, Umbria, 16th century. **Christ en croix et la Madeleine**, Antoine Rivalz. **Christ en croix, la Vierge, saint Jean et sainte Madeleine**, Anthony van Dyck. **Christ sur la croix**, Pierre-Paul Prud'hon. **Crucifix aux anges**, Charles Le Brun. **Crucifixion**, Naples, 14th century, Lorenzo Monaco, Master of the Madonna of San Pietro, Niccolo da Foligno, Andrea Solario, Taddeo di Bartolo.

Cambyse et Psamménite *(Cambyses and Psammetichus)*

Adrien Guignet

(Hist.) Cambyses II, emperor of Persia in the 6th century B.C., was reputed to be cruel and half insane. He conquered Egypt in 525 B.C. after Psammetichus III, the last Pharaoh of the XXVI dynasty, ascended to the throne. Psammetichus was betrayed by the leader of his Greek mercenaries and taken prisoner. Cambyses ordered him to commit suicide.

Camille livre le maître d'école de Faléries à ses écoliers *(Camillus and the Schoolmaster of Falerii)*

Nicolas Poussin

(Hist.) After capturing Falerii in Etruria in 394 B.C., Roman general Camillus was approached by the town's schoolmaster, who offered to deliver his pupils as hostages. Outraged by this gesture, Camillus turned the schoolmaster over to his pupils for chastisement.

Carlo et Ubaldo allant délivrer Rinaldo *(Carlo and Ubaldo Rescuing Rinaldo)*

Giovanni Bilivert

(Lit.) Rinaldo, a character in Tasso's epic poem, *Jerusalem Delivered*, disappeared from the encampment of the crusaders who were attacking the Saracens, under the command of Godfrey of Bouillon. Rinaldo had, in fact, gone to rescue his companions who were imprisoned by the beautiful witch Armida. In revenge, the lovely Armida cast her spell on him and Rinaldo stayed with her, forgetting his mission and enjoying the delights of an enchanted island. The valiant Carlo and the wise Ubaldo set off to rescue Rinaldo. They were assisted by a sorcerer who told them where to find the Fortunate Isle and how to avoid Armida's traps. The rescuers broke Armida's spell by giving Rinaldo a magic mirror, in which he saw himself decorated with jewels and silks, looking like a woman. Rinaldo immediately fled with his companions, leaving Armida in tears (see **Renaud et Armide**).

Carloman blessé à mort dans la forêt d'Yveline *(Carloman Mortally Wounded in the Forest of Yveline)*

Jean-Charles Rémond

(Hist.) Carloman was the second son of Louis the Stammerer, king of France in the 9th century. Conqueror of the Normans, he became king after the death of his elder brother Louis III, but his reign only lasted a few years as he was fatally wounded in a hunting accident.

Caron passant les ombres *(Charon Crossing to the Shades)*

Pierre Subleyras

(Myth.) For a coin, this fearsome boatman ferried the souls of the dead across the river Styx. He refused those who could not pay (which is why a coin was placed in coffins). He also refused to take the living (except for Ulysses, Aeneas, Dante and a few others), and those who had not been duly buried, condemning them to roam and suffer indefinitely.

Cène (La) *(The Last Supper)*

Joos van Cleve
Mathieu Le Nain
Philippe de Champaigne

(N.T.) The Last Supper was the final meal Jesus shared with his twelve disciples before his

La Cène, Giovanni
Battista Tiepolo

death. It was a festive dinner in celebration of
Passover when a lamb is sacrificed (hence the
symbolism of Jesus as the sacrificial lamb).
Jesus made his final recommendations to the
apostles, both in acts and in words:
— he announced his imminent death, saying
that one of them would betray him to the Jewish
leaders who sought to condemn him;
— he identified the traitor more or less explic-
itly. It was Judas, who then disappeared toward
the end of the meal;
— he washed the disciples'feet, commanding
them to continue to do so, meaning that they
should love one another;
— he broke bread and passed the wine saying,
" Take, eat; this is my body " and " Drink, this is
my blood. " This was the institution of the
Eucharist which led to the belief in transubstan-
tiation, implying that once the bread and wine of
communion have been consecrated, they become
the body and blood of Christ (see **Jésus-Christ
Instituant l'Eucharistie**). After the Last Supper,
Jesus and his disciples went to the Garden of
Olives (see **Christ au jardin des Oliviers**). Paintings of the Last Supper depict a particular
moment of the tragic evening, such as the washing of the disciples'feet, the institution of the
Eucharist or the denunciation of the traitor.

Frans Pourbus the Younger
Giovanni Battista Tiepolo

ce

Cène à Emmaüs (La) *(The Supper at Emmaus)*
See **Pèlerins d'Emmaüs**.

Giovanni Capassini

Céphale et l'Aurore *(Cephalus and Aurora)*

François Boucher

(Myth.) While hunting on Mount Hymettus, Cephalus was abducted by the goddess Aurora. He rejected her advances, reminding her that he was already married to Procris. Angered by his resistance, Aurora instilled doubts as to his wife's fidelity and told him to test her. Cephalus returned home in disguise and set out to seduce his wife. Procris fell into the trap. They quarreled and were reconciled. He later accidentally killed Procris while hunting.

Same subject: **Aurore et Céphale**, Pierre-Narcisse Guérin.

Céphée et Cassiopée remerciant Persée d'avoir sauvé Andromède *(Cepheus and Cassiopeia Thanking Perseus For Saving Andromeda)*
See **Persée délivrant Andromède**.

Pierre Mignard

Cérès protégeant Triptolème contre le roi Lyncus *(Ceres Protecting Triptolemus Against King Lyncus)*

Jacques Dumont

(Myth.) Ceres, goddess of the harvest, searched the entire earth for her missing daughter Proserpine (see **Enlèvement de Proserpine**). When she learned that her daughter had been abducted by Pluto and that she would never see her again, she relinquished her divine function and went to Eleusis where, disguised as an old woman, she offered her services as nurse. She was well received in the house of Celeus and nursed his young son Triptolemus. When he reached manhood she offered him a chariot drawn by winged dragons as a token of her gratitude. In the meantime, the harvests, abandoned by the goddess, had disappeared. Ceres ordered Triptolemus to travel the earth sowing corn. In certain regions he encountered harsh resistance. Lyncus, king of the Scythians, was jealous, and attempted to kill him. Ceres intervened and changed the king into a lynx, thus saving Triptolemus.

Charité de saint Martin *(The Charity of Saint Martin)*
See **Saint Martin donnant la moitié de son manteau.**

Touraine, 16th century

Charité de saint Nicolas de Bari (La) *(The Charity of Saint Nicholas of Bari)*
(Christ. Trad.) Saint Nicholas was bishop of Myra in the 4th century. His relics are enshrined in Bari. Famed for his generosity, he was said to have aided a nobleman whose poverty forced him to sell his three daughters as prostitutes. When he heard of their misfortune, Nicholas went to the poor man's house and, for three nights in a row, thrust bags of gold into the window as a dowry for the young women.

Giovanni Francesco da Rimini
Ambrogio Lorenzetti

Charité de saint Thomas de Villeneuve *(The Charity of Saint Thomas of Villanueva)*
(Christ. Trad.) Saint Thomas, born in 1488, entered the order of Augustine monks at a very early age and later became bishop of Valencia. His inexhaustible charity earned him the surname Thomas the Almsgiver.

Juan Carreno de Miranda

Charité romaine (La) *(Roman Charity)*, also known as **Cimon et Pero** *(Cimon and Pero)*
(Lit.) This painting was based on an anecdote told by Roman historian Valerius Maximus: Cimon was condemned to death and left in prison without food. However, his daughter was allowed to visit him daily and fed him with her own milk.

Charles Mellin

Charles Ier recevant une rose des mains d'une jeune fille au moment où il est conduit prisonnier au château de Carisbrook *(Charles I Receiving a Rose from a Young Girl as He Is Taken Prisoner to Carisbrooke)*

Eugène Lami

(Hist., Imag.) Charles I declared war on Parliament in 1642, but lost in 1646 and was imprisoned at Hampton Court in 1647. He escaped, but was recaptured and held at Carisbrooke Castle. Legend has it that a young girl, touched by his downcast air, gave him a rose.

Charles-Quint reçu par François Ier à l'abbaye de Saint-Denis (1540) *(Charles V Received by Francis I at the Abbey of Saint Denis, 1540)*

Antoine-Jean Gros

(Hist.) Charles V ruled over a vast empire: Germany, Flanders, Spain, Naples, Sicily, and Latin America. Because of its size, the empire was fragile and revolts were constant. When the population of Gand rebelled, Charles V asked Francis I for permission to cross France on his way to fight in Gand. During their meeting, Charles V promised the Milanese region to the Duke of Orléans, second son of Francis I.

Charon passant les ombres *(Charon Crossing to the Shades)*

Pierre Subleyras

See **Caron passant les ombres**.

Chasse de Diane *(Diana Hunting)*

Studio of Luca Giordano

See **Diane chasseresse**.

Chasse de Méléagre et d'Atalante *(Meleager and Atalanta Hunting)*

Charles Le Brun

(Myth.) Meleager was the son of the king of Calydon. After the harvest, the king sacrificed to the gods, but forgot the goddess Diana. In revenge she sent an enormous wild boar, which devasted the fields, to Calydon. Meleager formed a hunting party that included two of his uncles and the hunter Atalanta. Atalanta injured the beast, but it was Meleager who finally killed it (also see **Mort de Méléagre**).

Chaste Suzanne (La), also known as **Suzanne au bain** *(Susanna Bathing)*
See **Suzanne au bain**.

Théodore Chassériau

Chevalier et la Mort (Le) *(Death and the Knight)*, also known as **Chevalier, la Jeune Fille et la Mort (Le)**
(Imag.) The image of death began to haunt painters around the 14th century, following the black plague which had severely decimated Europe. Death became a frequent subject of spiritual meditation: beauty, grace and love were represented in flight, pursued by a grimacing skelton bearing a scythe.

Hans Baldung Grien

Choléra à Paris en 1832 (Le)
(The Cholera of Paris, 1832)
(Hist.) This epidemic claimed close to 20,000 lives. It was accompanied by rumors of poisoning which provoked unrest.

Prosper Lafaye

Christ à la colonne (Le) *(Christ at the Column)*
Same subject: Alexandre Dupuis, attributed to Simon Vouet (?).
See **Flagellation du Christ**.

Bartolomé Esteban Murillo

Christ apparaissant à la Madeleine (Le) *(Christ Appearing to Mary Magdalene)*
Christ apparaissant en jardinier à la Madeleine (Le)
See **Jésus apparaît à la Madeleine**.

Studio of Luca Giordano
Bronzino

Le Christ à la colonne,
Bartolomé Esteban
Murillo.

**Christ au désert servi par les anges
(Le)** *(The Angels Ministering to Christ in
the Desert)*

Charles Le Brun

(N.T.) After he was baptized (see **Baptême du
Christ**), Jesus retreated to the desert where he
fasted for forty days and forty nights. Believing
him to be weakened by hunger, Satan appeared
to tempt him, but in vain *(see* **Tentation du
Christ au désert** and **Tentation du Christ**). After
he was left alone, angels came to Jesus and
ministered to him.

Christ au jardin des Oliviers (Le) *(The
Agony in the Garden)*

Italian, 16th century
Francisco Goya
Lorenzo Monaco
Bartolomé Esteban Murillo
Niccolo da Foligno
Barnaert van Orley

(N.T.) At night, after the Last Supper with his
disciples (see **Cène**), Jesus went with several of
them to the hill of Gethsemane overlooking Jerusalem. Jesus knew that the hour of his death was

approaching and went to the Garden of Olives to pray. He moved away from the disciples and asked them to keep watch. He descended three times, found them sleeping and rebuked them. In the garden, he prayed to God asking him to save him, but an angel comforted him and he accepted his suffering and death. He was arrested in the garden in the early hours of the morning.

Same subject: **Jésus au jardin des Oliviers**, Théodore Chassériau.

Christ au tombeau *(Christ's Tomb)*　　　　Simone dei Crocifissi
See **Mise au tombeau**.

Christ aux outrages (Le) *(The Crown-*　　Master of the Annunciation
ing With Thorns)　　　　　　　　　　　　to the Shepherds
See **Christ couronné d'épines**.

Christ baptisant saint Jean-Baptiste　Dutch, 16th century
(Le) *(Christ Baptizing Saint John the Baptist)*
(Christ. Trad.) According to an apocryphal text, just after John the Baptist baptized Jesus (see **Baptême du Christ**), he asked Christ to baptize him. In the Gospel according to Matthew, it was John who asked to be baptized by Jesus, but Jesus insisted that John baptize him first.

Christ bénissant les enfants *(Christ*　Master H B
Blessing the Children)
See **Christ et les enfants**.

Christ chez Marthe et Marie (Le)　　Hendrick van Steenwyck
(Christ in the House of Martha and Mary)
See **Jésus-Christ chez Marthe et Marie**.

Christ couronné d'épines (Le) *(Christ*　Attributed to the Master
Crowned with Thorns)　　　　　　　　　of Madeleine Mansi
(N.T.) The chief priests and the elders rendered　Titian
Jesus to Pontius Pilate, the Roman procurator,

to be condemned to death. Unconvinced of Jesus'guilt, Pilate attempted to save him, but finally submitted to the determined resolution of the prosecutors, washing his hands in public to indicate that he was not responsible. He had Jesus whipped by the soldiers, as was the custom, before delivering him to be crucified. After the whipping the soldiers took Jesus to the courtyard and placed a purple (or scarlet) cloak over his shoulders (the royal mantle, here in derision), a crown of thorns on his head and a reed in his hand before paying mock tribute to him.

Same subject: **Christ aux outrages**, after Le Valentin, Master of the Annunciation to the Shepherds. **Christ de douleur, saint Agricol et un donateur**, Provence, 15th century. **Ecce Homo**, Bartolomeo Cincani, studio of Titian. **Couronnement d'épines**, Jan Janssens.

Christ de douleur, saint Agricol et un donateur (*The Man of Sorrows Standing in the Tomb, with Saint Agricolus Presenting a Donor*, known as the *Retable of Boulbon*)

Provence, 15th century

(Christ. Trad.) The suffering Christ is depicted after his flagellation. He was insulted by the Jews and mocked by the soldiers who adorned him with a pseudo-royal mantle and the crown of thorns. He is sometimes shown alone, overcome, stripped or still wearing the crown of thorns and the mantle.

Christ de la résurrection (Le) (*Christ Resurrected*)

School of Fra Angelico

See **Résurrection**.

Christ déposé de la croix (Le) (*Christ Descended From the Cross*)

Pieter van Mol

Christ descendu de la croix (Le)

Jacopo Bassano

See **Descente de croix**.

Le Christ couronné d'épines, Titian.

Christ devant Caïphe (Le) *(Christ before Caiaphas)*

Master of Messkirch

(N.T.) Caiaphas was the high priest of Judea. He presided over the Sanhedrin, the Jewish legislative council, which pronounced all sentences except condamnation to death: death sentences were under the jurisdiction of the Roman procurator. This is why there was considerable confusion during Jesus'trial, described rather ambiguously in the Gospels. Jesus appeared before Pilate, who thought he was innocent and hesitated to condemn him. Christ also appeared before Caiaphas who hated him for turning people away from the established religion. Many witnesses were called, and finally two were found who gave testimony of Jesus' "sacrilege": He said he would destroy the Temple and rebuild it in three days (symbolic words referring to the resurrection). This was a motive for incrimination and Jesus was condemned to death. All that remained was to convince Pontius Pilate to pronounce the sentence (see **Christ couronné d'épines, Ecce Homo**).

Christ devant Pilate (Le) *(Christ Before Pilate)*

Jean-François de Troy

See **Ecce Homo.**

Christ en croix *(Christ on the Cross)*

French, 19th century

See **Crucifixion**.
Same subject: Umbria, 16th century, Philippe de Champaigne, Eugène Delacroix, Michel Dorigny, Anthony van Dyck, El Greco, Antoine Revalz, Nicolas Tournier, Simon Vouet

Christ et la Cananéenne (Le) *(Christ Heals the Daughter of the Woman of Canaan)*

Germain-Jean Drouais

(N.T.) Jesus was resting with his disciples in Tyre, when a woman came to ask him to heal her daughter who was possessed by an evil spirit. Jesus replied, " I was sent only to the lost sheep of the house of Israel. It is not fair to take the children's bread and throw it to the dogs. " She responded, " Yes, Lord, yet even the dogs eat the crumbs that fall from their master's table. " Touched by her faith (and her sense of humor?), Jesus told her to return home where she would find her daughter healed.

Christ et la Femme adultère (Le) *(Christ and the Woman Taken in Adultery)*

Jacques Blanchard
Jobst Harrich
Lorenzo Lotto
Gabriel Metsu
Bonifacio de Pitati

(N.T.) According to Hebraic law, adulterous women were to be stoned to death. The Phari-

sees, enemies of Jesus, brought before him a
woman who had been caught in the act of adultery. Hoping to catch him breaking the Jewish
law, they asked him what should be done to her.
In reply, Jesus bent down and wrote in the sand.
He then said, "Let him who is without sin
among you be the first to throw a stone at her."
One by one, starting with the eldest, the Pharisees turned away (Had Jesus written their sins
in the sand?) The woman, surprised, remained
alone with Jesus who said to her, "Go, and do
not sin again."
Same subject: **Femme adultère**, Christian Wilhelm Ernst Dietrich, Nicolas Poussin, Emile
Signol.

Giovanni Domenico Tiepolo
Ippolito Scarsellino

Christ et la Madeleine (Le) *(Christ and
Mary Magdalene)*
See **Jésus apparaît à la Madeleine**.

Francesco Albani

Christ et la Samaritaine (Le) *(Christ
and the Woman of Samaria)*
See **Jésus et la Samaritaine**.

Juan de Flandes

Christ et les enfants (Le) *(Christ and
the Children)*
(N.T.) Christ preached to the crowds and healed
the sick. People came from all around with their
children so that Jesus could heal them. The disciples attempted to chase them away so that
Jesus could be left in peace, but Jesus said,
"Suffer the little children to come unto me, and
forbid them not: for of such is the kingdom of
Heaven."
Same subject: **Christ bénissant les enfants**,
Master H B. **Laissez venir à moi les petits
enfants**, Émile Champmartin.

Sébastien Bourdon

Christ et les pèlerins d'Emmaüs (Le)
(Christ and the Pilgrims to Emmaus)
See **Pèlerins d'Emmaüs**.

Giovanni Capassini

Christ guérissant le paralytique (Le)   Alessandro Magnasco
(Christ Healing the Paralytic)
See **Jésus guérissant le paralytique de Bethesda.**

Christ guérissant les aveugles (Le)   Nicolas Poussin
(Christ Healing the Blind)
See **Aveugles de Jéricho.**

Christ mort (Le) *(The Dead Christ)*   Carlo Crivelli
Christ mort couché sur son linceul   Philippe de Champaigne
(Le)   Lo Spagna
See **Crucifixion.**

Christ mort sur les genoux de la   Charles Le Brun
Vierge (Le) *(Christ on His Mother's Knees)*
See **Pietà.**

Christ portant sa croix (Le) *(Christ Bearing the Cross)*   Spanish, 17th century
Lorenzo Lotto
See **Portement de croix.**

Christ porté au tombeau (Le) *(The Bearing of the Body of Christ)*   Julio Cesare Amidano
See **Mise au tombeau.**

Christ ressuscité apparaissant à la   Theodoor van Thulden
Vierge (Le) *(The Appearance of Christ to His Mother)*
(Christ. Trad.) The apparition of Jesus to his mother is not mentioned in the Gospels; it is found in apocryphal texts. Here he appears surrounded by several companions and an angel carrying an extended standard. In the foreground are the instruments of the Passion.

Christ sur la croix (Le) *(Christ Crucified)*   Pierre-Paul Prud'hon
See **Crucifixion.**

Chryséis rendue à son père par Ulysse *(Ulysses Returning Chryseis to Her Father)*
See **Ulysse remettant Chryséis à son père**.

Claude Gellée, called Claude Lorrain

Chute des anges rebelles (La) *(Fall of the Rebel Angels)*

Master of the Rebel Angels

(Christ. Trad.) According to the Book of Henoch, an apocryphal text, after the creation of the earth, a group of angels led by Azazel and Semyaza descended to earth to unite with mortal women. They taught the women to adorn themselves and wear jewels and the men to build arms and make war. The union between the angels and the women produced terrible giants who devoured everything. Not particularly proud of their exploits, the rebel angels swore to stick together if their plot was uncovered. But the four gracious archangels, Michael, Uriel, Raphael and Gabriel saw everything and hurried to tell God. He ordered Michael to put Semyaza and his companions in chains, Raphael to seize Azaziel and Gabriel to kill the giants. The rebels were then thrown into an abyss at the bottom of the earth where they were joined by sinners (see **Saint Michel terrassant le démon**).

Cimon et Éphigène *(Cimon and Iphigenia)*
See **Vénus et les Grâces surprises par un mortel**.

Jacques Blanchard

Cimon et Pero *(Cimon and Pero)*
See **Charité romaine**.

Charles Mellin

Circé *(Circe)*

Studio of Guercino

(Myth.) In the *Odyssey*, Circe is the sorceress who received Ulysses' companions. She prepared a banquet for them and, using the magic potion that she carries in a vase, turned them into swine. Fortunately one of them, Eurylochus,

Circé, Studio of Guercino.

stayed behind to watch and returned to the ship to inform Ulysses. Armed with advice and an antidote given by Mercury, Ulysses set off for the witch's house. He drank the beverage she gave him, but it had no effect. He threatened Circe with his sword and she turned his companions back into men. Ulysses was then treated royally and stayed a year before continuing his voyage.

Circoncision (La) *(The Circumcision)*

(N.T.) Circumcision, carried out for medical and religious reasons, was practiced by the Egyptians and the Aztecs. Today it is performed by the Jews (on the eighth day) and the Muslims (around the age of thirteen). In the Bible, God ordered Abraham to respect the practice, saying that it would be a sign of the convenant between God and Abraham and his descendants; thus circumcision is included in Hebraic law. After the death of Christ, the first Christians abandoned the practice and replaced it by the "circumci-

Frederico Barocci
Il Garafalo
Master of Saint Severinus
Master of the Life
of the Virgin
Bartolommeo Veneto
Tommaso di Andrea Vincidor

sion of the heart." Jesus was circumcised when he was eight days old, probably by his foster father Joseph. However this scene is often combined with the Presentation in the Temple which took place when he was forty days old. Jesus may therefore be shown being circumcised by the High Priest, before a great crowd (see **Présentation au Temple**). When the circumcision is depicted separately from the Presentation in the Temple, Mary is not present.

Same subject: **Circoncision avec un donateur**, Bernardino Zenale.

Clélie passant le Tibre *(Cloelia Crossing the Tiber)*

(Hist.) Cloelia was a young Roman heroine and a descendant of the kings of Alba Longa. During the war between the Romans and the Etruscans, she was taken to King Lars Porsena of Etruria as

Abraham van Diepenbeeck
Jan van Noordt
Jacques Stella

Clélie passant le Tibre,
Jacques Stella.

a hostage. Cloelia fled, crossed the Tiber on horseback and returned to Rome with her companions who swam after her. The consul returned her to Porsena who, moved by her courage, released her and allowed her to return with the companions of her choice.

Cléopâtre avalant le poison (Cleopatra Swallowing the Poison)

Antoine Coypel

(Lit.) This is not Cleopatra, queen of Egypt, but a Syrian queen who appears in Corneille's tragedy *Rodogune*. She killed one of her sons and, out of hatred, pursued the other along with his beloved, Princess Rodogune. She was finally defeated, but died pronouncing a curse:
" Et pour vous souhaiter tous les malheurs ensemble,
Puisse naître de vous un fils qui me ressemble. "

Clorinde intervenant pour sauver Olinde et Sophronie (Clorinda Intervening to Save Olindo and Sophronia)

After Eugène Delacroix

(Lit.) This is an episode from *Jerusalem Delivered* by Tasso. The crusaders were at the gates of the Holy City. The magician Ismen, adviser to King Aladin of Jerusalem, suggested stealing the image of the Virgin from the Christian church and placing it inside the mosque. He promised that if the appropriate rites were performed the image of the Virgin would become a protectoress of the Muslims. The project was immediately carried out, but the next morning the image had disappeared from the mosque. Aladin was furious because he counld not find the culprit and decided to kill all the Christians. To save them, young Sophronia, who was innocent, confessed to the crime and was condemned to be burned at the stake. Her lover, Olindo, also confessed, hoping to save her. Aladin was relentless and condemned them both. Clorinda, a female warrior from the east, saw them and inquired of their fate. Her generous heart was moved and she obtained their release by promising to join the Saracen forces against the crusaders.

Clytemnestre et Égisthe s'apprêtant à frapper Agamemnon *(Clytemnestra and Aegisthus Preparing to Strike Agamemnon)*

Pierre-Narcisse Guérin

(Myth., Lit.) Agamemnon's wife, Clytemnestra, had several children: Iphigenia whom Agamemnon sacrificed to the gods, Orestes, Electra and Chrysothemis. Agamemnon returned triumphant from the Trojan War, but Clytemnestra could not forgive the sacrifice of Iphigenia; his affair with a Trojan captive, Chryseis; or his love

Combat de Minerve contre Mars, Jacques-Louis David.

for Cassandra, whom he brought back from Troy. She planned his assassination with her lover Aegisthus. Agamemnon's death was later avenged by his son, Orestes (see **Remords d'Oreste**).

Combat d'avant-garde dans le Darha *(Combat of the Advance Guard in the Darha)*

Jules Rigo

(Hist.) Here we see the spahis of Oran, commanded by Captain Fleury, fighting the sahrif Boumaza. This is an episode from the French colonization of Algeria.

Combat de Minerve contre Mars *(Combat Between Minerva and Mars)*

Jacques-Louis David

(Myth.) Mars is the god of War, but he was by no

means always victorious. His brutal and aggressive nature made him unpopular with the other gods and he was often opposed to the wisdom of Minerva. During the Trojan War they took opposite sides — Minerva with the Greeks, Mars on the side of the Trojans. They met and fought each on the plain of Ilium. Minerva won.

Combat de saint Georges contre le dragon *(Saint George Fighting the Dragon)*
See **Saint Georges terrassant le dragon**.

Rhine, 15th century

Combat des Lapithes et des Centaures *(The Battle of Lapiths and Centaurs)*
(Myth.) The Centaurs, half horse-half man, produced of a union between Ixion and a cloud, were monstrous cruel creatures (see **Ixion, roi des Lapithes**). The Lapiths, people of Thessaly, invited the Centaurs to the wedding of their king Pirithous. Pirithous' friend Theseus attended the banquet. The Centaurs, not accustomed to drinking wine, were soon drunk and havoc ensued; one of them even attempted to rape the bride Hippodamia. This led to a battle which the Lapiths finally won. They then chased the Centaurs from Thessaly forever.
Same subject: **Thésée poursuivant les Centaures**, Achille-Etna Michallon.

Johann Georg Platzer

Combat d'Hercule et d'Acheloüs *(Hercules and Achelous)*, also known as **Paysage avec Hercule combattant Acheloüs changé en taureau** *(Landscape with Hercules and Achelous)*
See **Hercule et Acheloüs**.

Domenichino

Combat livré sur les côtes d'Afrique par le chevalier des Augers à une escadre hollandaise *(Attack Led by the Knight of Augers Against a Dutch Fleet)*
(Hist.) The knight of Augers left Brest on March

Théodore Gudin

7, 1706, with a fleet of two vessels and two frigates. After stopping in Cape Verde, he set sail for the Island of Saint Helena. On April 12 he encountered three Dutch vessels and entered into combat. Holland was part of the coalition of European States against Louis XIV. Here we see the moment, on April 13, when the disabled Dutch vessel, *le Rochetet*, was forced to surrender.

Communion mystique de sainte Catherine de Sienne (La) *(The Mystic Communion of Saint Catherine)*

Fra Bartolommeo

See **Mariage mystique de sainte Catherine de Sienne**.

Concile de Trente (Le) *(The Council of Trent)*

Veneto, 16th century
Pier Francesco Mola

(Hist.) The Council of Trent, eagerly awaited by many Christians, was held in Trentino, Northern Italy. It could only be organized after the reconciliation of the king of France and the emperor of Germany by the peace of Crépy-en-Laonnais in 1544. Fathers of the Church, papal legates and theologians were to define the articles of faith to solve the problem of "intellectual anarchy and moral corruption." Despite positive proposals, the Protestants were not included. Twenty-five sessions were held between 1545 and 1563.

In terms of art, the Council of Trent was extremely important. It was decided that no images "inspired by incorrect dogma and liable to lead the innocent astray" should be placed in churches. The aim was to "avoid all impurity and to avoid attributing the saints with provocative traits." Nudity was also forbidden in religious paintings — but authorized for mythological themes, thus creating two distinct genres: sacred and profane art. Religious subjects were to be treated "seriously" and without unnecessary details. Veronese was criticized for his interpretation of **The Last Supper**. The painting was subsequently renamed **The Feast in the**

House of Levi. Figures were to be depicted with nobility and not in trivial poses like those found in Caravaggio's works.

Errors in depicting the Scriptures were also to be avoided, for example, the Virgin could not be shown swooning at the foot of the cross. The texts say *"stabat mater,"* i.e. his mother was standing.

The rigor that replaced the rich imagination of Renaissance painting with conventional images, must be placed in its correct context. The Catholic Church was faced with criticism by Protestants who cited several works as proof of the Catholic distortion. The Church did not censor earlier works, respecting them in the name of tradition. Contemporary artists generally acquiesced; controversy over scriptural dogma generally surpassed them and they considered the Council to be a guideline, not an instrument of repression.

Condamnation d'Aman (La) *(The Condemnation of Haman)*

Jean-François de Troy

(O.T.) The minister Haman denounced the Jews to King Ahasuerus and organized their massacre. His hatred stemmed mainly from his rivalry with Mordecai who, as the cousin of Queen Esther, had gained an important position in the palace. Certain of his victory, he had already made preparations to have Mordecai hanged, but Ahasuerus' eyes were opened by Esther's revelations and Haman was hanged on the gallows he had prepared (see **Aman irrité..., Évanouissement d'Esther, Repas d'Esther et d'Assuérus, Triomphe de Mardochée**).

Continence de Scipion (La) *(The Continence of Scipio)*

Niccolò dell'Abate
Giambattista Pittoni
Pieter-Joseph Verhagen

(Hist.) Scipio conquered New Carthage in Spain. His soldiers brought him a beautiful young maiden they had taken captive. On learning that she was engaged to Allucius, whom he had defeated, he returned her. The girl's aged parents knelt before him offering golden vessels as ransom. After refusing the ransom, he finally accepted, but gave it to the couple as a dowry.

Convalescence de Bayard *(The Convalescence of Bayard)*

Pierre Révoil

(Hist.) Bayard (1475-1524), a French soldier known as " le chevalier sans peur et sans reproche " (the knight without fear and without reproach), was the epitome of medieval French chivalry. After numerous glorious battles, he was severely wounded at the siege of Brescia in 1512, and was nursed back to health in a house that he had protected from pillage. After his recovery, the lady of the house offered him a large sum of money, but he refused and made her share it between her two daughters, thus providing them with dowries.

Conventionnel Merlin de Thionville à l'armée du Rhin *(Merlin de Thionville and the Rhine Army)*

Nicholas-Toussaint Charlet

(Hist.) Merlin de Thionville was twenty-seven at the outbreak of the French Revolution. He aligned himself with the far left of the National Convention and dedicated himself wholeheartedly to the new ideas. It was his task to recruit and supervise the Rhine army. He spoke out against the emigrés and personally fought in Mainz against the Prussians, defending the town in a display of heroism combined with strategic skill and compassion.

Conversion de saint Paul (La) *(The Conversion of Saint Paul)*

Italian, 16th century

(N.T.) Before his conversion, Paul was known as Saul. As a youth, he witnessed the stoning of Saint Stephen (see **Martyre de saint Étienne**), when the murderers laid their garments at his feet. Saint Stephen felt compassion for this youth who had unwittingly participated in the crime and prayed for him. In later life, Saul, who came from a Jewish background, became a bitter enemy of the Christian church. While on his way to Damascus to arrest any Christians he could find, he was struck by a blinding light, fell to the ground and heard Jesus asking "Saul, Saul, why do you persecute me?" He stood up dizzy and blinded, but enlightened. A disciple in Damascus, Ananias, restored his sight and baptized him Paul. From then on his Christian zeal was unfailing and he died a martyr.

Same subject: **Conversion de saint Paul sur le chemin de Damas**, Jan Speckaert.

Corésus et Callirhoé *(Coresus and Callirrhoe)*, also known as **Grand Prêtre Corésus se sacrifiant pour sauver Callirhoé (Le)** *(The High Priest Coresus Sacrifices Himself to Save Callirrhoe)*

Jean Honoré Fragonard

(Myth.) According to Pausanias, young Callirrhoe rejected the advances of Coresus, one of Bacchus'priests. Enraged, Coresus invoked his god for revenge, and the inhabitants of the region of Calydon were struck with madness. An oracle said that sacrificing Callirrhoe would lift the curse. As she approached the altar, Coresus was stricken with remorse and sacrificed himself in her place. Callirrhoe, touched by his love, took her own life.

Cornélie, mère des Gracques *(Cornelia, Mother of the Gracchi)*

Joseph-Benoît Suvée
Giuseppe Cades

(Hist.) Cornelia was a Roman aristocrat. After the death of her husband, she refused the hand of King Ptolemy of Egypt, devoting herself instead to the education of her sons, Tiberius and Gaius. In reply to a woman who was proudly displaying her jewels, she pointed to her sons and said, "These are my jewels." Encouraged by their mother to be heroic, the Gracchi undertook radical democratic reforms and fought against Consul Opimus. In the 11th century B.C., they were killed along with 3,000 of their followers. Their mother's only comment was, "They died for a noble cause."

Cortège de Thétis *(Thetis' Procession)*   Bartolommeo di Giovanni
(Myth.) In this painting Thetis, goddess of the
sea, is accompanied by sea gods: her father,
Nereus; her sister, Amphitrite, wife of Neptune,
lord of the sea; between fifty and one hundred
Nereids, her sisters, who personify the waves;
and several other gods.

Coucher de Desdémone *(Desdemona)*   Théodore Chassériau
(Lit.) Desdemona, heroine of Shakespeare's
Othello (see **Othello et Desdémone**), was prepar-
ing to retire after having been struck by Othello.
She loved Othello and was faithful to him, but
was unaware that, manipulated by the wicked
Iago, he was jealous and prepared to kill her.
Her premonitions led her to sing the melancholy
" song of willow. "

Courage des femmes de Sparte se   Jean-Jacques Le Barbier
défendant contre les Messéniens (Le)
(The Courage of the Spartan Women)
(Hist.) Aristomenes, leader of the Messenians,
learned that several women of the Greek town of
Sparta were gathered in Laconia to celebrate the
feast of Ceres. He decided to abduct them with
his troops, but did not reckon with their bravery
(the girls of Sparta were educated as boys). After
calling Ceres to their aid, they defended themselves with knives, skewers and sacrificial
torches. They held off the soldiers and were
ready to lynch Aristomenes, but the priestess Ar-
chidamia took pity on him and saved him from
her companions.

Couronnement d'épines (Le) *(The*   Jan Jansens
Crowning with Thorns)
See **Christ couronné d'épines**.

Couronnement d'Esther (Le) *(The*
Crowning of Esther)

Le Couronnement de la Vierge, Fra Angelico.

Couronnement d'Esther par Assuérus (Le) *(Esther Crowned by Ahasuerus)*
See **Toilette d'Esther**.

Jean-François de Troy
Jacopo del Sellajo

Couronnement de la Vierge (Le) *(The Coronation of the Virgin)*
(Christ. Trad.) The *Golden Legend* says that after Mary's death and assumption (see **Mort de la Vierge** and **Assomption**), Jesus called to her saying, "Come, my wife, and receive your crown." Blessed choirs, filled with joy, accompanied her to heaven, where she sat on the throne of glory at her son's right hand.
In other paintings, she is crowned by angels and not by Christ.
For details on the predella see **Histoire de saint Dominique**.
Same subject: **Couronnement de la Vierge au milieu d'anges**, Filippino Lippi.

Fra Angelico
Bologna, 14th century
Bernardo Daddi
Giovanni Lanfranco
Master of Santa Verdiana
Peter Paul Rubens
Michael Sittow

Courtisane amoureuse (La) *(The Courtesan Who Fell in Love)*

Pierre Subleyras

(Lit.) This episode is taken from a fable by La Fontaine. The courtesan, Constance, approaches Camille. She unbuttons his clothing and removes his shoes, but does not dare to touch his skin. He understands her feelings, but tests her before accepting to be her lover and later, her husband.

Crucifix aux anges (Le) *(The Crucifix and Angels)*

Charles Le Brun

See **Crucifixion**.

Crucifixion (La) *(The Crucifixion)*

(N.T.) Jesus was condemned to be crucified (see **Christ devant Caïphe, Ecce Homo**). Crucifixion was a humiliating sentence, not applied to Romans. Jesus was taken to Calvary with two condemned thieves (see **Portement de croix**) while a crowd of curious spectators gathered around them at Calvary or Golgotha (*"the place of a skull"*). Soldiers placed the condemned on the crosses and another group shared Jesus' garments, casting lots for his tunic. His followers formed a small group, including the holy women and his disciple Saint John, thought to be John the Evangelist. Near the group is Nicodemus, who helped take Jesus down from the cross and bury him, and Joseph of Arimathea, who provided a shroud and a temporary tomb.

The two thieves were crucified on either side of Jesus. The one on the left insulted Jesus and the one on the right repented and was converted. Jesus said he was thirsty and a sponge soaked in vinegar was held up to him on a reed. He cried "My God, My God, why hast thou forsaken me?" and died. Although it was afternoon, the sky darkened and the curtain of the temple was torn in two, from top to bottom. Later, soldiers came to break the legs of the crucified to ensure that they were dead. Seeing that Jesus was already dead they did not break his legs, but one of them pierced his side with a spear, and blood and water flowed from the wound.

Cologne, 16th century
French, 14th century
Naples, 14th century
Pedro Campana also known as Pietr de Kempeneer
Niccolo da Foligno
Lorenzo Monaco
Master of the Madonna of San Pietro
Lippo Memmi
Andrea Solario
Taddeo di Bartolo

Christ en croix, Philippe de Champaigne.

Same subject: **Calvaire**, Giovanni Bellini, Karel Dujardin, Josse Lieferinxe, Master of the Death of Saint Nicholas of Münster, Master of Saint Clare, Retable of the Parlement of Paris, David Téniers the Elder, Veronese. **Calvaire avec un moine chartreux**, Jean de Beaumetz. **Calvaire avec saint Dominique**, Fra Angelico. **Calvaire avec saint Job au pied de la croix**, Francesco Francia. **Christ en croix**, French, 19th century, Pierre-Charles Chuffer, Philippe de Champaigne, Michel Dorigny, Nicholas Tournier, Simon Vouet. **Christ en croix adoré par deux donateurs**, El Greco. **Christ en croix avec la Vierge, saint Jean et le bienheureux Gilles**, Umbria, 16th century. **Christ en croix et la Madeleine**, Antoine Rivalz. **Christ en croix, la Vierge, saint Jean et sainte Madeleine**, Anthony van Dyck. **Christ sur la croix**, Pierre-Paul Prud'hon. **Crucifix aux an-**

ges, Charles Le Brun. **Élévation de la croix**, Peter Paul Rubens. **Érection de la croix**, Peter Paul Rubens.

Cuisine des anges (La) *(The Angel's Meal)*

Bartolomé Esteban Murillo

(Christ. Trad.) Saint Diego of Alcalá de Henares was a Franciscan laybrother who cooked in a monastery. One day when there was nothing to prepare because the monks had given everything to the poor, he prayed with such fervor that his body was raised two feet off the ground. Angels then descended from heaven and prepared a meal for the monks.

Curius Dentatus refusant les présents des Samnites *(Curius Dentatus refusing the Samnites' presents)*

Bernardino Luini

(Hist.) Curius Dentatus was Roman consul in 290 B.C. when he defeated the Samnites, people in central Italy. They attempted to obtain clemency by giving him gold, but he refused, saying that it was more honorable to conquer those who had gold than to possess it oneself.

Cyrus condamné à périr par l'ordre d'Astyage *(Astyages Ordering Cyrus' Death)*

Jean-Charles-Nicaise Perrin

(Leg.) In a dream, Astyages, third king of Media, saw a vine emerging from his chest with branches that spread over all of Asia. Magi predicted that his grandson would take kill him and take his kingdom. Astyages summoned his pregnant daughter to the palace and when her child was born ordered a kinsman, Harpagus, to kill the child. Harpagus was upset and did not know what to do. Finally he gave the child to a shepherd and ordered him to abandon the child in the mountains. The shepherd substituted his wife's stillborn child and raised young Cyrus. Cyrus later overthrew his grandfather and seized the throne, proving that Fate cannot be crossed.

Dante et Virgile, Eugène Delacroix.

Dalila coupant les cheveux de Samson *(Delilah Cutting Samson's Hair)*
See **Samson et Dalila**.

Master H B

Dante et Virgile, conduits par Phlégias, traversent le lac qui entoure les murailles de la ville infernale de Dité *(Dante and Virgil Crossing the Lake That Surrounds the Infernal City)*, also known as **Barque de Dante (La)** *(The Barque of Dante)*

Eugène Delacroix

(Myth., Lit.) In his epic poem the *Divine Comedy*, Dante imagines that he descends to Hell and is guided by the Latin poet Virgil. Phlegyas, who ferries them across, was condemned to eternal suffering for having burned the Temple of Apollo after discovering that Apollo had seduced his daughter Coronis.

Daphnis and Chloé *(Daphnis and Chloe)*

François Gérard

(Lit.) Daphnis and Chloe were two children in a

Greek novel attributed to Longus (2nd and 3rd centuries A.D.). They were found by shepherds — one suckling a goat and the other a ewe — and were raised together. Later they experienced confusing emotions as they did not even know the word " love." Their innocent affection led to many adventures, but the tale ends with their marriage.

David et Bethsabée *(David and Bathsheba)* — Jan Massys
See **Bethsabée au bain**.

David sacré roi par Samuel *(David Anointed by Samuel)* — Claude Gellée, called Claude Lorrain
(O.T.) The young shepherd David was tending his flocks when the prophet Samuel called him and anointed him, promising that he would succeed King Saul who was unworthy and had displeased the Lord.

David tenant la tête de Goliath *(David Carrying Goliath's Head)* — Guido Reni
(O.T.) The Hebrews were at war with the Philistines and the two armies stood facing one another. The Philistine champion was a giant of terrifying size clad in heavy bronze armor. He defied the Hebrews to find a champion to kill him. David, future king of Israel, at the time still a shepherd, went to Saul and proposed his services. Saul was amazed, but finally gave in. David refused armor and a sword, instruments which were unfamiliar to him, and set off with his sling and five stones. Through his agility he was able to avoid Goliath's furious attacks and finally killed him by striking him in the forehead with a stone. He then took Goliath's sword and cut off his head.
Same subject: **Triomphe de David**, Matteo Rosseli.

Le Débarquement de Cléopâtre à Tarse, Claude Gellée, called Claude Lorrain.

Débarquement de Cléopâtre à Tarse (Le) *(The Landing of Cleopatra at Tarsus)*

Claude Gellée, called Claude Lorrain

(Hist.) Cleopatra, queen of Egypt, was dethroned by her brother Ptolemy XIII, and reinstated by Julius Caesar who took her victorious to Rome. After Caesar's death in 44 A.D., she used her charms to seduce his successor Marc Antony. In this scene, she goes to meet him, richly adorned, in a galley with silver oars and sails of purple silk.

Same subject: **Rencontre d'Antoine et de Cléopâtre**, Sébastien Bourdon, Gérard de Lairesse.

Décapitation de saint Barthélemy (La) *(The Beheading of Saint Bartholomew)*

Pietro di Giovanni d'Ambrogio

See **Prédication de saint Barthélemy**.

Décollation de saint Jean-Baptiste *(The Beheading of Saint John the Baptist)*

Fra Angelico
Claude Audran the Younger

(N.T.) The prophet John the Baptist was beheaded in his prison cell. Salome then brought his head to her mother, Herodias (see **Banquet d'Hérode**).

Same subject: **Salomé recevant la tête de saint Jean-Baptiste**, Giuseppe Caletti, Bernardino Luini.

Décollation de saint Paul *(The Beheading of Saint Paul)*
Louis de Boullongne

(N.T.) Saint Paul was imprisoned several times during his years of preaching. He was persecuted by both the Jews and the Romans and was finally beheaded in Rome around 63 A.D. It is said that milk, not blood, flowed from his head.

Décollation de sainte Catherine *(The Beheading of Saint Catherine)*
German, 15th century

(Christ. Trad.) Catherine of Alexandria lived in the 4th century. She was converted to Christianity by a desert hermit (see **Mariage mystique de sainte Catherine**) and distinguished herself at an early age by resisting the arguments of fifty pagan philosophers and then converting them. She was persecuted by the Roman governor of Egypt, Maxentius: she was to be put on a spiked wheel, but the wheel was struck by a thunderbolt from heaven; she was whipped and then imprisoned without food, but angels fed her and tended her wounds. Finally, she was beheaded and it is said that, as with Saint Paul and other martyrs, milk, not blood, flowed from her head.
Same subject: **Décollation de sainte Catherine d'Alexandrie**, Constance, 15th century.

Dédain de Mardochée envers Aman *(Mordecai and Haman)*
Jean-François de Troy

See **Aman irrité...**

Dédicace du Temple de Salomon (La) *(The Dedication of the Temple of Solomon)*
Jean Restout

(O.T.) After Solomon's death nothing remained of his kingdom, but two of his masterpieces survived: The Wisdom of Solomon and the first Hebrew Temple at Jerusalem of which only the Wall of Lamentations remained. Construction lasted seven years and resulted in a small, but magnificently decorated temple. As it was consecrated, the Lord signaled His presence by filling it with a cloud which consumed the sacrifices that had been placed on the altar.

Défaite de l'armée espagnole près du canal de Bruges *(The Defeat of the Spanish Army near Bruges Canal)*

Adam Frans van der Meulen

(Hist.) This painting celebrates the victory of Louis XIV, in 1667, over the Spanish troops occupying Flanders. Louis XIV is giving orders to the general riding next to him, hat in hand. In the background the French troops are crossing the canal. Behind the troops, one can see a calvary charge and the town of Bruges in flames.

Défaite des Cimbres *(The Defeat of the Cimbrians)*

Alexandre Gabriel Descamps

(Hist.) The Cimbrians were a Germanic people who, having invaded Spain and Gaul, were preparing to enter Italy when they were stopped by the armies of Marius (101 B.C.).

Défi des Piérides *(The Challenge of the Pierides)*

Rosso Fiorentino

(Myth.) The Pierides were the nine daughters of Pierus who sought to compete with the Muses. They went to Helicon, the mountain sacred to the Muses, and challenged them to a singing contest. The Muses won and punished the Pierides' presumptuousness by turning them into magpies.

Déjanire enlevée par le Centaure Nessus *(Deianira Abducted by the Centaur Nessus)*

Guido Reni

See **Déjanire et le Centaure Nessus**.

Déjanire et le Centaure Nessus *(Deia-nira and the Centaur Nessus)*
(Myth.) The Centaur Nessus ferried travelers across the river Evenus. Hercules and his wife Deianira signaled to him as they arrived at the riverbank. Nessus took Deianira across first and attempted to ravish her. Hearing her calls for help, Hercules shot a poisoned arrow and killed the Centaur. As he died, Nessus advised Deia-nira to collect his blood saying that if Hercules were ever unfaithful to her, she could use his blood as a love-potion. Unsuspecting, she dipped his tunic in the poisoned blood and later, believ-ing herself abandoned by Hercules, sent him the tunic. The blood was in fact an atrocious poison which burned him to death (see **Hercule sur le bûcher**).
Same subject: **Enlèvement de Déjanire par le Centaure Nessus**, Louis Lagrenée, François Marot.

Guido Reni

Délivrance miraculeuse de l'empe-reur Maximilien *(The Miraculous Res-cue of Emperor Maximilian)*
(Hist.) Maximilian I (1459-1519) was Holy Roman emperor and German king. His history consists mainly of alliances and wars with King Louis XI of France. In 1488, during a period of war, he was lured to Bruges and taken prisoner. His fa-ther Frederick III sent an army to free him.

Tobias Verhaecht

Déluge (Le) *(The Deluge)*
(O.T.) After creating man, God perceived his wickedness and determined to destroy the hu-man race by flooding. Rains, lasting forty days and forty nights, covered the earth. The only people saved were Noah, his wife, and three sons and daughters-in-law.
Same subject: **Scène du Déluge**, Théodore Géri-cault. **Entrée des animaux dans l'Arche**, Gero-lamo Bassano, Paul de Vos.

Antonio Carracci
Nicolas Poussin
Jean-Baptiste Regnault
Alessandro Turchi

Départ de Regulus pour Carthage
(Regulus Leaving for New Carthage)
(Hist.) Regulus was a Roman statesman and general during the wars with New Carthage (3rd century B.C.). Despite his brilliant victories, he was taken prisoner by the Carthaginians and subsequently sent to Rome, on his honor, to negotiate an exchange of prisoners. He dissuaded the Senate from accepting the exchange and thus condemned himself to be returned to the Carthaginians who tortured and killed him.

Augustin Pajou

Déploration *(The Lamentation)*
See **Déploration du Christ**.

German, 16th century
Francesco di Maria

Déploration du Christ (La) *(The Lamentation of Christ)*
(Christ. Trad.) The scene known as the Lamentation of Christ follows the Descent from the Cross and precedes the Entombment (see **Descente de croix** and **Mise au tombeau**). In this scene, the followers of Christ mourn over his dead body. Present are John the Evangelist, the three Maries: Mary, mother of Jesus, with her son's body resting on her knees; Mary Magdalene; and Mary, wife of Clopas or Salome (also see **Pietà**).
Same subject: **Déploration**, German, 16th century, Francesco di Maria. **Déploration sur le corps du Christ**, Francesco Albani, Key Willem.

Lubin Baugin
Dirck Bouts
Petrus Christus
Joos van Cleve
Wolf Huber
David Kindt
David Téniers the Younger
Otto van Veen

Déploration sur le corps du Christ
(Lamentation Over Christ's Body)
See **Déploration du Christ**.

Francesco Albani

Déposition de croix (La) *(The Deposition)*
Déposition du Christ (La) *(The Deposition)*
See **Descente de croix (La)**.

After Hugo van der Goes
José de Ribera

Derniers moments de la Grande Dauphine *(The Final Moments of the Great Dauphine)*

Joseph Beaume

(Hist.) Maria Anna of Bavaria was Louis XIV's daughter-in-law, as she had married his only son Louis, the Dauphin, called Monseigneur. The births of her three children and several miscarriages left her weak and she became ill and died in 1690 in the presence of her three sons and Mme. de Maintenon. Before she died, she kissed the youngest and said "Though your birth cost me my life, I have no regrets."

Louis XIV lost his son and two of his grandsons. His remaining grandson became king of Spain, so that after his death the French crown was inherited by his great-grandson Louis XV, aged five.

Descente aux limbes *(Descent into Limbo)*

Flanders, 16th century
French, 14th century

(Christ. Trad.) Limbo is a sort of border area to Hell in which the righteous who have not been baptized wait. Jesus' descent into limbo is not mentioned in the gospels. This descent poses a theological problem: Did Jesus descend before his resurrection, i.e. as a spirit and not in the flesh? Painters have always represented Him in the flesh. He is shown freeing the righteous, particularly Adam, who died before his ministry on earth.

de

89

Descente de croix *(The Descent from the Cross)*

Sébastien Bourdon
Jean Jouvenet
Rosso Fiorentino
Eustache Le Sueur
Master of Saint Bartholemew
Jean-Baptiste Regnault
Peter Paul Rubens

(N.T.) After the crucifixion and death of Jesus, a Jew named Joseph of Arimathea, member of the Sanhedrin (Jewish legislative council) and secret disciple of Jesus, obtained permission from the Roman procurator Pontius Pilate, to bury him. He assisted the disciples and the holy women in removing Jesus from the cross. According to a tradition dating from after the gospels, Joseph of Arimathea collected Christ's blood in the chalice which was used at the Last Supper (see

Descente de croix, Jean-Baptiste Regnault.

Cène). This chalice is the Holy Grail referred to in the legends of King Arthur.

Same subject: **Déposition de croix**, Pietro da Rimini. **Déposition du Christ**, José de Ribera. **Christ déposé de la croix**, Pieter van Mol. **Christ descendu de la croix**, Jacopo da Ponte Bassano.

Descente d'Énée aux Enfers *(Aeneas Descends into the Underworld)*

Antoine Coypel

((Myth., Lit.) During a series of adventures re-

counted by post-Homeric poets, particularly
Virgil, Aeneas disembarked at Cumae in Italy.
He visited the Sibyl, a prophetess of Apollo, who
guided him through Hell. Braving obstacles and
monsters, he crossed the river in Charon's boat
and found himself with the dead. He met Dido,
who had taken her life out of love for him; and
his father Anchises, who showed him a vision of
his descendants and their future exploits.

Descente du Saint-Esprit (La) *(The
Descent of the Holy Ghost)*
See **Pentecôte**.

Charles Le Brun

Desdémone *(Desdemona)*, also known
as **Romance du saule (La)** *(The
Romance of the Willow)*
See **Coucher de Desdémone**.

Théodore Chassériau

**Destruction de Jérusalem par les Ro-
mains (La)** *(Jerusalem Destroyed by the
Romans)*
(Hist.) Following the death of Herod Antipas
(during whose reign Jesus was crucified), Jerusalem revolted against Roman rule and was destroyed by the legions of Titus in 70 A.D. This
date marked the beginning of the Jews' dis-
persal. This painting depicts a particularly
tragic episode: on the advice of false prophets, a
large number of men, women and children took
refuge in the Temple of Jerusalem, believing
they would be saved, only to be massacred by
the Romans.

François-Joseph Heim

**Destruction de Troie (La) and Juge-
ment de Pâris (Le)** *(The Destruction of
Troy and The Judgment of Paris)*
(Myth., Lit.) The *Iliad* does not recount the entire
story of the Trojan War, merely Achilles' anger,
which led to the death of Hector. The Trojan
cycle was continued by Greek tragedians and la-

Mathis Gerung

ter by Virgil. After ten years of siege, the Greeks
devised a plan to enter the city. They built a huge
wooden horse, in which they hid several
soldiers, and left it outside the gates of the city.
Believing it to be a gift, the Trojans took the
horse into the city; the Trojan men were subsequently massacred and the women and children
taken hostage — all except for Astyanax,
Hector's son, who was thrown from the walls by
Ulysses. The city was then burned. Here the
Judgment of Paris (see **Jugement de Pâris**), a pre-
lude to the war, is associated with the destruction of the city.

Deux carrosses (Les) *(Two Carriages)*   Claude Gillot
(Lit.) This painting was inspired by a satire relat-
ing the story of two ladies whose carriages met
head on in a street that was too narrow for them
both to pass. Neither of the two women would
have her carriage retreat and they stayed there
until the commissioner came and had both carriages reverse at the same time.

Dévouement de Monseigneur de Bel-   Nicolas-André Monsiau
sunce pendant la peste de Marseille
(Le) *(The Devotion of Monseigneur de*
Belsunce During the Plague of Marseille)
(Hist.) A terrible plague ravaged Marseille from
1720 to 1721. At the height of the plague, Monseigneur de Belsunce, bishop of the town,
traveled the streets giving spiritual and material
aid to the needy. He risked his own life and encouraged the clergy and magistrates to support
his efforts.

Diane à la chasse *(Diana Hunting)*   French (?), 17th century
See **Diane chasseresse**.

Diane au bain *(Diana Bathing)*   Jean-Antoine Watteau
(Myth.) The usual traits of Diana, athletic and
ferocious, are subdued in this painting. In the

legends, Diana, when bathing or resting, is almost always accompanied by the nymphs or sometimes the satyrs, whom she considered harmless.

Diane chasseresse *(Diana the Huntress* or *Diana Goddess of the Hunt)*
(Myth.) Diana was Apollo's twin sister. He personified the sun, while she was associated with the moon which, like her, moved through the forest. She chose to remain a virgin and inhabit the forests where she hunted with the nymphs. She used her arrows to bring about sudden deaths, particularly those of women during childbirth. Mortals, like Acteon, who surprised her while she was resting or bathing were cruelly punished (see **Diane et Actéon**).
Same subject: **Chasse de Diane**, Luca Giordano.

School of Fontainebleau, 16th century
Bartolommeo Passaroti

Diane découvrant la grossesse de Callisto *(Diana Discovering Callisto's Pregnancy)*
See **Jupiter, sous les traits de Diane, et Callisto**.

Hendrick de Clerck
Paul Bril

Diane et Actéon *(Diana and Acteon)*
(Myth.) One day while Acteon was hunting with his companions, he suggested that they stop hunting and rest until the next day. He moved away from his companions and arrived in a clearing where Diana, goddess of the hunt, was bathing. The nymphs had removed her tunic and sandals and tied up her hair. They were pouring water over her naked body, but when they caught sight of Acteon, they moved around Diana, attempting to hide her. This proved to be impossible as goddesses are larger than other women. Having laid down her bow and arrows, Diana defended herself by throwing water on Acteon and transforming him into a stag. He was then chased and mortally wounded by his own dogs.
Same subject: **Actéon métamorphosé en cerf**, Francesco Albani.

Flanders, 16th century
Giuseppe Cesari
School of Fontainebleau, 16th century

Diane et ses nymphes au bain surprises par Actéon, Jacques-Antoine Vallin.

Diane surprise par Actéon, French, 17th century.

Diane et Endymion, detail, Jean-Baptiste Vanloo.

Diane et Endymion *(Diana and Endymion)*

(Myth.) (See **Sommeil d'Endymion**.) The painter substituted one goddess for another, without altering the legend. This was possible because the Roman goddess Diana was associated with the Greek goddess Artemis, but distinct from Selene, goddess of the moon, who figures in the story of Endymion. There were, however, cults worshiping Diana as the goddess of the moon, (who also roams the forests and the mountains) as there were those worshiping Apollo as god of the sun.

Jean-Bruno Gassies
Giovanni Antoni Pellegrini
Jean-Baptiste Vanloo

Diane et ses nymphes au bain surprises par Actéon. Effet de soleil couchant *(Diana and Her Nymphs Surprised by Acteon)*
See **Diane et Actéon**.

Jacques-Antoine Vallin

Diane sortant du bain *(Diana Leaving the Bath)*
(Myth.) The bath is not seen in the painting, but the river is doubtless intended to suggest it. Diana is obviously resting after the hunt as the catch hangs from her bow. When Diana is depicted bathing, the scenes are generally of her being surprised (see **Diane et Actéon**), but she may also be the one who surprises (see **Jupiter, sous les traits de Diane, et Callisto**).

François Boucher

Diane surprise par Actéon *(Diana Surprised by Acteon)*
See **Diane et Actéon**.

French, 17th century

Dicé offrant un banquet à Francus en présence de Hyanthe et de Climène *(Dice and Francus)*
See **Hyanthe et Climène à leur toilette**.

Toussaint Dubreuil and his studio

Didon. Énée racontant à Didon les malheurs de Troie *(Dido and Aeneas)*
(Myth., Lit.) After fleeing the burning city of Troy (see **Énée dans l'embrasement de Troie...**) and experiencing many trials, Aeneas tried to land on the coast of Italy, but a storm tossed him onto the African coast. There he climbed to the temple, leaving his companions on the shore, and met Dido, queen of Carthage, whose mercy he implored. Dido welcomed him and at this moment, the goddess Venus made her son, Aeneas, appear breathtakingly beautiful and steal Dido's heart. That evening Dido invited Aeneas and his son Ascanius to dine with her, and listened with great emotion to Aeneas'tale of the fall of Troy.

Pierre-Narcisse Guérin

Didon. Énée racontant à Didon les malheurs de Troie, Pierre-Narcisse Guérin.

Diogène brisant son écuelle
(Diogenes Breaking His Drinking Cup)
See **Diogène jetant son écuelle**.

Étienne Jeaurat

Diogène cherchant un homme
(Diogenes Looking for an Honest Man)
(Hist.) Diogenes was a Greek philosopher in the 4th century B.C., a contemporary of Plato and Alexander the Great, famous for advocating an austere lifestyle (he lived in a tub) and for breaking with conventional thinking. One day at noon, his contemporaries saw him carrying a lighted lantern. Seeing their surprised faces, he told them that he was looking for an honest man.

After Peter Paul Rubens

Diogène jetant son écuelle *(Diogenes Discarding His Drinking Cup)*
(Hist., Leg.) The philosopher Diogenes' (see **Diogène cherchant un homme**) only possession was a drinking cup, which he was about to use when he caught sight of a child drinking from his cupped hands. He immediately discarded the unnecessary object.
Same subject: **Diogène brisant son écuelle**, Étienne Jeaurat.

Nicolas Poussin

Dispute de Minerve et de Neptune Noël Hallé
(The Dispute Between Minerva and Neptune)
(Myth.) Minerva and Neptune were competing for the privilege of naming the future city of Athens. Each offered a gift: Neptune the horse and Minerva the olive tree. She won the contest and the city was named after her (Greek name: Athena).

Dispute de Trissotin et de Vadius Henri-Hippolyte Poterlet
(The Dispute Between Trissotin and Vadius)
(Lit.) This scene was taken from Molière's comedy *The Learned Women*. The bourgeois Chrysale was unpretentious, but some of the women in his family mistakenly prided themselves on their intelligence and culture.
They invited to their home a poet, Trissotin, and a pseudo-intellectual, Vadius, who charmed them, despite their priggishness. However, the guests soon revealed their true nature by becoming involved in a ridiculous dispute.

Doge de Venise sur le Bucentaure (Le) *(The Doge in the Bucentaur at San Nicolo di Lido on Ascension Day)* Francesco Guardi
(Hist.) The series of twelve views of Venice painted by Guardi in the 18th century depicts the celebrations in the city for the election of the doge Alviso IV Mocenigo in 1763. Formerly a hereditary position, in the 18th century the doge was elected by a council of eleven aristocrats (later the Council of Ten). The fact that he was merely a figurehead in no way detracted from the pomp of the ceremonies.

Don Pedro de Tolède, ambassadeur de Philippe II, baisant l'épée de Henri IV, also known as **Épée d'Henri IV (L')** *(The Sword of Henry IV)* Jean Auguste Ingres
(Hist.) Philip II of Spain, who was authoritarian

and fanatical, could have become the Christian king of Europe. He attacked France several times, taking advantage of its division, but his plans were thwarted by the conversion of Henry IV to Catholicism and his ascension to the throne in France, which resulted in French unity. Defeated, Philip was forced to send his ambassador to the king of France.

Don Quichotte attaché à une fenêtre par la malice de Maritorne *(Don Quixote Hanging from a Window)*

Studio of Antoine Coypel

(Lit.) In his obsession with chivalry Cervantes'famous hero, Don Quixote, mistook inns for castles, and servants for princesses whom he then proposed to free from their enemies. In Chapter XLIII, Don Quixote kept watch outside an inn which he thought was a fortress. The servant Maritornes decided to play a trick on him. She stood in the window and by her "chivalrous" flattery convinced Don Quixote to stand on his horse and hold out his hand to her. She then put a rope around his wrist and left him hanging from the window until he was rescued the next morning.

Don Quichotte guéri de sa folie par la Sagesse *(Don Quixote Cured of His Folly by Wisdom)*

Studio of Antoine Coypel

(Lit.) Don Quixote's imagination was fired by his reading of chivalrous romances and as a result, he wanted to set an example of love, honor and justice in a world that no longer understood these ideals. His obsession led him into dangerous and often ridiculous situations, but he always remained noble. On his deathbed, when Don Quixote realized that he was suffering from illusions and returned to reason, those around him tried to stop him, suggesting that we all need to live for ideals, without which existence becomes dull.

Douleur d'Andromaque (La) *(Andromache Laments)*

(Myth., Lit.) When Achilles single-handedly killed Hector, the eldest son of King Priam and leader of the Trojan army, he eliminated the main defender of Troy, but he also intended to avenge the death of his friend Patroclus by profaning Hector's body (see **Achille traînant le corps d'Hector devant les murs de Troie**). When Achilles finally returned the body to Hector's family, Andromache led the mourning. She grieved the loss of her beloved husband and also envisaged the plight in store for Troy without the incomparable warrior whose courage and intelligence had ensured the life and liberty of the inhabitants.

Douze scènes de la vie de la Vierge *(Twelve Scenes from the Life of the Virgin)*

Master of the Life of the Virgin

See explanations given under the title of each painting for more information. The group includes the following scenes:

— **Annonce à Zacharie** *(Announcement to Zacharias)* (see **Naissance de saint Jean-Baptiste**) ;

— **Naissance de la Vierge** *(The Birth of the Virgin)* ;

— **Présentation de la Vierge au Temple** *(The Presentation of the Virgin in the Temple)* (2 scenes) ;

— **Mariage de la Vierge** *(The Marriage of the Virgin)* (2 scenes) ;

— **Visitation** *(The Visitation)* ;

— **Nativité** *(The Nativity)* ;

— **Présentation de Jésus au Temple** *(The Presentation in the Temple)* ;

— **Circoncision** *(The Circumcision)* ;

— **Fuite en Egypte** *(The Flight into Egypt)* ;

— **Jésus parmi les docteurs** *(Jesus Among the Doctors)*.

Eberhardt, comte de Wurtemberg, dit le Larmoyeur, pleurant la mort de son fils *(Eberhard, Count of Württemberg, Mourning the Death of His Son)*

(Hist., Lit.) Eberhard II (1344-1392) established his reign in Württemberg at the expense of the neighboring towns. When they sided against him, he was forced to fight them. The legend of Eberhard, told in a ballad by Schiller (*Graf Eberhard der Greiner von Württemberg*), is part of German folklore. Ulrich led his father's troops in the battle of Reutlingen. The enemy attacked from behind and Ulrich was both defeated and injured. He returned home and was rejected by his father who cut the tablecloth in two to symbolize his rejection. Ulrich then went to battle hoping to regain his honor. Württemberg won the battle, but the soldiers brought Ulrich's body to his father who cried alone in his tent.

Ary Scheffer

Ecce Homo

(N.T.) Jesus was condemned to death by the Sanhedrin, the Jewish legislative council, and taken before the Roman procurator, Pontius Pilate, for sentencing. Pilate questioned Jesus and could not find him guilty, but was swayed by the determined resolution of the crowd and Jesus'refusal to defend himself. Before delivering Jesus, he had him whipped by the soldiers who adorned him with a purple (or scarlet) cloak and a crown of thorns, symbols of derision. In the Gospel according to John, Jesus was thus presented to the crowd by Pontius Pilate who said, *Ecce homo*, or "Behold the man."

Same subject: **Pilate présentant le Christ à la foule des Juifs**, Giovanni Battista Tiepolo.

Montagna
Guido Reni
Giovanni Battista Tiepolo
Studio of Titian

Écho et Narcisse *(Echo and Narcissus)*

(Myth.) The young nymph Echo fell in love with the handsome Narcissus. Juno had taken away her power of speech and she could only repeat the last words she heard. When she attempted to declare her love by repeating his words, Nar-

Nicolas Poussin

cissus spurned her. As punishment for having made so many young women unhappy, Narcissus was made to fall in love with his own reflexion. He gazed at himself in a pool and pined away. As he died he said "Farewell." Echo, who was nearby, could only repeat his final words (see **Narcisse contemplant son reflet dans l'eau**).

École d'Apelle (L') *(Apelles in His Studio)*

Jean Broc

(Hist.) In this painting we see the studio where the Greek painter Apelles (4th century B.C.) taught his pupils. There is a famous story about his portrait of Ptolemy I with ass's ears like those of King Midas. Apelles eloquently defended the painting which caused him difficulties with the prince.

Écho et Narcisse, Nicolas Poussin.

Édouard V, roi mineur d'Angleterre, et Richard, duc d'York, son frère puîné *(Edward V, King of England and his younger brother Richard, Duke of York)*

Paul Delaroche

See **Enfants d'Édouard**.

Éducation d'Achille par le Centaure Chiron *(The Education of Achilles by the Centaur Chiron)*
Jean-Baptiste Regnault

(Myth.) Achilles, hero of the *Iliad*, was the son of the goddess Thetis and Peleus. The legends vary as to Achilles' education: one says that he was educated in his home by the Centaur Chiron, whereas another version tells that his mother quarreled with Peleus and abandoned Achilles who was then entrusted to the Centaur. Chiron taught him to use a bow and to heal wounds, and fed him on lion marrow to make him brave and strong.

Éducation de la Vierge (L') *(The Education of the Virgin)*
Giovanni Battista Tiepolo
After Georges de La Tour

(Christ. Trad.) Mary is depicted learning to read with her mother Saint Anne. As she gave birth late in life, Saint Anne could not have been as young as she appears here; the painting was therefore thought to represent the education of Jesus. This was, however, a much rarer theme. Apocryphal texts emphasize the studious nature of young Mary reading the Scriptures. She may also be depicted sewing.

Élévation de la croix (L') *(The Elevation of the Cross)*
Peter Paul Rubens

See **Crucifixion.**

Éliézer et Rébecca *(Eliezer and Rebecca)*
Antoine Coypel
Nicolas Poussin

(O.T.) Abraham wanted to find a wife for Isaac, his son by Sarah, and sent his servant, Eliezer, to his kinsmen in Mesopotamia bearing gifts. Stopping at a well, Eliezer prayed to God for assistance and decided that the woman who drew water for himself and his camels would become Isaac's wife. When he discovered that the woman was Abraham's niece, Rebecca, he gave her a gold ring and two bracelets. She took him to her home and then, with her family's blessing, left with him to marry Isaac.

Same subject: **Rébecca recevant d'Éliézer les présents d'Abraham**, François Boucher. **Rébecca au puits.** Gian Domenico Tiepolo.

Embarquement de Théagène et Chariclée (The Embarkation of Theagenes and Charicleia)

Charles Poerson

(Lit.) Chariclea, the heroine of the Greek novel *Aethiopica* (*Ethiopian Tales*) by Heliodorus of Emesa (4th or 3rd century B.C.) is the daughter of the queen of Ethiopia, but she has white skin. He mother, who is afraid of being accused of adultery, exiles her. The daughter becomes a priestess of Apollo at Delphi and secretly becomes engaged to the young Thessalian Theagenes whom she follows on his ship. The two lovers are separated and finally reunited after a series of incredible adventures.

Embarquement pour Cythère (L') (The Embarkation for Cythera)

Jean-Antoine Watteau

See **Pèlerinage à l'île de Cythère.**

Empereur Héraclius en chemise et pieds nus rapporte la croix à Jérusalem (L') (The Emperor Heraclius Carries the Cross to Jerusalem)

Michele di Matteo Lambertini

(Christ. Trad.) Byzantine emperor Heraclius (575-641) defied King Chosroes II of Persia, and returned to Jerusalem with the wood of the true cross, found by Saint Helena. On his way he met an angel who told him to humble himself, hence his modest attire. Although he was not canonized, Heraclius is often considered as a saint.

Empereur Sévère reproche à Caracalla son fils d'avoir voulu l'assassiner (L') (Emperor Severus Reproaching His Son for Wanting to Assassinate Him)

Jean-Baptiste Greuze

(Hist.) Roman emperor Septimius Severus

granted both his sons the title of Augustus and shared his power with them. One of them, Caracalla, a madman (188-217), murdered his brother, saying that he had been threatened by him. Severus was probably justified in fearing for his life.

Empereur Théodose recevant son pardon de saint Ambroise, archevêque de Milan (L') *(Emperor Theodosius Being Pardoned by Saint Ambrose, Bishop of Milan)*

Pierre Subleyras

(Christ. Trad.) Saint Ambrose required public penance of Theodosius, who had been excommunicated for ordering a monstrously savage massacre at Thessalonica. Here the emperor is coming to be pardoned before fighting a tyrant whom he miraculously conquered.

Endymion. Effet de lune *(Endymion. Effect of the Moon)*

Anne-Louis Girodet

See **Sommeil d'Endymion.**

Énée, dans l'embrasement de Troie, voulant retourner au combat, est arrêté par sa femme Créüse *(Aeneas Held Back by His Wife Creusa)*

Joseph-Benoît Suvée

(Lit.) In the *Aeneid* by Virgil, Aeneas described this scene as he told Dido of the fall of Troy. The city was in flames and the image of Hector appeared to Aeneas, encouraging him to hurry on his way. Aeneas' father, Anchises, was reluctant to leave the city, so Aeneas took up arms and prepared to return to the fighting. His wife Creusa begged him not to go. At this moment, Jupiter sent a sign in the form of lightning and Anchises resigned himself to leaving with Aeneas, Creusa and the couple's young child, Ascanius. Aeneas carried his aged father on his back.

Énée, débarqué à Carthage, se pré-sente devant Didon *(Aeneas Presents Himself to Dido)* — Louis Galloche
See **Didon. Énée racontant à Didon les malheurs de Troie.**

Énée et Anchise *(Aeneas and Anchises)* — Lionello Spada
(Lit.) Aeneas fled Troy as it burned, with his wife Creusa (in certain texts she is said to be absent, transformed into a goddess by the gods), his young son Ascanius and his aged father Anchises, whom he carried on his back. Thus depicted, Aeneas personifies filial piety (also see **Énée dans l'embrasement de Troie, voulant...**)
Same subject: **Énée portant Anchise**, Carle van Loo.

Énée et ses compagnons combattant les Harpies *(Aeneas and His Compan-ions Fighting the Harpies)* — François Perrier
(Lit.) Aeneas fled Troy as it burned and sailed toward Italy. He suffered many misfortunes on his journey, including an encounter with the Harpies. He was attacked and driven away by these winged monsters who had the body of a woman, vulture's wings and hooked claws.

Énée portant Anchise *(Aeneas Car-rying Anchises)* — Carle van Loo
See **Énée et Anchise.**

Enfance de Bacchus (L') *(The Educa-tion of Bacchus)*, also known as **Nourri-ture de Bacchus (La)** *(The Nurture of Bacchus)* or **Petite Bacchanale (La)** — Nicolas Poussin
(Myth.) Bacchus, god of the vine, was the son of Jupiter and the princess Semele. Jupiter's wife Juno, jealous of Semele, suggested that the young woman ask him to appear before her in all his splendor. Jupiter attempted in vain to dis-

suade her from asking this favor. She insisted and, having sworn by the river Styx, he was compelled to grant the request. When he appeared surrounded by thunder and lighting, she was overcome and died at the sight. Jupiter took the child she was expecting (she was six months pregnant) and hid him in his thigh. Three months later Bacchus was born. To protect him from Juno's wrath, Jupiter entrusted him to nymphs in Nysa and, as further protection, turned him into a kid goat.

Enfant prodigue (L') *(The Prodigal Son)*

Frans Francken the Younger

See **Parabole de l'enfant prodigue**.

Enfants d'Édouard (Les) *(King Edward's Sons)*

Paul Delaroche

(Hist., Lit.) King Richard III of England was the younger brother of Edward IV. He set about eliminating those who stood between him and the throne. His most unpopular crime was the murder of his brother's children. He had the children imprisoned in the Tower of London and then killed (1483).

Les Enfants d'Édouard,
Paul Delaroche.

L'Enlèvement d'Hélène,
Guido Reni.

Enlèvement de Déjanire par le Centaure Nessus *(Deianira Abducted by the Centaur Nessus)*
See **Déjanire et le Centaure Nessus**.

Louis Lagrenée
François Marot

Enlèvement d'Europe (L') *(The Rape of Europa)*
(Myth.) The young princess Europa was playing on the beach with her companions when an amazingly white bull with horns shaped like crescent moons lay down at her feet. The bull was in fact Jupiter, transformed to seduce her. The unsuspecting Europa sat on the back of the animal, which carried her off despite her cries. The bull rushed to the island of Crete where Jupiter resumed his natural form and ravished her under the plane trees. In gratitude he promised that these trees could keep their leaves all year round.

François Boucher
Liberale da Verona

Enlèvement d'Hélène (L') *(The Abduction of Helen* or **The Rape of Helen)**
(Myth.) Helen, the most beautiful woman in the world, was married to King Menelaus of Sparta.

Guido Reni
Jean Tassel

However, Venus had promised her to the shepherd Paris (see **Jugement de Pâris**). Paris went to Sparta where he was received by Menelaus, but when left alone for a moment with Helen, he abducted her along with treasures and slaves. Homer and most of the post-Homeric poets said that she consented. This abduction is said to have caused the Trojan War.

Enlèvement de Proserpine *(The Rape of Proserpine)*

Niccolò dell'Abate

(Myth.) Proserpine, the daughter of Jupiter and the goddess of agriculture, Ceres, was gathering flowers with nymphs when her uncle Pluto abducted her. He was apparently aided by Jupiter as the two rogues chose a moment when Ceres was absent. Ceres heard her daughter's cry from afar and rushed to find her daughter. She searched the whole world, but was unable to find her. She then left the heavens and, disguised as an old woman, offered her services as nurse. Because the corn goddess abandoned her functions, there was no corn on earth. Jupiter then ordered Pluto to return Proserpine, but this was not possible as, having eaten a pomegranate, she was condemned to remain in the

Enlèvement de Proserpine, Niccolò dell' Abate.

underworld. A compromise was found: Proserpine would live six months in the underworld and six months with her mother. She would appear at the beginning of spring and descend to the underworld at the end of the summer, thus leaving the land barren.

Same subject: **Proserpine cueillant des fleurs avec ses compagnes dans la plaine d'Enna**, Nicolaas Verkolje.

Enlèvement de Psyché (L') *(The Abduction of Psyche)*

Pierre-Paul Prud'hon

See **Amour et Psyché (L')**.

Enlèvement de Rébecca *(The Abduction of Rebecca)*, also known as **Rébecca enlevée par le templier** *(Rebecca Abducted by the Templar)*

Eugène Delacroix

(Lit.) Rebecca is a character in Walter Scott's novel *Ivanhoe*. The novel takes place in England during the reign of Richard the Lion-Hearted (12th century). The Saxons, who have the author's sympathy, were constantly fighting the Normans. Rebecca, a young Jewish woman who was a friend of the Saxons, refused the advances of a Norman knight, the Templar Bois-Guilbert. He discovered her tending Ivanhoe's wounds in the castle of Front-de-Boeuf which he had just set on fire. Paying no heed to her cries, Bois-Guilbert abducted her and later delivered her to the Inquisition. She was condemned to be burned at the stake, but Ivanhoe came to her rescue.

Enlèvement des Sabines (L') *(The Rape of the Sabine Women)*

Nicolas Poussin

(Hist.) The Romans needed women to ensure the growth of their population and asked their neighbors for women, but were refused and mocked. The Romans then organized a festival and invited their neighbors, the Sabines. At a given signal, the Roman soldiers abducted the

Sabine women. This incident led to wars between the two peoples (see **Les Sabines arrêtant le combat entre les Romains et les Sabins**).

Ensevelissement du Christ (L') *(The Burial of Christ)*
See **Mise au tombeau**.

Quentin Varin

Entrée d'Alexandre dans Babylone or **Triomphe d'Alexandre (Le)** *(Alexander Entering Babylon* or *The Triumph of Alexander)*
(Hist.) After conquering Greece, Syria and Phoenicia, Alexander the Great went on to Mesopotamia to conquer Babylon. As king of Asia, he used it as his capital.

Charles Le Brun

Entrée de la duchesse d'Orléans dans le jardin des Tuileries le 4 juin 1837 *(The Duchess of Orléans Entering the Tuileries Gardens on June 4, 1837)*
(Hist.) Princess Helen of Mecklenburg married Louis Philippe's son, the duke of Orléans. The ceremony took place on May 30, 1837. The crown prince was initially reproached for having married a Protestant, but the Duchess soon won over the population with her charm.

Eugène Lami

Entrée des animaux dans l'Arche *(The Animals Entering the Ark)*
Entrée des animaux dans l'Arche de Noé *(The Animals Entering Noah's Ark)*
(O.T.) When God flooded the earth, he decided to save Noah along with his wife, his three sons and their wives. He commanded Noah to build an ark and enter it with his family and a male and female of every species of bird and beast.
Also see **Déluge**.

Gerolamo Bassano?
Paul de Vos

Entrée des croisés à Constantinople
(Entry of the Crusaders into Constanti-nople on April 12, 1204.)
See **Prise de Constantinople par les croisés**.

Eugène Delacroix

Entrée du Christ à Jérusalem (L')
(Christ Entering Jerusalem)
(N.T.) Jesus entered Jerusalem to fulfill God's will. He sent two of his disciples before him, saying that they would find an ass ticd and a colt with her which they should bring to him. "If any one says anything to you, you shall say, 'The Lord has need of them.'" The disciples brought him the animals and laid their clothing on the ass's back as a saddle. Jesus then entered Jeru-salem on the back of the animal and was received triumphantly. The crowd laid garments and palm branches on the road and shouted, "Blessed is he who comes in the name of the Lord." He was received less favorably by the Jewish leaders.

Bernard-Joseph Wampe

Épée de Henri IV (L') *(The Sword of Henry IV)*
See **Don Pedro de Tolède, ambassadeur de Phi-lippe II, baisant l'épée de Henri IV**.

Jean Auguste Ingres

Épisode de l'affranchissement des communes sous Louis le Gros *(The Liberation of the Communes under Louis the Fat)*
(Hist.) This painting is a tribute to the French king, Louis VI "the Fat" (1081-1137) who liber-ated the communes. In fact, he did so to reduce the power of the barons. The liberation of the communes resulted in insurrections against tyrannical nobles.

Clément Boulanger

Épisode de la retraite de Russie (1812)
(Retreat From Russia, 1812)
(Hist.) During the Franco-Russian conflict,

Denis-Auguste-Marie Raffet

Emperor Napoleon I left France with a powerful army of 600,000 men. He advanced to Smolensk and then entered Moscow. The Russians abandoned their towns after burning them, making it impossible for Napoleon to find supplies for his soldiers. He was finally forced to retreat, but it was too late. He was badgered by the enemy and also faced atrocious climatic conditions. Many of the men and horses died of hunger and the cold; only 40,000 soldiers returned to France.

Érection de la croix (L') *(The Raising of the Cross* or *The Elevation of the Cross)*
See **Crucifixion**.

Pierre-Paul Prud'hon

Érigone, Léon Riesener.

Érigone *(Erigone)*

Léon Riesener

(Myth.) When Bacchus descended to earth to bring the vine and wine, he was received by the Athenian Icarius and fell in love with his daughter, Erigone. In order to seduce her, he transformed himself into a bunch of grapes and she became his lover.

Bacchus offered wine to Icarius who drank it with shepherds; they became drunk and killed him.

When Erigone discovered her father's body, she hanged herself in grief. Bacchus, enraged by the murder, made young Athenian women go mad and hang themselves. The Athenians killed the shepherds and instituted a ceremony during which they suspended young women from trees. Later, the young women were replaced by small disks decorated with a portrait. In Rome, where this practice was also common, the disks were called *oscilla*.

Ermitage de Vaucouleurs (L'). **Jeanne d'Arc consultant l'ermite sur la mission qu'elle doit accomplir** *(Joan of Arc Consulting the Hermit About Her Mission)* — François-Richard Fleury

(Christ. Trad.) During the period when France was divided and occupied by the English, Joan of Arc heard "voices" urging her to fight the enemy (see **Jeanne d'Arc au sacre de Charles VII...**). The painter imagined that to confirm her mission, Joan of Arc consulted a monk from the Abbey of Vaucouleurs, a town in her native province.

Ermite (L') or **Frère Luce (Le)** *(The Hermit or Brother Luce)* — Pierre Subleyras

(Lit.) This tale by La Fontaine mocks the tricks used by a monk who convinced a widow to entrust him with her daughter. The daughter became pregnant and her mother took her away. In an attempt to smooth things over the monk predicted a magnificent future for the daughter's son, however she later gave birth to a baby girl.

Esther et Assuérus *(Esther and Ahasuerus)* — Claude Vignon

See **Salomon et la reine de Saba**.

Esther se parant pour être présentée à Assuérus *(The Toilet of Esther)*
See **Toilette d'Esther**.

Théodore Chassériau

Et in Arcadia ego
See **Bergers d'Arcadie**.

Nicolas Poussin

Été (L') *(Summer)*, also known as **Ruth et Booz** *(Ruth and Boaz)*
See **Ruth et Booz**.

Nicolas Poussin

Eurydice mordue par le serpent *(Eurydice Bitten by the Serpent)*
See **Orphée et Eurydice dans un paysage**.

Nicolas Poussin

Éva prima Pandora
(Myth., O.T.) Pandora is the mythological equivalent of Eve. She was the first mortal woman and received gifts from the gods at her birth. One gift consisted of a box (or urn) which she was told not to open. Jupiter sent her to earth where she married Epimethus, Prometheus' brother. Pandora could not resist temptation and opened the box; out flew the evils which spread over the earth. Only hope remained inside the box. This was Jupiter's punishment of the human race for Prometheus'theft of the fire from heaven.

Jean Cousin the Elder

Éva prima Pandora, Jean Cousin the Elder.

Évandre pleurant la mort de son fils Pallas *(Evander Mourning the Death of His Son Pallas)*

Antoine Coypel

(Lit.) Pallas was one of Aeneas' companions in Virgil's *Aeneid*. He was killed in battle and Aeneas had his body, escorted by a thousand warriors, carried to his father, Evander.

Évanouissement d'Armide au départ de Renaud (L') *(Renaldo and Armida)*

Antoine Coypel

See **Renaud et Armide**.

Évanouissement d'Esther (L') *(The Swooning of Esther)*

Antoine Coypel
Jean Restout
Jean-François de Troy
Veronese

(O.T.) The minister Haman, a bitter enemy of the Jews, convinced Ahasuerus that they should be massacred. To save the Jews, Esther decided to reveal to her husband that she herself was Jewish. She knew Ahasuerus loved her, but it was forbidden to enter the king's presence without being summoned. She swooned with relief at the sign that he accepted her.

Also see **Aman irrité de ce que Mardochée...**

Exposition du corps de saint Bonaventure (L') *(The Lying-in-State of Saint Bonaventure)*

Francisco de Zurbarán

(Christ. Trad.) Saint Bonaventure, bishop of Albano in the 13th century, played a prominent role in the Council of Lyons. He became ill and died during the council. In the painting he is surrounded by James I of Aragon (or King Michael VIII of the Palaeologus dynasty) — who was not present, but who is referred to in the *Golden Legend* — Pope Gregory X and the bishop of Lyons. The body of Saint Bonaventure was laid out in Lyons and caused numerous miracles. When the body was burned, the heart remained intact.

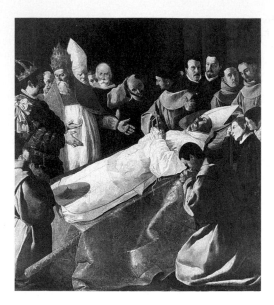

L'Exposition du corps de saint Bonaventure, Francisco de Zurbarán.

Extase du père Birelle *(The Ecstasy of Father Birelli)*

Vicente Carducho

(Christ. Trad.) Father Birelli, born in Limoges, was the twenty-fourth general of the order of Saint Bruno. He refused to be cardinal (hence the red tasseled hat abandoned on the ground) as he was a contemplative. He experienced ecstasy and levitation. In the background is an incident involving another monk, Father Molin. One night a voice from heaven informed Father Molin that the devil was trying to persuade another monk to flee the monastery. Molin rushed to convince the monk to follow his vocation.

Extérieur d'un hôpital militaire
(Exterior of a Military Hospital)
See **Français en Italie**.

Nicolas-Antoine Taunay

Famille de Darius aux pieds d'Alexandre (La) *(The Family of Darius Before Alexander)*

Francesco Trevisani

(Hist., Lit.) Darius, king of Persia, fled when he was defeated by Alexander the Great, but his wife and daughters were taken captive. They believed Darius to be dead and grieved for him. Alexander promised them that they would have the same riches and be treated with the same respect as in Persia. This noble behavior was particularly remarkable for the period. He respected their honor and allowed them to live in private apartments. Plutarch emphasizes his merit saying that Darius' wife was extremely beautiful.

Famille de Loth fuyant Sodome (La) *(Lot and His Family Fleeing Sodom)*
Famille de Loth quittant Sodome (La)
See **Fuite de Loth**.

Studio of Veronese
Peter Paul Rubens

Famille de Priam pleurant la mort d'Hector (La), Pâris jure de la venger *(Priam's Family Mourning Hector's Death, Paris Swearing to Avenge Hector's Death)*

François-Louis Dejuinne

(Myth., Lit.) After killing Hector, Achilles initially refused to return the body to his family (see **Achille traînant le corps...**). Hector's aged father, Priam, encouraged and protected by Jupiter, ventured into the Greek camp, and pleaded with Achilles for the return of the body. Achilles finally relented. Paris later avenged his brother's death by shooting an arrow into Achilles' heel.

Faucon (Le) *(The Falcon)*

Pierre Subleyras

(Lit.) In this tale by La Fontaine a young aristocrat ruined himself out of unrequited love for a married woman. All that remained of his possessions was a farm, an aged servant and a magnificent hunting falcon. The young woman's husband died and shortly after her son fell ill and asked his mother for the famous falcon. After her initial hesitation, she went to see her admirer to ask him for the falcon. The flustered young man, not knowing what to give her for dinner, had the falcon prepared and served, before she could make her request.

La Femme adultère,
Nicolas Poussin.

Femme adultère (La) *(The Woman Taken in Adultery)*
(N.T.) According to Hebraic law, adulterous women were to be stoned to death. The Pharisees, enemies of Jesus, brought a woman who had been caught in the act of adultery before him. They asked him what they should do, testing him, hoping to make him break Jewish law. But Jesus bent down, wrote in the sand and then said "Let him who is without sin among you be the first to throw a stone at her." One by one, starting with the eldest, the Pharisees turned away (Had Jesus written their sins in the sand?) The woman, surprised, remained alone with Jesus who said to her, "Go, and do not sin again."
Same subject: **Le Christ et la femme adultère**, Jacques Blanchard, Jobst Harrich, Lorenzo Lotto, Gabriel Metsu, Bonifacio de Pitati, Ippolito Scarsellino, Giovanni Domenico Tiepolo.

Christian Dietrich
Gabriel Metsu
Nicolas Poussin
Emile Signol

Femmes souliotes (Les) *(The Women of Souli)* — Ary Scheffer
(Hist.) Despite heroic resistance, the Greek town of Souli was conquered by the Turks during the War of Independence (1821). Rather than fall into the hands of the victors, the women of Souli threw themselves from a cliff along with their children.

Festin de Bacchus et d'Ariane *(The Feast of Bacchus and Ariadne)* — Daniel Vertangen
See **Ariane abandonnée**.

Festin de Balthasar (Le) *(Belshazzar's Feast)* — Nicola Bertuzzi
See **Mane, Thecel, Pharés: le festin de Balthasar**.

Festin de l'enfant prodigue (Le) *(The Feast of the Prodigal Son)* — David Téniers the Younger
See **Parabole de l'enfant prodigue**.

Fête donnée en l'honneur de la trêve de 1609 *(Allegory of the Truce of 1609 between the Archduke of Austria, Governor of the Southern Netherlands, and the States-General of the Northern Netherlands)* — Adriaen van de Venne
(Hist.) This truce lasted twelve years and resulted in the recognition of the United Provinces of the Netherlands by various European countries. It was the basis of the Holland's prosperity in the 17th century and its hegemony at sea.

Fiancée d'Abydos (La) *(The Bride of Abydos)* — Eugène Delacroix
(Lit.) In this poem by Lord Byron, Selim and Zuleika believed they were brother and sister, but Selim discovered that Giaffir, who had raised him, was his uncle and that he had mur-

dered his father. The young couple confessed their mutal love and fled the palace to await rescue by their friends. However, instead of their friends, it was Giaffir's soldiers who disembarked. Selim kissed Zuleika for the last time and attacked the soldiers with his father's scimitar. As he turned to look for Zuleika, he was shot in the back. Zuleika died of sorrow at the same moment.

Fingal visite Cuchullain dans la caverne de Tura *(Fingal Visits Cuchulain in a Cave in Tura)*
French, 19th century

(Myth.) Fingal was the father of Ossian, a legendary Scottish hero, and Cuchulain was a mythical Irish hero. After the death of his son, Cuchulain retreated to a cave where he was visited by Fingal and his companions, who wished to comfort him.

Flagellation *(The Flagellation)*
Niccolo da Foligno
See **Flagellation du Christ**.

Flagellation de saint Georges (La) *(The Flagellation of Saint George)*
Bernardo Martorell
See **Scènes de la légende de saint Georges**.

Flagellation du Christ (La) *(The Flagellation of Christ)*
French, 14th century
Thuringian, 15th century
Giuseppe Cesari
Jaime Huguet
Niccolo da Foligno
Master of Saint Elizabeth
Master LCZ

(N.T.) The chief priests and the elders handed Jesus over to Pontius Pilate, the Roman procurator, to be condemned to death. Unconvinced of Jesus' guilt, Pilate attempted to save him, but finally submitted to the determined resolution of the prosecutors and the crowd, washing his hands in public to indicate that he was not responsible. He had Jesus whipped by the soldiers, as was the custom, before delivering him to be crucified. Jesus was tied to a column or post.

Same subject: **Christ à la colonne**, Alexandre Dupuis, Bartolomé Esteban Murillo, Simon Vouet (?).

La Flagellation du Christ, Master LCZ.

Flagellation du Christ (La) et Quatre symboles des Évangélistes (Les) (The Flagellation; The Four Symbols of the Evangelists)
(N.T.) See **Flagellation du Christ**. The four symbols of the Evangelists are: Matthew, the angel; Mark, the lion; Luke, the winged bull; John, the eagle.

Forêt hantée (La) *(The Enchanted Forest)*

Henry Singleton

(Lit.) This painting depicts a tale by Bocaccio. Nastagio degli Onesti was in love with one of the young women of the Traversare family. He spent large sums of money on her, but to no avail. One day as he was leaving the town, he saw a knight murder a woman and throw her heart to the dogs. Nasagio attempted to rescue the woman, but the knight told him not to interfere and explained why. When he was alive, he had loved this hard-hearted woman. He subsequently killed himself and was condemned to hell. The woman was overjoyed at his death, but then she too died. As punishment for her cruelty, she was condemned to reenact the scene of her death and the knight's feeding her heart to the dogs. They met every Friday at the same place.

Nastagio told the Traversare family that he no longer wished to marry their daughter, but that he wanted to hold a farewell feast. He set up tables in the place in country where the visitors witnessed the terrifying scene. When Nastagio told the story of the hard-hearted woman, his beloved was overcome with fear and agreed to marry him. She never regretted her decision for they were happy for the rest of their lives.

Forges de Vulcain (Les) *(Vulcan's Forge)*, also known as **Vulcain présentant à Vénus des armes pour Énée** *(Vulcan Presenting Venus with Arms for Aeneas)*

François Boucher

(Myth., Lit.) After many adventures, Aeneas, hero of the *Aeneid*, arrived in Latium where Fate decreed he would found the city of Rome. The Rutulians and their leader Turnus resisted. As he was preparing to fight, Aeneas' mother, Venus, went to her husband, Vulcan, the divine blacksmith, and asked him to forge arms for her son. He forged magnificent arms, including a shield on which he engraved the future of Rome and the glorious exploits of Aeneas' descendants.

Français en Italie (Les), also known as **Extérieur d'un hôpital militaire** *(The French in Italy)*

Nicolas-Antoine Taunay

(Hist.) This painting depicts an episode from Bonaparte's Italian campaign (1796-1797). Although the French were victorious, they suffered heavy losses during the war. Here we see a cart serving as a ambulance and bringing the wounded to a place that was used as a military hospital.

Francesca et Paolo *(The Ghosts of Paolo and Francesca Appear to Dante and Virgil)*

Ary Scheffer

(Hist., Lit.) Francesca da Rimini was the daughter of a lord of Ravenna (13th century). She was given in marriage to Gianciotto, a deformed dwarf. Gianciotto feared that she would reject him and sent his handsome brother, Paolo, in his place. Francesca believed him to be her future husband and fell in love with him. One day Gianciotto surprised the lovers embracing and stabbed them both. In the *Divine Comedy*, Dante and Virgil meet the lovers in Hell. They are described more as victims than sinners. Francesca describes the beginning of their love and her sad tale makes the narrator faint.

Frappement du rocher *(Moses Striking the Rock)*

Studio of Jacopo Bassano
Valerio Castello
Charles Le Brun

(O.T.) Moses and his brother Aaron were chosen by God to lead the Israelites out of Egypt, but the Exodus was difficult and the Israelites constantly complained about their guides. While camped at Rephedim and thirsty, they once again found fault with Moses. He feared they would stone him and asked for God's help. God told him to strike the rock of Horeb with his staff. When he did so, water flowed from the rock.

Frère Junipero et le pauvre *(Brother Juniper and the Beggar)*

Bartolomé Esteban Murillo

(Christ. Trad.) This painting was long thought to depict a monk being attacked by a bandit but, in fact, it shows Brother Juniper and a beggar. Brother Juniper's superior found his charity excessive and forbade him to give away his garments. When Juniper met a beggar who was suffering from the cold, he told him to remove his tunic, so that he would not disobey his superior. Here the beggar is shown undoing Brother Juniper's belt.

Fuite de Loth *(Lot's Flight)*, also known as **Famille de Loth quittant Sodome (La)** *(Lot and His Family Fleeing Sodom)*

Peter Paul Rubens

(O.T.) Abraham's nephew, Lot, lived in Sodom. He took two angels to his house and protected them from the crowd. The angels announced that God intended to destroy Sodom and Gomorrah, two evil cities. They told Lot to flee with his family before the city was destroyed. One of the angels led Lot, his wife and their two daughters (the husbands did not want to leave) out of the flaming city. They had been warned not to look behind, but Lot's wife could not resist the temptation and was turned into a pillar of salt. She is sometimes taken to represent those who joined the orders and renounced their worldly possessions, but who regret what they have left behind.

Fuite en Égypte (La) *(The Flight into Egypt)*

Rhine, 15th century
Sébastien Bourdon
Noël Hallé
Hans Memling
Louis-Étienne Watelet

(N.T.) After hearing of the miraculous birth of Jesus in Bethlehem, Herod, king of the Jews, was troubled by prophecies that this child was to be the king of Israel, and ordered all newborn males in Judea to be killed. Having been warned of this in a dream, Joseph immediately departed for Egypt with Mary and the Christ Child. They remained there until after the death of Herod four years later. (Also see **Repos de la Sainte Famille pendant la fuite en Égypte**.) Apocryphal texts and even the Koran have described this episode in detail.

Same subject: **Paysage avec la fuite en Égypte**, Domenichino.

Funérailles de l'Amour (Les) *(Cupid's Funeral)*

Attributed to the studio of Antoine Caron

(Myth., Imag.) Cupid, stretched out on a coffin without his wings, is carried to the Temple of Diana surrounded by putti, while his mother, Venus, observes the scene from the sky in her chariot drawn by doves. This painting may represent the death of Love following the demise of Diane de Poitier, mistress of Henri II, in 1566. It may also represent the period when Ronsard abandoned his *Amours* and *Odes* to write the *Discours*. In the left corner we see three classical poets and on the right the seven poets of the Pléiade.

Funérailles d'Atala (Les) *(The Burial of Atala)*

Anne-Louis Girodet

See **Atala portée au tombeau**.

Funérailles de Miltiade (Les) *(The Funeral of Miltiades)*

Pierre Peyron

(Hist.) Miltiades was one of the ten generals who led the Greek army at the Battle of Marathon (490 B.C.). He then went to war in the Cycladic islands to cut the Persians off from the Aegean Sea. He was defeated and subsequently accused of treason. After having been condemned to death, he was offered the possibility of salvation if he paid a fine of ten talents. He could not pay and was imprisoned, but died of a battle wound which became gangrenous. As he had not served his sentence, he did not have the right to a decent funeral. His son, Cimon, served the remainder of the sentence to allow his father to have a fitting funeral.

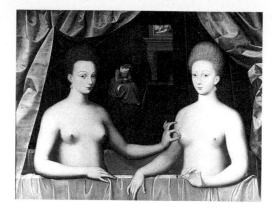

Gabrielle d'Estrées et une de ses sœurs, School of Fontainebleau.

Gabrielle d'Estrées et une de ses soeurs *(Gabrielle d'Estrées and One of Her Sisters)*

School of Fontainebleau, 16th century

(Hist.) Gabrielle d'Estrées was one of Henry II's mistresses. She had several sisters; the one depicted in the painting is either the Duchess of Villars or the wife of the Marshal of Balagny. Her sister is touching her breast to invoke the birth of an illegitimate son of the king.

Galilée devant le Saint-Office au Vatican *(Galileo Before the Holy Office in the Vatican)*

Joseph-Nicolas Fleury

(Hist.) Galileo was an astronomer, mathematician and physicist. At the beginning of the 17th century, he published his theory on the movement of planets, which confirmed Copernicus' ideas of a century earlier that the sun, and not the earth, was the center of the universe. He was condemned by theologians and forced to recant his theory after twenty days before the Inquisition.

Ganymède enlevé par Jupiter *(Ganymede Abducted by Jupiter)*

Eustache Le Sueur

(Myth.) Ganymede was a young shepherd who was so beautiful that even Jupiter fell in love with him. Jupiter transformed himself into an eagle and carried Ganymede off to Olympus where he made him his cup-bearer. As compensation, Jupiter gave Ganymede's father a pair of divine horses or, according to another version, a golden image of vines made by Vulcan.

Gascon puni (Le) *(The Punishment of The Gascon)*

Nicolas Lancret

(Lit.) This painting depicts a tale by La Fontaine in which a Gascon was punished for his bragging. He was in love with Phillis who did not reciprocate his love, but boasted of having won her affection. To teach him a lesson, she asked him to do her a favor. Disguised as a woman, he was to spend the night with her neighbor's jealous husband, thus allowing the neighbor to meet her lover. The Gascon accepted and spent the night huddled in bed, afraid that the husband might become aroused. In the morning light, he realized that he had, in fact, spent the night next to Phillis whose beauty increased his regret.

Gédéon incendiant le camp des Madianites *(Gideon Defeating the Midianites)*

Jérémie Le Pileur

(O.T.) Gideon was one of the judges of Israel (12th — 11th centuries B.C.) and was also a powerful military leader. The Israelites were constantly at war with the neighboring nomadic tribes who attacked them and destroyed the crops they had planted. The great battle between the Israelites and the Midianites is told in Judges. Thousands of Israelites volunteered to fight, but only 300 were chosen. Following God's instructions, Gideon led all the volunteers to the water and watched them drink. Those who lapped water from their cupped hands were chosen while the rest, who knelt down, were sent home. Gideon set out with the chosen men, each armed with a trumpet and a torch in any empty jar. The soldiers surrounded the enemy camp, blew their trumpets, broke the jars and brandished the torches crying, " A sword for the Lord and for Gideon." The frightened Midianites fled.

Général Bonaparte au pont d'Arcole *(Bonaparte on the Bridge at Arcola on November 17, 1796)*
Antoine-Jean Gros

(Hist.) Bonaparte was particularly illustrious during the Italian campaign at Arcola in Veneto (1796). His brilliant strategy won the battle, although his 15,000 men were outnumbered by the enemy's 40,000.

Grand prêtre Corésus se sacrifiant pour sauver Callirhoé (Le) *(The High Priest Coresus Sacrifices Himself to Save Callirrhoe)*
Jean-Honoré Fragonard

See **Corésus et Callirhoé.**

Grappe de raisin rapportée de la Terre promise (La) *(The Grapes from the Promised Land)*, also known as **Automne (L')** *(Autumn)*
Nicolas Poussin

(O.T.) God entrusted Moses with the mission of leading the Hebrews out of Egypt to the Promised Land of Canaan. The journey was long and full of trials; the Hebrews were discouraged and constantly complained. Moses sent men on ahead to the Promised Land and they returned with a bunch of grapes that was so large it took two men to carry it. However, the emissaries' glorious description did little to calm the crowd's fear in the face of adversity, nor did it prevent their revolt.

Guéhazi retournant de la maison de la Sunamite et allant à la recontre d'Élisée *(Gehazi Going To Seek Elisha)*
Rombout van Troyen

(O.T.) Elisha, a prophet in the 9th century B.C., retreated to the desert with other hermits and performed many miracles, often to help the poor. Whenever he visited the town of Shunem, a wealthy woman offered him food and lodging. He wanted to repay her hospitality and was told that her only desire was to have a son. Unfortunately her husband was old. Elisha told her that she would have a son and she gave birth the following year. One day her son was taken ill and died in her lap. The mother went to find Elisha, who sent his servant Gehazi on ahead with his staff. Gehazi returned saying that he had been unable to revive the child. Elisha went to the house and lay on the child "putting his mouth upon his mouth, his eyes upon his eyes, and his hands upon his hands." The child sneezed seven times and opened his eyes.

Guérison de saint Bonaventure enfant par saint François *(Saint Bona-venture Healed by Saint Francis)*
See **Saint Bonaventure enfant guéri par saint François**.

Francisco de Herrera

Guérison miraculeuse de don Carlos par saint Diego d'Alcala *(The Miraculous Healing of Don Carlos by Saint Diego of Alcalá)*
(Christ. Trad.) Don Carlos (1545-1568) was the crown prince of Spain, son of Philip II. This painting, which depicts his miraculous healing, has not been fully explained. We only know that the body of Saint Diego of Alcalá was removed, perfectly preserved, from the tomb and carried under a canopy to a sickroom. It was placed on the bed of Don Carlos and then removed, but the winding sheet which enshrouded the body was used to wipe the prince's face and he was healed.

Louis Licherie

Guillaume de la Marck, surnommé le Sanglier des Ardennes *(William de la Marck, known as the Wild Boar of Ardennes)*
See **Assassinat de l'évêque de Liège**.

Eugène Delacroix

Hamlet et Horatio au cimetière, Eugène Delacroix.

Hamlet et Horatio au cimetière
(Hamlet and Horatio in the Cemetery)

Eugène Delacroix

(Lit.) In Shakespeare's tragedy *Hamlet,* the hero, obsessed by thoughts of life, death and revenge, goes with Horatio to the cemetery where Ophelia's grave is being dug (see **Mort d'Ophélie**). There Hamlet discovers the skull of a court jester who had played with him when he was a child. "Alas, poor Yorick!... Where be your gibes now?"

Hamlet et Ophélie *(Hamlet and Ophelia)*

Eugène Delacroix

(Lit.) When Hamlet's father, the king, died, his uncle Claudius ascended to the throne and married his mother. Hamlet, already distraught over the death of his father and the haste with which his mother remarried, then discovered that Claudius had murdered his father. He was torn between his desire for revenge and his conscience, and also his love for his mother and horror at her behavior. He made his young and innocent fiancée, Ophelia, the victim of his suffering, thus causing fits of madness.

Héliodore chassé du Temple *(Heliodorus Driven Out of the Temple)*

Francesco Solimena

(O.T.) Heliodorus, a minister of King Seleucus of Syria (2nd century B.C.), was sent with the army to recover great sums of money, which the king had been told were in the treasury of the Temple of Jerusalem. The High Priest Onias intervened in vain and Heliodorus was about to accomplish his deed when a knight in golden armor appeared and struck him down. Two angels dealt him such strong blows that he was on the brink of death, but Onias, fearing reprisals from the king, prayed for him and saved him. The angels ordered Heliodorus to express gratitude to both Onias and the Lord. Heliodorus made a sacrifice on the altar and then left with his soldiers.

Henri III à son lit de mort *(Henry III On His Deathbed)*

Joseph Beaume

(Hist.) The reign of Henry III of France, who became king after the death of his brother Charles IX in 1574, was troubled by conflicts between three groups: the king's followers; the Catholic League led by Henry, 3rd duc de Guise, whose aim was to suppress Protestantism; and a force of Protestants and moderate Catholics led by Henry of Navarre. Having been expelled from Paris, Henry III was preparing to retake the capital when he was murdered by Jacques Clément, a fanatical monk. He died without an heir and is depicted here on his deathbed, giving the crown to Henry of Navarre who became Henry IV of France. He had the members of the court approach and instructed them to recognize Henry of Navarre as their king. Some knelt before him while others refused to give their word.

Henri IV faisant entrer des vivres dans Paris *(Henry IV Having Food Brought to Paris)*   François-André Vincent

(Hist.) After the assassination of Henry III, Henri de Navarre (later to become King Henry IV) was the rightful heir to the crown, but the Catholic League proclaimed the Cardinal of Bourbon king of France under the name of Charles X. Henry laid siege to Paris, but did not want the inhabitants to starve to death (see **Henri III à son lit de mort**). He was famous for his concern for the common people.

Hercule assommant Cacus *(Hercules and Cacus)*   François Le Moyne

(Myth.) As Hercules was returning from his expedition against Geryon whose cattle he had stolen, he stopped along the banks of the Tiber to rest and allow the cattle to graze. Cacus, a fire-breathing giant, stole four bulls and four cows. Hoping to throw Hercules off their trail, he dragged them backwards to his cave, but Hercules, discovering what had happened, sought out Cacus and struck him with his club.

Same subject: **Paysage avec Hercule tirant Cacus de sa caverne**, Domenichino.

Hercule combat les Centaures *(Hercules Fighting the Centaurs)*   Bon Boullongne

(Myth.) Hercules was the guest of Pholos, one of the good-natured Centaurs. Pholos possessed a jar of wine, but feared to open it lest he attract the Centaurs, as the wine belonged to all the Centaurs. Hercules encouraged him to open the wine, and lured by the smell of the wine, the Centaurs attacked Pholos' cave with rocks and pine trees. Hercules killed several of the monsters and drove the others away.

Hercule délivrant Hésione *(Hercules Delivering Hesione)*   Netherlandish, 18th century
                                                                                    Charles Le Brun

(Myth.) King Laomedon of Troy employed Neptune and Apollo to build the walls of Troy, but refused to pay them once they completed their work. As punishment, Neptune sent a sea monster which devoured the inhabitants of the city. An oracle announced that the monster would be calmed if Laomedon's daughter, Hesione, were sacrificed to it, and she was consequently tied to a rock. When Hercules passed through the city, he offered to kill the monster and asked Laomedon for horses as a reward (the Trojans were famous horse tamers). Hercules freed Hesione, but her father gave him two old nags instead of the reward they had agreed on. When Hercules discovered Laomedon's treachery he attacked Troy and captured Hesione, whom he gave to one of his friends as a wife.

Hercule délivrant Prométhée *(Hercules Delivering Prometheus)*

Nicolas Bertin

(Myth.) Prometheus formed man from clay and then stole Jupiter's fire to give him life. As punishment Jupiter had Prometheus bound to a rock in Caucasus where an eagle came and pecked at his liver. Each day his liver was regenerated and the torture repeated. After several thousand years, Hercules, who was passing through the region, killed the eagle with an arrow. Jupiter was proud of his son and his feats and finally decided to free Prometheus under one condition: he had to wear on his finger a ring made of the steel chains used to bind him and a piece of the rock to which he had been tied.

Hercule enfant étouffant deux serpents dans son berceau *(The Infant Hercules Killing Two Snakes in His Cradle)*

Hugues Taraval

(Myth.) Jupiter desired Alcmena, but she was so faithful to her husband, Amphitryon, that Jupiter appeared as her husband to seduce her. Juno was jealous of Alcmena and resolved to kill her son Hercules. When he was eight months old and lying in his cradle with his half-brother Iphicles, she sent two enormous snakes which wrapped themselves around the two infants. Iphicles screamed and Amphitryon came running, but young Hercules had already taken a snake in each hand and squeezed them both to death.

Same subject: **Hercule enfant étouffant les serpents**, Annibale Carrachi.

Hercule et Acheloüs *(Hercules and Achelous)*, also known as **Hercule luttant avec Acheloüs** *(Hercules Wrestling with Achelous)*

Guido Reni

(Myth.) Hercules wanted to marry Deianira who had been promised to him by her brother Meleager. In order to win the young woman, he wrestled with the river Achelous who was also in love with her. Achelous transformed himself into a bull, but Hercules still managed to defeat him.

Same subject: **Combat d'Hercule et d'Acheloüs**, Domenichino.

Hercule et Omphale *(Hercules and Omphale)*

French, 18th century
François Lemoyne
Peter Paul Rubens

(Myth.) Hercules suffered from fits of madness. During his first fit of madness he killed his own children, believing them to be the children of another man, and was condemned to undertake his Twelve Labors. After killing his friend Iphitus in another fit of madness, he was sold to Omphale, queen of Lydia. He gloriously accomplished all the tasks she set him and she subsequently became his mistress. They exchanged clothing, which is why she is wearing the lion's skill and carrying the club and he is draped in long robes and holding the distaff.

Hercule luttant avec Acheloüs *(Hercules Wrestling with Achelous)*

Guido Reni

See **Hercule et Acheloüs**.

Hercule et Omphale,
Peter Paul Rubens.

Hercule sur le bûcher *(Hercules on the Pyre)*

Guido Reni

(Myth.) In an attempt to regain Hercules'affection, Deianira sent him Nessus' tunic, believing it to have been soaked in a love potion (see **Déjanire et le Centaure Nessus**). When Hercules put on the tunic, the poisoned blood burned his flesh. Realizing that he would not recover and wishing to put an end to his agony, he built a pyre and laid down on it. From the midst of the flames he was carried up to heaven on a cloud.

Hercule tuant l'Hydre de Lerne *(Hercules Vanquishing the Hydra)*, also known as **Hydre de Lerne (L')** *(The Lernaean Hydra)*

Guido Reni

(Myth.) This painting depicts one of Hercules' Twelve Labors. The Lernaean hydra had been raised by Juno to test the hero. It was a serpent with seven (or nine) heads which terrorized the country. When one of the heads was cut off, two grew back in its place. Hercules vanquished the monster by cutting off its heads and cauterizing them with a burning torch; he then dipped his arrows in its blood.

Hercule tuant l'Hydre de Lerne, Guido Reni.

Herminie chez les bergers *(Erminia with the Shepherds)*, also known as **Hermine chez les bergers sous les armes de Clorinde**

Domenichino

(Lit.) This painting depicts an episode from Tasso's *Jerusalem Delivered*. Erminia was the daughter of the king of Antioch and had been well treated by the Christian knight, Trancred, while she was his prisoner. Although she should have been his enemy, she was secretly in love with him. When she learned that he was wounded, she slipped out of the Saracen camp at night wearing the armor of her warrior cousin

Clorinda. She attempted to enter the crusader's camp because she knew how to heal with plants. She was immediately followed by sentinels and fled on her horse. She lost control of the animal, which raced until it reached the Jordan river where she fell onto the riverbank exhausted. She awoke to find herself being attended by shepherds and subsequently stayed with them for a period of time, keeping their flocks.

Herminie et Valfrino secourent Tancrède blessé après le combat d'Argante *(Erminia and Vafrino Tending the Wounded Tancred)*
Pier Francesco Mola

(Lit.) This painting depicts an episode from Tasso's *Jerusalem Delivered*. Tancred was wounded as he single-handedly fought the Saracen giant Argantes. Before the duel began, he sent Vafrino, disguised, to the Saracen camp to discover the preparations for an attack against the Christians. Vafrino was recognized by Erminia, daughter of the king of Antioch, who was secretly in love with Tancred. She asked Vafrino to take her to the crusaders' camp. On the way, Erminia provided Vafrino with details of the attack. After traveling the whole night they discovered Tancred's body. Erminia's tears awoke him and she healed his wounds with plants, tore her veil and cut her hair to make bandages.

Herminie gardant ses troupeaux grave sur un arbre le nom de Tancrède *(Erminia Carving Tancred's Name in a Tree)*
Pier Francesco Mola

See **Herminie chez les bergers**.

Héro et Léandre *(Hero and Leander)*, also known as **Poète et la Sirène (Le)** *(The Poet and the Siren)*
Théodore Chassériau

(Myth.) Leander, who lived in Abydos on the shores of the Hellespont, was in love with Hero, a priestess of Apollo, who lived on the opposite bank. Every night he swam across the strait to meet his beloved who guided him by lighting a torch at the top of the tower. One stormy night, the torch went out and Leander, who was unable to find the shore, drowned. When Hero saw his body washed up on the shore, she threw herself from the tower.

Héroïsme de l'amour conjugal (L')
(The Heroism of Marital Love)

Pierre Peyron

See **Alceste se dévouant à la mort pour sauver son époux Admète**.

Hersilie séparant Romulus et Tatius
(Hersilia Separating Romulus from Tatius)

Guercino

See **Sabines arrêtant le combat**.

Histoire de David *(The History of David)*

Hans Sebald Beham

(O.T.) - **The Women Coming out of Jerusalem to Meet Saul and David**. David had just killed the giant Goliath and the Philistines had been vanquished. David entered Jerusalem with King Saul, but the women came mainly to greet David, singing hymns of praise to the accompaniment of various instruments.
— **Bathsheba at Her Bath** (see **Bethsabée au bain**).
— **The Siege of Rabbah** (see **Bethsabée au bain**).
— **The Prophet Nathan Before David**.
In the name of God, Nathan reproached David for coveting Bathsheba and sending Uriah on the dangerous military mission that resulted in his death. Nathan told the parable of a rich man and a poor young shepherd: When the rich man had to make a sacrifice, he took the shepherd's only ewe lamb and had it prepared in place of one of his own animals. David responded that the rich man should have been killed and that four lambs should be given to the poor shepherd.

Histoire d'Esther et d'Assuérus *(The Story of Esther)*

Filippino Lippi

See **Évanouissement d'Esther. Triomphe de Mardochée.**

Histoire de Psyché *(The Story of Psyche)*

Hendrick de Clerck

See **Amour et Psyché**.

Histoire de saint Dominique *(History of Saint Dominic)*

Fra Angelico

(Christ. Trad.) Saint Dominic was the founder of the Dominicans, officially named the Order of Preachers.

— **Saints Peter and Paul Appear to Saint Dominic**. The saints present him with a staff and a book, symbolizing the Gospels.

— **The Dispute of Saint Dominic and the Miracle of the Book**. Saint Dominic wrote a treaty against the heretics and gave it to one of them who gathered his friends around a fire. They put the manuscript into the flames, but it sprang out intact. They repeated their attempts three times, but in vain. The heretics wanted to keep this miracle secret, but it was revealed by a soldier who witnessed the event.

— **The Dream of Innocent III**. Saint Dominic asked Pope Innocent III for permission to found the Order of Preachers. The Pope initially refused, but then dreamed that he saw the collapsing Lateran church being held up by Saint Dominic. As a result of the dream, he granted his permission.

— **Christ Rises from the Tomb**. In Rome, Saint Dominic saw Christ above him armed with three arrows to destroy Pride, Avarice and Lust.

— **Saint Dominic Revives Napoleon Orsini**. In this painting, Saint Dominic revives Napoleon Orsini, the nephew of Cardinal Stephano di Fossanuova, who was killed when he fell from his horse.

— **The Angels Serve Food to the Monks**. One evening in the monastery of Saint Sixtus in

Rome there was not enough bread. Saint Dominic sent for bread and two young men appeared bearing bread in their robes. They served the bread and then disappeared; Saint Dominic told the monks to eat the bread, which had been sent by God.

— **The Death of Saint Dominic**. When Saint Dominic was ill in the monastery of Bologna, Christ appeared to him. Saint Dominic then called twelve monks to him and gave them his last commandments. He comforted them by saying that he would be more use to them after his death than while alive.

Hiver (L') *(Winter)*
See **Déluge**.

Nicolas Poussin

Honneurs funèbres rendus à Titien mort à Venise pendant la peste *(The Funeral of Titian)*

Alexandre Hesse

(Hist.) Titian is said to have died at the age of ninety-nine in 1576 at the height of the plague or Black Death, which claimed up to three quarters of the population of Europe. The convoy accompanying him stopped at Saint Mark's square in front of the Doges' palace.

Hyanthe et Climène à leur toilette *(The Toilet of Hyanthe and Climène)*

Toussaint Dubreuil and his studio

(Lit.) The figures are characters from Ronsard's unfinished epic *La Franciade*. Francus, son of Hector, escaped from the Greeks. A storm tossed him up on the shore of Crete where he was received by King Dicé. Dicé's two daughters, Hyanthe and Climène, both fell in love with the young hero. Climène, who was jealous of her sister, threw herself into the sea. Hyanthe, a prophetess, revealed the future to Francus by showing him a vision of all the kings of France, from Pharamond to Charlemagne.

Hyanthe et Climène à leur toilette, Toussaint Dubreuil and his studio.

Hyanthe et Climène offrant un sacrifice à Vénus *(Hyanthe and Climène Offering a Sacrifice to Venus)*
See **Hyanthe et Climène à leur toilette**.

Toussaint Dubreuil and his studio

Hydre de Lerne (L') *(The Lernaean Hydra)*
See **Hercule tuant l'Hydre de Lerne**.

Guido Reni

Immaculée Conception (L') *(The Immaculate Conception)*
(Christ. Trad.) The belief in the Immaculate Conception of the Virgin Mary was declared an article of faith by Pope Pius IX in 1854, but it was already widespread, as is clear in the iconography of the Virgin. Mary was said to have been conceived without the Original Sin which has tainted all men since Adam and Eve and that is said to be removed by baptism. This idea was symbolized by Mary crushing the head of the serpent that tempted Eve. Mary is the Second Eve, since Eve was also born without sin. Some have associated EVA with its inversion AVE in the angel's greeting "Ave Maria."

Giuseppe Maria Crespi
Bartolomé Esteban Murillo
Juan de Valdés Leal

Imposition de la chasuble à saint Ildefonse *(Saint Ildefonso Receiving the Chasuble)*
(Christ. Trad.) Saint Ildefonso was archbishop of Toledo in the 12th century and defended the belief in Mary's perpetual virginity against attacks by Helvidius. One night as he was praying before the altar in his church, he saw a bright light at the episcopal throne. He recognized the Virgin Mary and knelt before her. She placed the heavenly chasuble on his shoulders.

Master of Saint Ildefonso

Incendie des drapeaux dans la cour des Invalides *(The Burning of Flags in the Court of the Invalides)*
(Hist.) After Paris was captured on March 30, 1814, Marshal Sérurier had the flags which had been captured from the enemy burned to avoid returning them to the allied armies which defeated Napoleon I.

Émile De Frenne

Incrédulité de saint Thomas *(The Incredulity of Saint Thomas)*
(N.T.) Thomas was one of Jesus' twelve disciples. When the disciples told him of Jesus' resurrection, he said that he would not believe it until he

Italian, 14th century
Salviati
Simon de Châlons

touched the wounds himself. A week after his death, Jesus appeared again to his disciples when Thomas was present, and told him to put his finger in the wounds.

Innocence de Suzanne reconnue (L'), also known as **Jugement de Daniel** *(The Judgment of Daniel)*
See **Suzanne au bain**.

Le Valentin

Inspiration du poète *(The Inspiration of the Poet)*
(Myth.) Apollo, god of poetry and fine arts, dictates his text to the poet for whom laurels have already been prepared. The *Odyssey* is in the hands of one of the genii, the *Iliad* is under Apollo's foot. The poet may be Virgil and the woman standing behind Apollo is Calliope, the Muse of epic poetry.

Nicolas Poussin

Inspiration du poète, Nicolas Poussin.

Instruction pastorale (L') *(Saint Gery Preaching)*
See **Prédication de saint Géry**.

Master of the view of Saint Gudule

Iris envoyée à Turnus par Junon *(Iris Sent to Turnus by Juno)*

Claude-François Beaumont

(Myth., Lit.) This is an episode from the *Aeneid*. Aeneas arrived in Italy where he had to defeat Turnus, king of the Rutulians, in order to conquer Latium. Juno, who was against the Trojans, sent her winged messenger, Iris, to Turnus with encouragement, rousing him for combat and informing him that he was better armed than Aeneas. Although this was true, Turnus was nevertheless defeated.

Isaac bénissant Jacob *(Isaac Blessing Jacob)*

Jan Victors

(O.T.) Esau and Jacob were the twin sons of Isaac. The elder of the two was a hunter and Jacob a farmer. Returning hungry from the hunt one day, Esau was offered a dish of red lentils by his brother, in exchange for his birthright.

On reaching adulthood, Esau chose foreign wives and thus displeased his mother Rebecca, whose favorite was Jacob. One day, realizing that death was near, Isaac wanted to bless Esau, whom he still considered as his heir. He asked him to prepare a savory dish of wild game and Esau immediately left for the hunt. Rebecca seized the occasion to prepare a succulent dish of kid goat and told Jacob to put on his brother's clothing. Isaac, who was almost blind, could not tell the difference between the two sons (nor between the wild game and the kid goat). Isaac unwittingly blessed Jacob and made him head of the household. When Esau learned of this ruse, his anger forced Jacob to flee. During his exile Jacob married. He returned fourteen years later with his wives. Esau met him with an army of 400 men. However, Jacob bowed to the ground and the two brothers were reconciled.

Isabelle d'Aragon implorant Charles VIII *(Isabella of Aragon Imploring Charles VIII)*

Attributed to
Giovanni Bilivert

(Hist.) Isabelle of Aragon was married to Giovanni Sforza, duke of Milan, whose power had been usurped by Ludovico the Moor. In 1494, Ludovico encouraged King Charles VIII of France to invade Italy, hoping to strengthen his own position. Isabelle intervened and convinced the king to grant the duchy to Sforza, but her husband died shortly after.

Israélites recueillant la manne dans le désert (Les) *(The Israelites Gathering Manna in the Desert)*

Nicolas Poussin

(O.T.) Moses led the Israelites out of Egypt where they had been prisoners. They had been traveling through the desert for fifteen days and complained that their leader and his brother Aaron were leading them on a dangerous journey. At least in Egypt they had had enough to eat. Moses called to the Lord who promised to intervene. That evening a flock of quails descended on the camp and the next morning the dew was transformed into a white, flake-like matter which tasted of honey and satisfied them. Each morning they gathered a fair portion of "manna."

Same subject: **Israélites recevant la manne**, Giovanni Francesco Romanelli.

Ixion, roi des Lapithes, trompé par Junon *(Ixion, King of the Lapiths, Tricked by Juno)*

Christiaen van Couwenbergh
Peter Paul Rubens

(Myth.) King Ixion of Thessaly married the daughter of King Eioneus, promising gifts to her father. When Eioneus came to collect the presents, Ixion threw him into a pit filled with burning coals. This was a sacrilegious crime as families were considered to be linked by a sacred bond; no mortal could pardon Ixion and the gods were horrified. Finally Jupiter pardoned him and put an end to the calamity caused by his crime. Far from being appreciative, Ixion even tried to rape Jupiter's wife, Juno. Jupiter and Juno formed a cloud which resembled Juno and sent it to Ixion who lay with it. The cloud then

Ixion, roi des Lapithes,
trompé par Junon,
Christiaen van
Couwenbergh.

gave birth to the Centaurs. Convinced of Ixion's
guilt, Jupiter punished him by fastening him to a
burning wheel which revolves forever through
the heavens.

Same subject: **Ixion trompé par Junon**, Christiaen van Couwenbergh.

146   **Ixion trompé par Junon** *(Ixion Tricked*   Christiaen van Couwenbergh
by Juno)
See **Ixion, roi des Lapithes, trompé par Junon**.

Jacob envoyant son fils Joseph chercher ses frères à Sichem *(Jacob Sending His Son To Look For His Brothers),* earlier known as **Jeune Tobie recevant des instructions de son père (Le)** *(Young Tobias Receiving Instructions From His Father)*
See **Joseph et ses frères.**

Eustache Le Sueur and his studio

Jacob, Rachel et Léa (Paysage avec) *(Landscape with Jacob, Rachel and Leah)*
See **Jacob venant trouver les filles de Laban.**

Nicolaes Berchem
Guercino

Jacob reprochant à Laban de lui avoir donné pour femme Lia au lieu de Rachel *(Jacob Reproaching Laban For Having Given Him Leah and Not Rachel)*
(O.T.) Jacob was sent by his father, Isaac, to stay with his uncle Laban and marry one of his daughters. Jacob met the beautiful Rachel at the well and wished to make her his wife. Laban was in no hurry to marry his youngest daughter and required seven years service from Jacob in return for the hand of his beloved. On the day of their wedding, Laban substituted Rachel's elder sister, Leah. Jacob protested, but Laban demanded that he spend a week with her and said that if he worked another seven years for him, he could also marry Rachel. After fourteen years of service, Jacob was finally able to marry Rachel. They had two sons, Joseph and Benjamin.

Antoine Coypel

Jacob venant trouver les filles de Laban *(Jacob and Laban's Daughters)*
(O.T.) To escape the wrath of his brother, Esau (see **Isaac bénissant Jacob**), Jacob went to stay with his uncle Laban. His father had advised him to marry one of Laban's daughters. He met the two sisters at a well with their sheep. Rachel

Louis Gauffier

Jacob venant trouver les filles de Laban, Louis Gauffier.

was waiting until all the sheep were gathered to water them. Jacob rolled away the stone protecting the well and watered the animals. He kissed her and wept aloud.

Same subject: **Paysage avec Jacob, Rachel et Léa,** Guercino. **Paysage avec Rachel, Jacob et Léa,** Nicolaes Berchem.

Jason présentant la Toison d'or dans le temple de Jupiter *(Jason Presenting the Golden Fleece in the Temple of Jupiter)*

Pierre Toutain

(Myth.) Jason was raised by Chiron, the wisest of the Centaurs. As an adult he returned to his native city, Iolcos, and discovered that his uncle Pelias had usurped the kingdom which he should have inherited from his father. Jason claimed his kingdom and Pelias proposed to return it in exchange for the Golden Fleece that was kept under guard by King Aeëtes of Colchis. Pelias only made this promise as he was sure that Jason would not return alive from the expedition.

Jason set out with fifty heroes, the Argonauts. Aeëtes had the Golden Fleece protected by a dragon and imposed many challenges which Jason overcame with the help of the king's daughter, Medea, a sorceress (also see **Médée furieuse**).

The Golden Fleece has its own story. Phrixus and his sister, Helle, were pursued by the hatred of their stepmother. Their father was persuaded to sacrifice them, but Jupiter sent a winged ram with a fleece of pure gold to carry them off. Helle fell into the strait that separates Europe from Asia (afterwards named the Hellespont) and was drowned. Phrixus arrived safely in the land of king Aeëtes who gave him his daughter's hand in marriage. As a token of gratitude, Phrixus sacrificed the ram to Jupiter and gave the Golden Fleece to Aeëtes.

Jeanne d'Arc au sacre de Charles VII dans la cathédrale de Reims *(Joan of Arc at the Coronation of Charles VII in the Cathedral of Reims)*   Jean Auguste Ingres

(Hist.) Joan of Arc was born in 1412 to a family of peasants. When she was thirteen, she claimed to have heard heavenly "voices" (those of Saints Michael, Catherine and Margaret) ordering her to free France from English occupation. She obtained an escort and went to see Charles VII at his court in Chinon. Charles disguised himself in order to observe the young girl, but she recognized him immediately and persuaded him to give her the command of an army, which she led in a long string of victories. Joan also convinced Charles VII, whose legitimacy was in question, to be crowned in the cathedral of Reims (where French kings were crowned). She accompanied him to Reims after numerous victories, one of which liberated the city.

Jeanne d'Arc, devant Charles VII, répond aux prélats qui l'interrogent *(Joan of Arc, Before Charles VII, Examined by the Prelates)*   Gillot Saint-Evre

(Hist.) Inspired by heavenly "voices" (see **Jeanne d'Arc au sacre de Charles VII dans la cathédrale de Reims**), the young shepherdess Joan of Arc went to see the king from whom she hoped to obtain an army to drive the English out of France. Charles VII was suspicious and would not grant her request until she had been questioned by Church authorities. She passed the examination (when asked in which language the "voices" spoke, she purportedly replied "one better than yours!").

Jésus apparaît à la Madeleine, Eustache Le Sueur.

Jésus apparaît à la Madeleine *(Jesus Appearing to Mary Magdalene or Noli Me Tangere)*

French, 14th century
Eustache Le Sueur

(N.T.) Jesus'apparition to Mary Magdalene is described in the Gospel according to John. Three days after his burial, Mary Magdalene went to the tomb and, to her surprise, found the stone rolled aside and the tomb empty. She rushed to tell two of the disciples, Peter and John, who were equally astonished. They visited the tomb and went away convinced that Jesus had been resurrected, but Mary Magdalene remained behind, in tears. Suddenly a man appeared before her and, mistaking him for the gardener, asked if he had taken away the body. When he spoke her name, she recognized him and rushed toward him. Jesus drew back, saying "Touch me not (*Noli me tangere*) for I am not yet ascended to my Father" and sent her to tell the disciples that she had seen him risen from the dead.

Same subject: **Christ apparaissant à la Madeleine**, studio of Luca Giordano. **Christ apparaissant en jardinier à la Madeleine**, Bronzino. **Christ et la Madeleine**, Francesco Albani. **Noli me tangere**, Fra Bartolommeo, Lorenzo di Credi.

Jésus apparaît à saint Pierre *(Jesus Appearing to Saint Peter)*

Dirck Barendsz

(Christ. Trad.) Traditionally there is only one description of Jesus appearing to Saint Peter after his death. The scene took place outdoors, not in Peter's room, as depicted in this painting. The painting is an adaptation of the texts.

Jésus au jardin des Oliviers *(Agony in the Garden)*

Théodore Chassériau

See **Christ au jardin des Oliviers**.

Jésus chassant les marchands du Temple *(Jesus Chasing the Moneylenders from the Temple)*

Bernardo Bellotto
Jacob Jordaens
Simon Julien

(N.T.) Arriving in Jerusalem, where he was to be condemned to death, Jesus entered the Temple of Solomon. There he discovered money-changers and sellers of sacrificial animals. He drove them out saying, "It is written, 'My House shall be called a house of prayer; but you make it a den of robbers.'" According to Saint Matthew, he overturned the tables and chairs.

Same subject: **Jésus chassant les vendeurs du Temple**, Giovanni Benedetto Castiglione. **Marchands chassés du Temple**, Giovanni Paolo Pannini.

Jésus chassant les vendeurs du Temple *(Christ Chasing the Moneylenders from the Temple)*
See **Jésus chassant les marchands du Temple**.

Giovanni Castiglione

Jésus chez Marthe et Marie *(Jesus in the House of Martha and Mary)*
See **Jésus-Christ chez Marthe et Marie**.

Hendrick van Steenwyck

Jésus et la Samaritaine *(Jesus and the Woman of Samaria)*
(N.T.) On his way through Samaria, Jesus met a Samaritan woman at a well. As the Samaritans and the Jews did not usually speak to each other, she was surprised when Jesus asked her for water. He spoke to her of the living water saying, "Every one who drinks of this water will thirst again, but whoever drinks of the water that I shall give him will never thirst." He then revealed to her that he was the Messiah.

Pierre Mignard

Jésus et les disciples d'Emmaüs *(Jesus and the Disciples of Emmaus)*
See **Pèlerins d'Emmaüs**.

Dirck Barendsz

Jésus guérissant le paralytique de Bethesda *(Jesus Healing the Paralytic)*
(N.T.) Jesus was in Jerusalem for a feast of the Jews. He visited a nearby pool called Bethesda where the sick and the invalid lay under the colonnades. From time to time an angel descended into the pool, stirring the water. The first to be dipped in the water after the angel's passing was healed. Jesus met a paralytic, who had been ill for thirty eight years and who was unable to find someone to help him into the water. Jesus said to him, "Rise, take up your pallet, and walk" and the man immediately did so. This act created difficulties with the Jewish leaders who said that the event had taken place on the Sabbath, the day of rest, and that the man should not have carried his bed.

Alessandro Magnasco
Gian Domenico Tiepolo

Jésus guérissant les aveugles de Jéricho *(Jesus Healing the Blind)*
See **Aveugles de Jéricho**.

Étienne Villequin

Jésus guérissant les malades *(Jesus Healing the Sick)*
(N.T.) The period of Jesus' preaching, from his baptism to the Passion, included many miraculous healings.

Jean Jouvenet
Alexander Ubeleski

Jésus guérissant un sourd-muet, Bartolomeus Breenberg.

Jésus guérissant un sourd-muet
(Jesus Healing the Deaf-mute)
(N.T.) Jesus was asked to heal a deaf man who had difficulty speaking. Jesus took him aside, put his fingers in his ears, touched his tongue with his own saliva and then breathed on him. The man's ears were immediately opened, his tongue was loosened and he began to speak.

Bartolomeus Breenberg

Jésus parmi les docteurs *(Jesus Among the Doctors)*
(N.T.) When Jesus was twelve, his parents took him to Jerusalem for the Passover. On their way home, Mary and Joseph realized that Jesus was

After Hieronymus Bosch
Master of the Life of the Virgin
Giovanni Serodine

Jésus parmi les docteurs, after Hieronymus Bosch.

not with them. After searching for three days, they found him in the Temple debating with the doctors. When they reproached him, he replied "How is it you sought me? Did you not know that I must be in my Father's house?"

Jésus portant sa croix *(Jesus Bearing the Cross)*
See **Portement de croix**.

Charles Le Brun
Eustache Le Sueur

Jésus prêchant *(Jesus Preaching)*
(N.T.) The crowds that gathered to hear Jesus preaching were so large that he sometimes climbed onto a boat to address them. Here we see Peter at the prow and Andrew and James pulling in their nets. On the horizon is the town of Capernaum.

Bolognese, 14th century

Jésus succombant sous le poids de la croix *(Jesus Collapsing Under the Weight of the Cross)*
Jésus sur le chemin du Calvaire *(Jesus on the Road to Calvary)*
See **Portement de croix**.

Veronese and his studio
Pierre Mignard

Jésus sur le lac de Génésareth *(Jesus on the Sea of Galilee)*
(N.T.) After crossing the sea with Jesus, the disciples left him to pray. Their boat was already halfway across when they noticed that he was walking toward them on the water. They were afraid, but Jesus reassured them. Peter tried to imitate Jesus and took a few steps, but he suddenly became afraid and sank. Jesus helped him and reproached him for doubting.

Alexandre Gabriel Descamps

Jésus-Christ chez Marthe et Marie *(Jesus in the House of Martha and Mary)*
(N.T.) In Bethany, Jesus often visited Martha and Mary, the sisters of Lazarus whom he had raised from the dead. Mary is often assumed to be Mary Magdalene, but is most often called Mary of Bethany. One day as Martha was preparing to serve Jesus, she complained that her sister, who was meditating at Jesus' feet, was not helping her. Jesus defended Mary, and the merits of contemplation.

Jean Jouvenet
Hendrick van Steenwyck

Jésus-Christ, conduit au Calvaire, tombe sous le poids de la croix *(Jesus Collapsing Under the Weight of the Cross)*
See **Portement de croix**.

Étienne-Barthélemy Garnier

Jésus-Christ donnant les clefs à saint Pierre *(Jesus Giving the Keys of Paradise to Saint Peter)*
(N.T.) When Peter recognized Jesus as the

Giambattista Pittoni

Christ, Son of the living God, Jesus said to him,
"And I tell you, you are Peter (from the Greek
word *petros* meaning rock), and on this rock I
will build my church, and the power of death
shall not prevail against it." He added, "I will
give you the keys of the kingdom of Heaven, and
whatever you bind on earth shall be bound in
Heaven, and whatever you loose on earth shall
be loosed in Heaven."

Jésus-Christ instituant l'Eucharistie
(The Institution of the Eucharist)
(N.T.) Jesus told his disciples several times that his flesh was food and his blood a drink. These remarks surprised, and even shocked, some of his disciples who preferred to leave him. At the Last Supper (see **Cène**), Jesus broke bread and passed the wine saying, "Take, eat; this is my body" and "Drink, this is my blood." He instructed the disciples to repeat the ceremony in remembrance of him. The first Christians met to celebrate the Lord's Supper, the Eucharist.

Nicolas Poussin

Jésus-Christ montant au Calvaire
(Jesus Christ on the Road to Calvary)
See **Portement de croix**.

Francesco Bassano

Jésus-Christ reçoit la Vierge dans le ciel *(Jesus Receiving Mary in Heaven)*
See **Couronnement de la Vierge**.

Jacques Stella

Jeune Pyrrhus à la cour de Glaucias (Le) *(Young Pyrrhus at the Court of Glaucus)*
(Myth., Lit.) After the death of his father Achilles, young Pyrrhus was saved by soldiers who had remained faithful to his father (see **Jeune Pyrrhus sauvé**). They crossed the river and went see King Glaucus who they found seated in his home. They placed the child on the ground before the king who remained silent for a long while. In the meantime, little Pyrrhus lifted himself up and leaned on the king's knees. The king broke into a smile and decided to take Pyrrhus under his protection.

French, 19th century

Jeune Pyrrhus sauvé (Le) *(The Rescue of Pyrrhus)*
(Myth., Lit.) After Achilles was killed by an arrow shot into his heel by Paris during the Trojan war, a revolution seemed imminent. Soldiers

Nicolas Poussin

who feared for the life of Achilles's son, Pyrrhus, hurried him away from the Greek camp. They traveled all day, chased by their enemies, and were halted by a flooding river, not far from the city of Megara. They sent a message on two strips of bark tied to a stone which they attached to a javelin, and the Megarians came to their rescue.

Jeune Tobie recevant des instructions de son père (Le) *(Young Tobias Receiving Instructions from His Father)*
New title: **Jacob envoyant son fils Joseph.**

Eustache Le Sueur and his studio

Jeune Tobie rend la vue à son père (Le) *(Young Tobias Restores His Father's Sight)*
See **Archange Raphaël quittant la famille de Tobie.**

Jan Sanders van Hermessen

Job tourmenté par les démons *(Job Tested by the Devil)*
(O.T.) The book of Job is a popular tale. Job, the rich, beloved father of seven sons and three daughters, was righteous and pious. God asked Satan if he knew Job and the Devil laughed, saying that it was easy for a man who had everything to be pious. God allowed him to test Job, who subsequently lost his house, his children and his health, but remained faithful to the Father. God rewarded him by restoring his riches and his heath.

After Peter Paul Rubens

Josabeth exposant Moïse sur le Nil *(Josabeth Exposing Moses on the Nile)*
See **Moïse sauvé des eaux.**

Pierre Patel the Elder

Joseph d'Arimathie et Nicodème sur le chemin du Calvaire *(Joseph of Arimathaea and Nicodemus on the Road to Calvary)*

Niccolo da Foligno

(N.T.) Joseph of Arimathaea was a secret disciple of Jesus who obtained permission to bury him and provided a temporary tomb. Nicodemus, another disciple, helped remove the body from the cross and embalm it (see **Crucifixion** and **Calvaire**).

Joseph et ses frères *(Joseph and His Brothers)*

Jules Richomme

(O.T.) Jacob had ten children by Lea and two handmaids, but his favorite wife, Rachel, remained barren. Late in life she gave birth to a son, Joseph, who was his father's favorite and the envy of his elder brothers (half-brothers). One day Joseph went to the fields where they were working and they decided to kill him. The eldest, Ruben, dissuaded them and, intending to return and rescue him, advised them to throw Joseph into a dry pit. However, they decided to sell him as a slave to a caravan of Ishmaelite merchants who subsequently took him to Egypt. Believing themselves rid of him, they dipped his coat in kid's blood and sent it to their father, pretending to have found it. When he saw the coat, Jacob believed that Joseph had been devoured by a wild beast.

Joseph expliquant les songes *(Joseph Interpreting the Dreams)*

Antonio Burrini

(O.T.) After considering killing him, Joseph's brothers sold him to a caravan of merchants who were on their way to Egypt (see **Joseph et ses frères**). He was bought by a captain, Potiphar, whose wife attempted to seduce him. Humiliated by his refusal, she took revenge by accusing him of rape and he was imprisoned. While in prison he interpreted the dreams of the Pharaoh's butler and baker. Two years later, when the Pharaoh was troubled by dreams that no one could interpret, the butler advised him to send for Joseph. In his dream, seven fat cows were swallowed by seven thin cows and seven plump ears of grain were consumed by seven thin ears of grain. Joseph told him that there would be seven years of prosperity and seven years of famine in Egypt and that the Egyptians should make provisions during the plentiful years. The Pharaoh rewarded Joseph richly for his interpretation.

Josué arrêtant le soleil *(Joshua Halting the Sun)*
Jacques Courtois

(O.T.) During the conquest of Canaan, the Israelites, led by Moses' successor, Joshua (see **Josué défait les Amalécites**), drove away an army formed of five enemy kings and their troops. They pursued them and sought revenge. As night was falling, Joshua prayed to God, asking Him to halt the sun and the moon until the enemy had been exterminated and his prayer was answered.

Josué défait les Amalécites *(Joshua Defeating the Amalkites)*
Jacques Courtois

(O.T.) Moses led the Israelites out of Egypt, where they had been prisoners, but he died before they arrived in the Promised Land, Canaan. Moses chose Joshua as his successor for the military qualities he had demonstrated against the Amalkites, a nomadic people. Joshua then led the Israelites through obstacles and pitfalls.

Judith tranchant la tête d'Holopherne, Jacopo Palma the Younger.

Judith tenant la tête d'Holopherne
(Judith Bearing Holofernes' Head)
See **Judith tranchant la tête d'Holopherne**.

Jan Massys

Judith tranchant la tête d'Holopherne *(Judith Beheading Holophernes)*
(O.T.) The town of Bethulia in Judea was besieged by the army of Holofernes, a general of the Assyrian king Nebuchadnezzar. As the town was on the verge of surrendering, a widow named Judith was inspired by God. She went to the Assyrian camp with a handmaid and captivated Holofernes by her beauty. When she was alone with him and he was drunk, she took a sword and cut off his head which she took back to Bethulia. The Jews displayed the trophy on the town walls and the Assyrians, terrified, were defeated.

Jacopo Palma the Younger

Jugement de Daniel *(The Judgment of Daniel)*
See **Suzanne au bain**.

Le Valentin

Jugement de Pâris *(The Judgment of Paris)*
(Myth., Lit.) The young Trojan Paris was guarding his sheep when he caught sight of three goddesses, Juno, Minerva and Venus coming toward him. They were fighting over the golden apple that was marked *For the Fairest* (see **Noces de Thétis et Pélée**). Jupiter had told Mercury to take them to Paris, who was watching his father's sheep on Mt. Ida, and that he would judge which of them should receive the apple. The three goddesses attempted to bribe him: Juno offered him the kingdom of Asia, Minerva wisdom and victory and Venus the most beautiful woman in the world, Helen. Without hesitating, he gave the apple to Venus. He was rewarded with Helen, but invoked the wrath of the other two goddesses who subsequently sided with the Greeks against Troy.

Girolamo di Benvenuto
Charles Poerson
Jean-Antoine Watteau

Jugement de Pâris et la destruction de Troie *(The Judgment of Paris and the Destruction of Troy)*
See **Jugement de Pâris et Destruction de Troie**.

Mathis Gerung

Le Jugement de Salomon, Nicolas Poussin.

Jugement de Salomon (Le) *(The Judgment of Solomon)*

Le Valentin
Andrea Mantegna
Nicolas Poussin

(O.T.) Solomon was famous for the magnificence of his reign and for his wise judgments. Two prostitutes were fighting over a baby. They had given birth several days apart and one of them had accidently suffocated her child and taken the other woman's baby. The matter was brought before Solomon, who ordered a soldier to cut the baby in two. The true mother's identity was revealed when one of the women said that the child should be given to the other, to spare it. The child was then returned to its rightful mother.

Jugement dernier (Le) *(The Last Judgment)*

Jean Cousin the Younger
Jacob Jordaens

(N.T.) This scene is described in the Gospel according to Matthew. Jesus will appear in his glory and place the righteous, who will be granted eternal life, on his right and the wicked, who will be condemned to eternal suffering, on his left. According to tradition, archangel

Michael will weigh men's souls in a set of scales and then direct them to heaven or hell. According to the Apocalypse of Saint John, the final judgment, whose hour has never been revealed, will be preceded by great disasters, the destruction of the world, the renewal of all nature and the resurrection of the dead.

Junon confiant Io à Argus *(Juno Entrusting Io to Argus)*
Jan van Noordt
Gregorio de Ferrari
Junon et Argus *(Juno and Argus)*
See **Mercure et Argus**.

Junon, Iris et Flore *(Juno, Iris and Flora)*
François Lemoyne
(Myth.) Juno was both the sister and the wife of Jupiter and also the most powerful of the goddesses of Olympus. She was the protectress of marriage and was particularly jealous of her husband. She was famous for the wrath with which she pursued her husband's lovers. Iris was the messenger of the gods and had wings and transparent veils. She was the personification of the rainbow linking heaven and earth. Iris was responsible for conveying messages from Jupiter and Juno and was sometimes depicted as Juno's servant. Flora was the goddess of vegetation responsible for flowering and blossoming. Juno was irritated by the fact that Jupiter had conceived a child on his own (see **Naissance de Minerve**) and asked Flora to assist her. Flora gave her a plant and said that she would become pregnant if she touched it. The goddess did so and conceived the god Mars. At Juno's feet is the peacock with Argus' eyes set in his tail (see **Mercure et Argus**).

Jupiter en satyre avec Antiope et leurs jumeaux *(Jupiter, Antiope and Their Twins)*
Vincent Sellaer
See **Jupiter et Antiope**.

Jupiter enfant nourri par la chèvre Amalthée *(Jupiter Suckled by Amalthea)* — Jacob Jordaens

(Myth.) Jupiter's father, Saturn, devoured his children, as he had been told that one of them would dethrone him. Jupiter's mother, Earth, saved him by entrusting him to Amalthea. According to various legends Amalthea was either a nymph who had the child suckled by a goat, or the goat itself. The goat was a fine nurse, but a terrifying beast. Later, while at war with the Titans, Jupiter wore the goat's skin, the aegis, as majestic armor.

Jupiter et Antiope *(Jupiter and Antiope)* — Hendrick Goltzius / Jean-Antoine Watteau

(Myth.) Jupiter seduced the daughter of Nycteus, a king of Thebes, by disguising himself as a satyr. Antiope became pregnant and left home. Her father took his life in despair after ordering Lycus to avenge the misdeed. Lycus pursued Antiope and the twin boys to whom she gave birth. Same subject: **Jupiter en Satyre avec Antiope et leurs jumeaux**, Vincent Sellaer.

Jupiter et Danaé *(Jupiter and Danaë)* — Joachim Wtewael

(Myth.) Danaë was the daughter of Acrisius, king of Argos. An oracle had prophesied that Danaë's son would kill Acrisius. The king built a bronze underground chamber (in other versions a tower) as a prison for Danaë. Jupiter entered in the form of a rain of gold through a crack in the roof. Danaë became pregnant and gave birth to Perseus. Acrisius locked both mother and child in a trunk and threw them into the sea, but Jupiter protected them from harm.

Jupiter foudroyant les Titans *(Jupiter Striking the Titans)* — Charles Lamy

(Myth.) The six Titans were the sons of Uranus (heaven) and Gaea (Mother Earth). Uranus was constantly stretched out over Gaea and the offspring were smothered as no life was possible between heaven and earth. Gaea managed to rescue young Saturn who castrated his father (Uranus'genitals fell into the sea and resulted in the birth of the prodigious Venus). The Titans were in power, but a new generation, the gods of Olympus, led by Jupiter, whose attribute was thunder, opposed the Titans and vanquished them.

Jupiter, sous les traits de Diane, et Callisto *(Jupiter, Disguised as Diana, and Callisto)*

François Marot

(Myth.) Callisto was a woodland nymph. She was one of Diana's companions, and sworn to virginity. Jupiter fell in love with her and disguised himself as Diana in order to seduce her. One day as she undressed to bathe with the other nymphs, her advanced state of pregnancy was revealed. As punishment, Diana turned her into a bear, but Jupiter transformed her into a constellation, Ursula Major or the Great Bear.

Justice d'Othon (La) *(The Judgment of Otto)*

Luca Penni

(Hist.) The wife of the Holy Roman Emperor Otto III, who ruled from 983 — 1002, was secretly in love with a count of the court. He was an honest man and resisted her advances. She took revenge by claiming that the count had dishonored her; he was subsequently condemned to death and beheaded. Before dying, he convinced his wife of his innocence and asked her to prove it to others. The count's widow underwent an ordeal by red-hot iron and proved his innocence. The emperor condemned his wife and had her burned at the stake.

Laban cherchant ses idoles *(Laban Searching for His Idols)*

After Bourdon
Gabriel de Saint-Aubin
Laurent de La Hyre

(O.T.) Jacob and his two wives, Leah and Rachel, lived with their father (see **Jacob reprochant à Laban de lui avoir donné pour femme Lia au lieu de Rachel**). During his stay with Laban, he amassed considerable wealth and his brothers-in-law were jealous of him. However, Jacob felt he had been wronged by Laban who continuously cheated on his wages and the sharing of ewes. Inspired by God, Jacob decided to return to his native land, Canaan, with his wives and animals. They left in secret and, unknown to Jacob, Rachel stole her father's teraphim, or household gods. Laban discovered their departure and pursued them; he reproached Jacob for not allowing him to kiss his daughters farewell. He looked for his idols that Rachel had hidden in the camel's saddle she was sitting on. She excused herself, saying, "Let not my lord be angry that I cannot rise before you, for the way of women is upon me." The two men reproached one another, but finally Laban proposed an alliance. They built an altar of large stones, sacrificed and made a covenant.

Same subject: **Alliance de Jacob et de Laban**, Pietro da Cortona.

la

166

Laban cherchant ses idoles, after Bourdon.

Lady Macbeth somnambule *(Lady Macbeth)*

Johann Heinrich Fuseli

(Lit.) In Shakespeare's play *Macbeth*, the hero kills the king of Scotland to accelerate his ascension. However, the murder is not sufficient to ensure his security as monarch and he launches upon a bloodbath, killing all who could betray him. While Macbeth becomes increasingly ruthless, Lady Macbeth, who encouraged the initial crime, begins to suffer from remorse. She sleepwalks, wringing her hands in a desperate attempt to remove imagined blood stains. Her servant asks the doctor to witness one of these crises and, comprehending its cause, they decide to remain silent.

Laissez venir à moi les petits enfants *(Suffer the Children to Come Unto Me)*
See **Christ et les enfants**.

Emile de Champmartin

Lapidation de saint Étienne *(The Stoning of Saint Stephen)*
See **Martyre de saint Étienne**.

Jan Pynas
Annibale Carracci
Cornelis van Poelenburgh

Lara

Jules Jollivet

(Lit.) Lara, the hero of Lord Byron's poem of the same title, is a quiet, disenchanted, sometimes cruel pirate. He spends many of his evenings absorbed in contemplation of a skull.
"Why gazed he so upon the ghastly head
Which hands profane had gather'd from the dead,
That still beside his open'd volume lay,
As if to startle all save him away?"
Only his page understands and accompanies him wherever he goes. He is a young foreigner who became attached to Lara. On Lara's death, the page throws himself on his master's body and tears his clothes in despair, thus revealing that Lara was in fact a woman disguised as a man.

Larmes de saint Pierre (Les) *(The Tears of Saint Peter)*
See **Reniement de saint Pierre**.

Guercino

Latone métamorphosant les paysans de Lycie en grenouilles *(Latona Turning the Lycian Peasants into Frogs)*
(Myth.) Latona (or Leto) was the mother of Apollo and Diana, who she conceived with Jupiter. Juno, jealous as usual, forbade all regions of the earth to help her in any way. When, after numerous adventures, Latona finally managed to give birth to the twins, she took them to Lycia in Asia Minor. One day when she was thirsty and wished to drink from a lake, the local peasants tried to prevent her. She pleaded with them, but to no avail. In the end she lost her temper and said, "Live then for ever in that lake of yours!" and turned them into frogs.

Pietro Paolo Bonzi

Lecture de la Bible *(The Reading of the Bible)*, also known as **Anne et Tobie** *(Anne and Tobit)*
(O.T.) In recent translations of the Bible, Tobias is called Tobit to distinguish him from his son Tobias. Tobit, like Job, was an honest man who suffered many misfortunes. He was exiled and became blind, but always remained faithful to the Lord.

Gérard Dou

Léda *(Leda)*
(Myth.) Leda was the wife of Tyndareus, king of Sparta. The legends recount that Jupiter visited her in the form of a swan and that she laid two eggs: Castor and Pollux were hatched from one, Helen and Clytemnestra from the other.

Clément Belle

Légende de saint Georges *(The Legend of Saint George)*
See **Scènes de la légende de saint Georges**.

Bernardo Martorell

Léda, Clément Belle.

Légende de sainte Ursule *(The Legend of Saint Ursula)*

Master of the Saint Ursula Legend

(Christ. Trad.) Ursula was the daughter of a king of Brittany. A pagan king asked her father for her hand in marriage for his son. She accepted on the condition that she could first spend three years on a pilgrimage to Rome with a number of virgins, traditionally eleven thousand. The first reference to the virgins, speaks of ten and these eleven virgins may have become "eleven thousand" because one of them was named Undecimilla (mistakenly read as undecim millia, eleven thousand) or because of an inscription which read "*Ursula et XI M.V.*" which stood for "Ursula and eleven virgin *martyrs*" and not eleven *thousand* virgins. The young women set off for Rome, traveling through Gaul and up the Rhine to Cologne. On their way home, they were captured by the Huns who had laid siege to Cologne. All but Ursula were massacred. Attila the Hun found her so beautiful that he wanted to marry her, but she refused and he had her shot with an arrow.

Léonidas aux Thermopyles, Jacques-Louis David.

Léonidas aux Thermopyles *(Leonidas at Thermoplyae)*

Jacques-Louis David

(Hist.) Leonidas, king of Sparta, was defending the pass of Thermoplyae against the Persians.

This mission was so dangerous that, before leaving, the soldiers and their families celebrated funeral rites. When King Xerxes of Persia sent an ultimatum to Leondias demanding that he surrender his arms, Leondias retorted, "Come and get them yourself." The Persians, informed by a shepherd, discovered a path that led them behind the camp. When Leonidas discovered what had happened, he ordered a dinner and told the soldiers that they would all dine with Pluto (in the underworld) that evening. He led them on a desperate mission against the enemy and they were all massacred (480 B.C.), but he and his 300 soldiers defended Thermoplyae against Xerxes' huge army for several days.

Libéralité de Cimon l'Athénien invitant le peuple à prendre les fruits de ses jardins *(Cimon, of Athens, Inviting the People to Gather Fruit in His Gardens)* (Hist., Lit.) Cimon was an Athenian general and contemporary of Pericles (5th century B.C.). He was famous for his successful military campaigns against the Persians, his important public works and his generosity.

Noël Hallé

La Liberté guidant le peuple, Eugène Delacroix.

Liberté guidant le peuple, le 28 juillet 1830 (La) *(Liberty Guiding the People, July 28, 1830)*

Eugène Delacroix

(Hist., Imag.) The painting evokes the "three glorious days" of the July Revolution: July 27, 28 and 29, 1830, when the Parisians took to the streets and dethroned King Charles X, whose absolutism was increasingly unpopular. The adolescent to the right is identified as Gavroche, the Parisian urchin, a character from Victor Hugo's *Les Misérables*, who was killed on the barricades (of 1832) after a gallant display of courage and valiant resistance.

Licteurs rapportant à Brutus le corps de ses fils (Les) *(The Lictors Bringing Brutus His Sons' Bodies)*

Jacques-Louis David

(Hist.) Lucius Junius Brutus was appointed the first Roman consul. He learned that his two sons were plotting the restoration of the Tarquins, enemies of the Republic. He himself had to condemn them to death. The lictors were officials who accompanied the magistrates bearing fasces, bundles of rods containing an axe with its blade protruding. (This Brutus, who lived in the 6th century B.C., should not be confused with Marcus Junius Brutus, nephew of Cato, Julius Caesar's adopted son and assassin (Also see **Brutus condamnant ses fils à mort**).

Lion de Florence (Le) *(The Lion of Florence)*

Nicolas-André Monsiau

(Lit.) The painting is dedicated to "mothers." It was inspired by a news item that was recounted as a legend. A lion, which had escaped from a zoo, terrified the inhabitants of Florence. As she was fleeing, a woman dropped the child she was carrying and the lion picked it up in its mouth. The mother fell before the lion, pleading with it to return the child. The lion stopped, stared at her and then placed the child on the ground and turned away.

Lit de Justice tenu au Parlement à la majorité de Louis XV (Le) *(Royal Session in the Court at the Majority of Louis XV)*

Nicolas Lancret

(Hist.) This event took place on February 22, 1723, when the majority of Louis XV was declared. He became king at the age of five and France was governed by several regents during the years of his minority.

Loth et ses filles *(Lot and His Daughters)*

Antwerp or Leiden,
16th century
Bernardo Cavalino
Guercino
Jean-Baptiste Greuze

(O.T.) After fleeing Sodom and Gomorah (see **Fuite de Lot**), in flames, Lot went to the hills with his daughters. The young women were convinced that mankind had been entirely destroyed and that they had to ensure the descendance of their father. They made him drunk

Loth et ses filles,
Antwerp or Leiden,
16th century.

and then lay with him, one after the other. Both of the daughters gave birth to a son, the ancestors of the Moabites and the Ammonites.

Louis XIII couronné par la Victoire (siège de La Rochelle, 1628) *(Louis XIII Crowned by Victory — Siege of La Rochelle, 1628)*

Philippe de Champaigne

(Hist.) This painting is a tribute to Louis XIII for having obtained the surrender of La Rochelle (see **Siège de La Rochelle par Louis XIII**).

Louis-Philippe prêtant serment à la Charte constitutionelle le 9 août 1830 *(Louis Philippe Swearing Loyalty to the Constitutional Charter, August, 9, 1830)*

French, 19th century

(Hist.) Louis Philippe descended from the Orléans branch of the French royal family and embraced the Revolutionary ideas of 1789. After the Revolution, the Bourbons (Louis XVIII and Charles X) were restored to the throne. In 1830, Charles X was driven from Paris and Louis Philippe installed in power by the bourgeoisie. He swore loyalty to the Charter, thus becoming a constitutional monarch with the title "King of the French." He reigned from 1830 to 1848.

Lucrèce et Tarquin *(Lucretia and Tarquin)*

Studio of Luca Giordano

(Hist.) Lucretia was the wife of Tarquin Collatinus (5th century B.C.), brother of the king Lucius Tarquinus Superbus (Tarquin the Proud). The royal princes were away at battle, but they returned home one night to observe their wives'behavior during their absence. They discovered that their wives had not hesitated to take advantage of their absence, except for the beautiful, chaste Lucretia, who was spinning with her servants. Her nephew, Sixtus Tarquinus, was aroused by the sight of her. Several days later he visited her in her apartment. Finding her alone, he threatened her into submitting to him. The next day she summoned her father and husband and told them how she had been violated and then stabbed herself. This episode had political consequences that marked the end of the Etruscan reign. Junius Brutus, who later became the first Roman consul, seized the bloody dagger and incited the people to rebel against the unpopular Tarquins, who were definitively driven out of Rome (also see **Brutus condamnant ses fils à mort**).

Madeleine *(Mary Magdalene)*
Madeleine à la veilleuse (La) *(The Magdalen with the Nightlight)*
See **Sainte Madeleine repentante renonce à toutes les vanités du monde**.

Jean-Marc Nattier
Georges de la Tour

Madeleine aux pieds du Christ (La), also known as **Repas chez Simon (Le)** *(The Feast in the House of Simon)*
(N.T.) Saint John recounts that when Jesus was dining in Bethany in the house of Simon the Pharisee, a woman threw herself at his feet, wet them with tears and wiped them with her hair and an expensive ointment. According to Saint Matthew, she stood behind him and poured the ointment on his head. The woman was Mary of Bethany, sister of Martha and Lazarus, but it is difficult to determine whether she was also Mary Magdalene. The scent of the ointment spread throughout the house and the disciples complained of the waste, saying that the ointment could have been sold and the money used to help the poor. According to John, it was Judas, the steward who guarded the purse, who made this remark. Jesus defended the woman, saying that she had demonstrated her faith by embalming him as a sign of his imminent death.
Same subject: **Onction de Béthanie**, Dirck Barendsz. **Repas chez Simon**, Juan de Valdes Léal.

Pierre Subleyras

Madeleine pénitente (La) *(The Repentant Magdalene)*
See **Sainte Madeleine repentante renonce à toutes les vanités du monde**.

Guy François

Mane, Thecel, Pharès: le festin de Balthasar *(Mane, Tekel, Parsin: Belshazzar's Feast)*
(O.T.) Belshazzar, who is presented in the Book of Daniel as the son of Nebuchadnezzar and the king of Babylon, held a feast and invited a thousand of his lords. He ordered the golden and

Nicola Bertuzzi

silver vessels that his father had stolen from the Temple of Jerusalem to be brought for the wine. In the middle of the feast, Belshazzar saw the fingers of a man's hand writing on the wall. He was terrified and asked for an explanation, but no one could interpret the writing. His wife advised him to call for Daniel who refused the rewards which Belshazzar offered him and reproached him for profaning the vessels from the Temple. He then explained the mysterious writing. There were three words in the inscription: mene, tekel and parsin (counted, weighed and divided). Daniel explained, saying, "*Mene*, God has numbered the days of your kingdom and brought it to an end; *tekel*, you have been weighed in the balances and found wanting; *peres*, your kingdom is divided and given to the Medes and the Persians." That night, Belshazzar was killed and Darius the Mede took possession of his kingdom.

Same subject: **Festin de Balthasar**, Frans Francken the Younger.

Marchands chassés du Temple (Les) *(The Merchants Driven Out of the Temple)*

Paolo Giovanni Pannini

See **Jésus chassant les marchands du Temple**.

Maréchal Ney à la redoute de Kovno (Le) *(Marshal Ney at the Redoubt of Kovno)*

Denis-Auguste-Marie Raffet

(Hist.) In 1812 Marshal Ney, surnamed the "Brave of the Braves," accompanied Napoleon on the Russian campaign that ended with the disastrous winter retreat by the French army. Kovno, a city in western Russia, was sacked by the French.

Mariage de la Vierge (Le) *(The Marriage of the Virgin)*

Italian, 16th century
Jan van Coninxloo the Younger
Charles de La Fosse
Luca Giordano
Master of the Life of the Virgin

(Christ. Trad.) According to apocryphal texts, Mary served in the Temple from the age of four (see **Présentation de la Vierge au Temple**). At the

age of fourteen she was betrothed because women were not allowed to remain there. As she
had taken a vow of virginity, her husband's role
was to guard her virginity. Mary's family was
rich, she herself virtuous, and consequently the
suitors, summoned by the high priest, were
numerous. Following divine inspiration, the
high priest told the suitors to bring a rod. The
man whose rod produced a dove (according to
another legend, whose rod flowered) would become her husband. Each of the men brought a
rod, but no miracle occurred. It was later discovered that one man, Joseph, had not presented
himself. He had stayed back because he was
poor and much older than Mary. However, when
he took up his rod, a dove appeared, designating
him as Mary's divinely chosen husband.

Mariage de Psyché et de l'Amour
(The Marriage of Psyche and Cupid)
See **Amour et Psyché**.

François Boucher

**Mariage mystique de sainte
Catherine d'Alexandrie (Le)** *(The
Mystic Marriage of Saint Catherine)*
(Christ. Trad.) Saint Catherine of Alexandria (4th
century), a pagan, was converted to Christianity
by a hermit who promised her the most wonderful husband. After her baptism, the Infant Jesus
appeared to her, in the arms of the Virgin, and
chose her as his bride by slipping a ring onto her
finger.
Same subject: **Mariage mystique de sainte
Catherine**, Umbrian, 16th century, Orazio di Alfani, Bon Boullongne, Hans Memling.

Correggio

**Mariage mystique de sainte
Catherine de Sienne** *(The Mystic Mar-
riage of Saint Catherine of Siena, with
Eight Saints)*
(Christ. Trad.) At the age of eight, Saint
Catherine of Siena had decided Jesus would be

Fra Bartolommeo

her only husband. He appeared to her as a young child and slipped a ring, which was visible only to her, onto her finger.

Marie de Médicis

Peter Paul Rubens

(Hist., Imag.) This series of historical paintings is by no means objective. It was commissioned by Marie de Médicis for the Palais du Luxembourg to celebrate her virtue and the success of her reign.

1. **Les Trois Parques filent la destinée de Marie de Médicis** *(The Destiny of Marie de Médicis)*.

Marie has not yet been born, but the rulers of heaven, Jupiter and Juno, watch over the Three Fates who are determining her fate.

The Fates (Moirae in Greek) are the goddesses who spin human destiny: Clotho draws out the thread of life, Lacheis determines the destiny and Atropos cuts the thread at the moment decreed by Fate.

2. **La Naissance de Marie de Médicis, 26 avril 1573** *(The Birth of Marie de Médicis, April 26, 1573)*.

The city of Florence is personified by the young woman who is receiving the infant princess from Juno, the goddess of childbirth. They are surrounded by the Horae (Hours), the river Arno and the lion of Florence.

3. **L'Éducation de Marie de Médicis** *(Marie's Education)*.

Minerva, Apollo and Mercury take turns teaching the child to read and instructing her in music and the sciences. The three Graces offer her beauty and charm.

4. **Présent du portrait de Marie de Médicis à Henry IV** *(Henry IV Receives the Portrait)*.

Hymen and Cupid present the portrait of Marie de Médicis to Henry IV under the watchful eyes of Jupiter and Juno. Henry IV, depicted in his magnificent armor, is seduced by her irresistible beauty.

5. **Le Mariage par procuration de Marie de Médicis à Florence, 5 octobre 1600** *(The Marriage)*.

Les Trois Parques filent la destinée de Marie de Médicis, Peter Paul Rubens.

The marriage took place in Florence on October 5, 1600, by proxy. The grand duke of Toscany placed the wedding ring on the finger of the beautiful princess.

6. **Débarquement de Marie de Médicis à Marseille, 3 novembre 1600** *(The Landing at Marseille).*

Marie landed in Marseille on November 3, 1600, accompanied by the duchess of Mantua. In the painting she is announced by winged Fame and welcomed by the king's messenger. In the foreground are Neptune and the three Sirens.

7. **Première entrevue du roi et de Marie de Médicis à Lyon, 9 novembre 1600** *(The Meeting at Lyons).*

The first meeting of Marie de Médicis and the king took place in Lyons on November 9, 1600. The relatively prosaic encounter was glorified by the painter.

L'Éducation de Marie de Médicis, Peter Paul Rubens.

8. **La Naissance de Louis XIII, à Fontainebleau**
(The Birth of Louis XIII).
Louis XIII was born at Fontainbleau on September 27, 1601. His mother looks on tenderly as he is welcomed by the gods, including his godmother, Justice.

9. **Henri IV confie la régence à la reine, 20 mars 1610** *(Institution of the Regency).*
This politically motivated painting was intended to demonstrate that Marie de Médicis received the government from the king himself and had not usurped power, as was widely assumed.

10. **Le Couronnement de la reine à Saint-Denis, 13 mai 1610** *(Coronation of Marie de Médicis).*
Marie convinced the king to crown her in Saint-Denis. The coronation took place on May 13, 1610. In this scene, as in **The Marriage**, Rubens painted real portraits of members of the court.

Le Couronnement de la reine à Saint-Denis, Peter Paul Rubens.

11. **L'Apothéose du roi Henry IV et la régence de Marie de Médicis, 14 mai 1610** *(Apotheosis of Henry IV).*
Henry IV has just been assassinated by a madman; Time helps him ascend to Jupiter. Nobility kneels before the tearful queen and presents her with the orb of government.

12. **Le Gouvernement de la reine**, also known as **Le Conseil des dieux pour les mariages espagnols** *(The Council of the Gods).*
Princess Elizabeth, daughter of Henry IV and Marie de Médicis, was engaged to King Philip III of Spain. Her brother, Louis XIII, was to marry the daughter of Philip III, Anne of Austria, who was only fourteen.

13. **La Prise de Juliers, 1er septembre 1610** *(The Capture of Juliers).*
Juliers, a city in western Germany, was claimed by both the Holy Roman Emperor and the king of France. By capturing this city, Marie de Médicis proved that she could conquer, as did her late husband.

14. **L'Échange des princesses à Hendaye, 9 novembre 1615** *(The Exchange of Princesses).*
The princesses of France and Spain were "exchanged" on the river Bidassoa in Hendaye, on the French-Spanish border. France and Spain, depicted as friendly and helmeted messengers, present them.

15. **La Félicité de la régence** *(The Happiness of the Regency).*
Beauty, Love and the Arts triumph; Time is enchanted.

16. **La Majorité de Louis XIII, 20 octobre 1614** *(The Majority of Louis XIII).*
When Louis XIII came of age, Marie entrusted the Ship of State to him. Strength, Faith, Justice and Prudence hold the oars. Despite the show of enthusiasm, the king was determined to reign alone and exile his mother.

17. **La Reine s'enfuit du château de Blois, 21-22 février 1619** *(The Flight from Blois).*
Marie escaped from her exile in the castle of Blois on the night of February 21-22, 1619 (in reality she slipped through a window and jumped into the moat). The gods are shown protecting her flight and the painter pays tribute to maternal love.

18. **La Reine reçoit des offres de paix, 30 avril 1619** *(The Treaty of Angoulême).*
The treaty sealed the reconciliation of Marie and her son. Here Mercury brings the olive branch, the symbol of peace, to Angoulême. The painter makes no reference to the role of Cardinal Richelieu, the instigator of the reconciliation.

19. **La Conclusion de la paix, 10 août 1620** *(The Peace of Angers).*
Mercury leads Marie up the steps of the Temple of Concord while a woman protects her from

evil figures, perhaps representing supporters of the Duke of Luyne, who was hostile to the Queen.

20. La Réconciliation de la reine et de son fils *(The Queen's Reconciliation with Her Son).*
Mother and son are reconciled. The fact that Louis XIII wished to stop Marie and imposed her exile in Blois has been practically forgotten.

21. Le Triomphe de la Vérité *(The Triumph of Truth).*
The queen and her son are in heaven, holding a flaming heart crowned with laurels, while Time helps naked Truth climb up to them. Shortly after commissioning this idyllic image of her life, Marie was again sent into exile, this time definitively.

Marius défait les Cimbres dans la plaine située entre Belsanettes et la Grande Fugère (Provence) *(Marius Defeating the Cimbrians)*
See **Défaite des Cimbres**.

Alexandre Gabriel Descamps

Marius prisonnier à Minturnes *(Marius Imprisoned at Minturnae)*

Germain-Jean Drouais

(Hist.) Gaius Marius was a Roman statesman and general (2nd century B.C.), famous for his heroic actions and the clumsy intrigues that set him at odds with all the parties. He was, however, extremely popular: when the Senate granted his rival, Sulla, the command of the forces against Mithriades VI, the people voted to grant it to Marius instead. Sulla had already left Rome, but when he heard the news, returned with the legions. Marius, seized by fear, took flight and hid in the marshes of Minturnae. He was discovered and condemned by the Senate, but no one was willing to carry out the death sentence. The magistrates summoned a Cimbrian cavalryman. He went to Marius who asked in an awesome voice, "My man, do you dare make an end of Gaius Marius?" Marius had defeated the Cimbrians in a memorable battle (see **Défaite des Cimbres**). The cavalryman fled crying, "I cannot kill Gaius Marius." His reaction astonished everyone and Marius was eventually allowed to go to Africa. Later, after regaining favor, he returned to Rome.

Mars enlaçant Vénus *(Mars Embracing Venus)*
Mars et Vénus *(Mars and Venus),* also known as **Le Parnasse** *(Parnassus)*
See **Parnasse**.

French, 18th century
Andrea Mantegna

Mars et Vénus dans la forge de Vulcain *(Mars and Venus in Vulcan's Forge)*
(Myth.) Venus, although the wife of Vulcan, blacksmith and god of fire, was in love with Mars. Cupid, the god of love, was born of Venus' infidelity (also see **Mars et Vénus surpris par Vulcain**).

Luca Giordano

Mars et Vénus dans la forge de Vulcain, Luca Giordano.

Mars et Vénus surpris par Vulcain *(Mars and Venus Surprised by Vulcan)*
(Myth.) Venus was married to Vulcan by her father, Jupiter, but was in love with the god Mars. One of their adventures was told by Ovid and Homer. The Sun, who sees all, caught sight of

Louis Lagrenée

them embracing and informed Vulcan. The husband arrived, not with a blanket as depicted here, but with an invisible net which he threw over the lovers; they were caught in the net and mocked by the gods who Vulcan had summoned to witness the event. Neptune interceded on behalf of the lovers and convinced Vulcan to set them free.

Martyre de saint André (Le) *(The Martyrdom of Saint Andrew)*

Luca Giordano

(Christ. Trad.) Like many other martyrs, Saint Andrew was persecuted for refusing to worship idols. He also converted the wife of Egeas, the Roman governor of Patras, Greece. As punishment for this unpardonable crime, the governor decreed that he be crucified. Andrew, who glorified the cross, was overjoyed to be bound to it himself. He remained alive for two days, while the people, who were against his torture, wanted to take him down. He pleaded with them to leave him there and their arms were paralysed. The troubled governor pardoned him, but Andrew prayed to die on the cross. He was surrounded by a blinding light and as the light ascended to heaven, he took his final breath.

Martyre de saint Côme et saint Damien, Fra Angelico.

Martyre de saint Côme et saint Damien *(The Martyrdom of Saints Cosmas and Damian)*

Fra Angelico

(Christ. Trad.) Cosmas and Damian, were inseparable twins, persecuted under Diocletian around 287 because they refused to worship idols. After being condemned to death, they were cast into the sea, thrown into a fire, tortured and stoned, but could not be killed. As with many other martyrs, the final recourse was beheading, which no one survived. They were beheaded with their three brothers, Antinus, Leonce and Eutrope.

Martyre de saint Denis *(The Martyrdom of Saint Denis)*

Henri Bellechose

(Christ. Trad.) Saint Denis, bishop in the 3rd century, was beheaded at Montmartre in Paris where was serving as a missionary. He is said to have stood up before his executioners bearing his severed head in his hands (this legend may have originated from a statue from which the head became separated and was placed in its arms).

Martyre de saint Érasme *(The Martyrdom of Saint Erasmus)*

After Nicolas Poussin

(Christ. Trad.) Saint Erasmus is said to have been martyred under Diocletian (3rd century), but is often confused with other martyrs of the same name. According to legend he was disemboweled and his intestines wound around a windlass, but this version was probably the result of a misinterpretation; a windlass and a rope were his symbols in primitive art.

Martyre de saint Étienne *(The Martyrdom of Saint Stephen)*

Jean-Baptiste Mauzaisse

(N.T.) Saint Stephen was the first of the seven deacons of the Christian Church chosen by the apostles help them administer the new community of the converted. Stephen was also the first

Christian martyr. He was preaching in Jerusalem when the Jews, angered by his conversions, had him captured and brought before the Sanhedrin, the Jewish legislative council. False witnesses were produced, who accused him of having spoken against Hebraic law, and after a mock trial, he was stoned. Stephen, like Christ, prayed for his executioners. Young Saul, who later became Saint Paul, approved of this murder. According to the Bible, the executioners laid their garments at Saul's feet (see **Conversion de saint Paul**).

Same subject: **Lapidation de saint Étienne**, Anibale Carraci, Cornelis van Poelenburgh. **Saint Étienne conduit au martyre**, Michel-Ange Houasse.

Martyre de saint Jacques le Majeur (The Martyrdom of Saint James the Greater)

Lorenzo Monaco

(Christ. Trad.) Saint James the Greater, one of the twelve disciples, was persecuted by Herod Agrippa, king of Judea, who sentenced him to be beheaded. On the way to his execution, he healed a paralytic, converted a Pharisaic scribe and baptized them both just before they were executed. According to legend, James' followers, fearing the Jews, were hesitant to provide him with a grave and put his body on a boat, which they cast out into the water. Guided by an angel, the boat landed in Spain, the origin of the pilgrimage to the shrine at Santiago de Compostela.

Martyre de saint Janvier (The Martyrdom of Saint Januarius)

Luca Giordano

(Christ. Trad.) Saint Januarius was a bishop in the 3rd century, at the beginning of Diocletian's persecution of the Christians. He was led to Pozzuoli and beheaded in 301. Several towns claim his relics, consisting of two phials containing his coagulated blood, which liquefies at varying intervals and attract crowds of pilgrims.

Martyre de saint Jean l'Évangéliste
(The Martyrdom of Saint John the Evangelist)

Master of the Martyrdom of Saint John

(N.T.) Saint John the Evangelist was persecuted under Domitian, Roman emperor in the 1st century. Domitian had him thrown in boiling oil, but he escaped unharmed. Domitian then exiled him to the island of Patmos where he wrote the Apocalypse.

Martyre de saint Sébastien, Andrea Mantegna.

Martyre de saint Pierre *(The Martyrdom of Saint Peter)*

Pierre Subleyras

(N.T.) Simon-Peter, one of the twelve disciples, was martyred under Nero. He asked to be crucified upside down, saying that it was fitting that the Son who descended from heaven was crucified upright, but that his own head should point to the ground. When the population revolted against Nero and attempted to take him down, Peter ordered them to leave him to die.

Martyre de saint Sébastien *(The Martyrdom of Saint Sebastian)*

Camille Corot
Anthony van Dyck
Andrea Mantegna
Michele Manzoni
Hans Memling
Perugino

(Christ. Trad.) Saint Sebastian was an officer in the Roman Imperial guard in the 3rd century. Emperor Diocletian put him in charge of a company, but he comforted the Christians he saw collapsing under torture. His behavior was reported to the emperor who ordered that he be taken to the middle of a field and pierced by arrows. He was left to die but, according to tradition, was either healed by a local widow, Irene or by angels, or revived by Christ. Several years later, he was martyred for a second time, battered to death.

Same subject: **Saint Sébastien martyr**, Sebastiano Ricci. **Saint Sébastien martyr dans un paysage**, Guido Reni. **Saint Sébastien secouru par les anges**, Anthony van Dyck. **Saint Sébastien soigné par Irène**, Georges de la Tour.

Martyre de sainte Irène *(The Martyrdom of Saint Irene)*

Carlo Francesco Nuvolone

(Christ. Trad.) Irene was martyred in Salonika (today called Thessaloniki) in 304. Roman governor Dulcitius forced her to witness the burning of her sisters, Agape and Chionia, but offered to pardon her if she worshiped pagan gods. She refused and was condemned to be exposed naked in a brothel. Irene was protected by the Holy Ghost, so that no man dared approach her. Dulcitius finally condemned her to be burned alive like her sisters. She went to the stake singing.

Martyre des chartreux d'Allemagne *(The Martyrdom of the German Carthusians)*, previously known as **Martyre des chartreux à Bourg-Fontaine** *(The Martyrdom of the Carthusians at Bourg-Fontaine)*

Vincente Carducho

(Christ. Trad.) The title of this painting was changed as the attackers are obviously Turks. The European Carthusians were massacred in the 16th century when the Turkish army arrived in the area surrounding Vienna.

Martyre des vénérables Vincent Herck et Jean Léodieux de la chartreuse de Ruermonde *(The Martyrdom of the Venerables Vincent Herck and Jean Léodieux of the Charterhouse of Roermond)*

Vincente Carducho

(Christ. Trad.) This is an episode from the Dutch uprising against Spain on July 8, 1572. William, prince of Orange, called William the Silent, crossed the Rhine with an army he raised in Germany to reconquer Roermond in the Netherlands. The army was not able to enter the town, but besieged it and forced its surrender. The sieging troops pillaged and massacred; twelve of the twenty-three Carthusian monks were savagely killed. It is said that the head of Father Vincent Herck, sexton of the community, was split open and his blood flowed on to the altar.

Massacres de Scio *(The Massacre at Chios)*
See **Scènes des Massacres de Scio**.

Eugène Delacroix

Massacre des Innocents *(The Massacre of the Innocents)*

Émile Champmartin

(N.T.) Herod the Great, the first to receive the title "King of the Jews" from the Romans, should not be confused with his son Herod Antipas, who was responsible for the beheading of Saint John the Baptist. Herod became alarmed when he heard that the Magi had paid homage to the Infant Messiah, born in Bethlehem. He had all the children under the age of two killed, but Mary and Joseph, who had been forewarned in a dream, had already fled to Egypt with the child.

Same subject: **Massacre des Innocents devant Hérode**, Rhine, 15th century.

Massacres du triumvirat (Les) *(The Massacres of the Triumvirate)*

Antoine Caron

(Hist.) This episode involves the Second Triumvirate formed by Octavian (future emperor Augustus), Marc Antony and Lepidus in 43 B.C. The First Triumvirate (Julius Caesar, Pompey and Marcus Licinius Crassus) had been indulgent with its enemies, but this leniency proved to be detrimental. The Second Triumvirate therefore began with severe repression. Three hundred senators and two thousand knights were executed; even members of the rulers' families were not spared. Marc Antony ordered the assassination of Cicero, statesman, writer and orator, and commanded that his head be hung above the rostra in the Forum from which the leaders harangued the people. Here Cicero's assassin is depicted bearing Cicero's head, impaled on his sword, to the triumvirs.

Médée enlevée sur son char après avoir tué ses enfants *(Medea Born Away in Her Chariot After Killing Her Children)*

Jean-François de Troy

See **Médée furieuse**.

Médée furieuse *(Medea)*

Eugène Delacroix

(Myth., Lit.) Medea, who had magical powers, was the granddaughter of the Sun. She helped Jason capture the Golden Fleece (see **Jason présentant la Toison d'or dans le temple de Jupiter**). They were married and she followed him to Corinth. The king of Corinth, Creon, wanted Jason to banish Medea and marry his daughter,

Creusa. Medea appeared to accept the plan and even sent her rival a beautiful robe and jewels. The gifts had, however, been dipped in a poison which burned the young woman and her father who came to her aid. Medea set fire to the palace and then killed her two children by Jason to avoid their enslavement. She then soared off to Athens in her chariot drawn by winged dragons.

Méléagre présentant à Atalante la hure du sanglier de Calydon *(Meleager Presenting the Head of the Calydonian Boar to Atalanta)* **Méléagre supplié par sa famille de prendre les armes pour défendre la ville de Calydon** *(Meleager Entreated by His Family to Defend Calydon)* See **Chasse de Méléagre et d'Atalante**.

Attributed to Caspar Netscher
François-Guillaume Ménageot

Mercure, amoureux de Hersé, change en pierre Aglaure qui voulait l'empêcher d'entrer chez sa soeur *(Mecury Changing Aglauros Into Stone)* (Myth.) The three sisters, Herse, Aglauros and Pandrosos were Athenian princesses. After Mercury fell in love with Herse, the most beautiful, Aglauros prevented him from entering her sister's chamber out of jealousy. According to some legends, Herse gave birth to Cephalus after being seduced by Mercury (see **Céphale et Aurore**), but there are varying accounts of his origin.

Jean-Baptiste-Marie Pierre

Mercure endormant Argus *(Mercury Lulling Argus to Sleep)* **Mercure endormant Argus au son de la flûte** *(Mercury Lulling Argus to Sleep with the Pipes)* See **Mercure et Argus**.

Charles de Steuben
Rhine, 17th century

Mercure et Argus *(Mercury and Argus)*   Jean Honoré Fragonard
(Myth.) Ovid recounts this tale of Juno's jealousy of Io with whom Jupiter had fallen in love. Jupiter changed the young woman into a cow, but Juno was not deceived. She tricked Jupiter into having the cow watched over by Argus, whose 100 eyes kept a constant watch over her. The frustrated Jupiter ordered Mercury to free the unfortunate Io. Mercury lulled Argus to sleep with the reed pipes and then deepened his sleep using his magic wand. Once all the eyes had closed, he killed Argus. Juno was inconsolable and set Argus' eyes in the tail of her favorite animal, the peacock.

Same subject: **Mercure endormant Argus**, Charles de Steuben. **Mercure endormant Argus au son de la flûte**, Rome, 17th century.

Mercure ordonne à Énée d'abandonner Didon *(Mercury Ordering Aeneas to Abandon Dido)*   Orazio Samacchini
See **Mort de Didon**.

Mère Catherine-Agnès Arnauld et la soeur Catherine de Sainte Suzanne Champaigne *(Mother Catherine Agnes Arnauld and Sister Catherine de Sainte*   Philippe de Champaigne

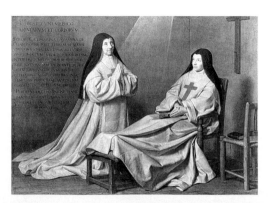

Mère Catherine-Agnès Arnauld et la sœur Catherine de Sainte-Suzanne Champaigne, Philippe de Champaigne.

Suzanne, the Artist's Daughter, also known as **Ex-Voto de 1662** *(The Ex-Voto of 1662)*

(Hist.) This incident took place in the Convent of Port Royal during the reign of Louis XIV, when there was considerable laxity in the religious orders. The mother superior, Angélique Arnaud, reestablished total austerity and a cloistered life for the sisters. Her sister, Mother Agnes, was a member of the community. In early January, 1662, Sister Catherine de Sainte Suzanne, the artist's daughter, who had been unable to walk for fourteen months, was miraculously healed. She went to the chapel where she knelt for mass and then descended a flight of forty steps to the amazement of the community. The artist painted this work as an expression of gratitude for this miracle.

Messe de fondation des ordres trinitaires (La) *(The Mass for the Foundation of the Order of the Trinitarians)*

Juan Carreno de Miranda

(Christ. Trad.) This scene took place at the end of the 12th century. Saint John of Matha was celebrating mass in the Lady Chapel of the archdiocese of Paris attended by gentlemen and monks. When he raised the host, a vision of the Trinity accompanied by angels appeared directly above his head. One angel, dressed in white and bearing a blue and red cross on its chest, placed its crossed arms on the heads of two kneeling slaves. The slave, dressed in red, was a Christian and the other, dressed in blue, was a Saracen. As a result of this vision, John of Matha founded the order of Trinitarian friars in 1198 to free captives. The members of the order, who wore a red and blue cross on the scapular, were also dedicated to caring for the sick.

Messe de saint Basile (La) *(The Mass of Saint Basil)*

Pierre Subleyras

(Christ. Trad.) Roman emperor Flavius Valens (4th century) was a Christian who adhered to the beliefs of Arius. Arianism differed from the original beliefs of Christianity in claiming that Jesus was not of the same substance as the Father. Valens wished to convince Saint Basil, bishop of Caesarae, to follow this doctrine. One day he fainted when he saw the saint celebrating mass.

Messe de saint Grégoire, Amiens or Burgundy, 15th century.

Messe de saint Grégoire *(The Mass of Saint Gregory)*

Amiens or Burgundy, 15th century

(Christ. Trad.) Pope Gregory the Great became a monk at the age of thirty-five and transformed the palace he inherited from his rich family into a monastery. He was elected pope by popular acclaim in 590. One day while he was celebrating the Easter mass, Christ appeared to him surrounded by the Instruments of the Passion, and a chalice collecting his blood (the numerous objects known as the "Instruments of the Passion" include the nails and the hammer, the lance, the sponge, the rods and the crown of thorns). The scene traditionally takes place in the Church of Santa Croce di Gerusalemme in Rome.

Messe de saint Martin (The Mass of Saint Martin)

Eustache Le Sueur

(Christ. Trad.) On his way to the church one day, Saint Martin, the bishop of Tours, met a beggar who was almost naked. He ordered the archdeacon to dress him, but the deacon did not react quickly enough and Saint Martin gave the poor man his own tunic. He then said mass during which a ball of fire appeared above his head.

Minerve chassant les Vices du jardin de la Vertu (Minerva Chases the Vices from the Garden of Virtue)

Andrea Mantegna

(Myth.) Inspired by Ovid and Pindar, the artist used mythological figures to depict a Christian subject. Three chaste goddesses lead the combat: Minerva, armed with a lance; Diana, with her bow; and a third goddess (Aurora? or Ceres?), bearing a torch. Behind them is the laurel-woman, Daphne, the symbol of abandoned virtue. In heaven the three Cardinal Virtues support the goddesses: Justice with the scales and the sword; Fortitude, with the club and the column; and Temperance, bearing a jar of wine and a jar of water with which she dilutes the wine. The fleeing figures include: bacchante and putti, who represent carnal love; the satyrs and Centaurs, one of whom is carrying the Venus Vulgaris on his back, are symbols of lust; Idleness, without arms, Sloth, dressed in rags, Ignorance, carried by Ingratitude and Avarice, and particularly the hermaphrodite with a monkey's head, are symbols of treachery, hatred and wickedness.

Minerve chez les Muses *(Minerva and the Muses)*

Jacques Stella

(Myth.) The nine Muses lived on Mt. Helicon where the winged horse Pegasus struck a rock with his hoof and made a source rise. The fountainhead, Hippocrene, was the source of poetic inspiration. The Muses were not distinguished from one another at the time of their creation, but at a later date (3rd-1st centuries B.C.) they each specialized in one domain. The Muses were followers of Apollo, god of Fine Arts and Truth, and accompanied him to Mt. Parnassus. Here they are visited by Minerva, the goddess of Wisdom.

Mirabeau devant Dreux-Brézé *(Mirabeau Before Dreux-Brézé)*

Alexandre-Évariste Fragonard

(Hist.) Louis XVI summoned the States-General, consisting of deputies elected by the three orders of nobility, clergy and the third estate. Difficulties were encountered from the first meet-

Le Miracle de la Vraie Croix, followers of Simon Marmion.

ing on May 5,1789. The third estate remained behind to deliberate. The marquis of Dreux-Brézé, master of ceremonies to the French king, gave the group's leader, Mirabeau, the order to disperse. Mirabeau, famous for his eloquence, replied, "Go and tell those who sent you that we are here by the will of the people and that we will not leave unless forced out by bayonets."

Miracle de la Vraie Croix (Le) *(The Miracle of the True Cross)*, also known as **Invention de la Croix (L')** *(The Invention of the True Cross)*

Followers of Simon Marmion

(Christ. Trad.) Saint Helena, mother of Emperor Constantine (3rd-4th centuries), discovered the cross on which Jesus was crucified. Excavations on Golgotha, undertaken after she had a dream, uncovered three crosses. When a recently deceased young woman was revived after being touched by one of the crosses, the identity of true cross of Jesus was ascertained.

Miracle de saint Éloi (Le) *(The Miracle of Saint Eloi)*

Gaetano Gandolfi

(Christ. Trad.) Before he chose a saintly life, Eloi was a master smith. Proud of his craft, he wrote on his sign: "Eloi, master of masters, master of all, who forges a shoe in two heats" (i.e., heating it only twice or very quickly). Jesus decided to teach him a lesson in humility and appeared to him as a fellow smith traveling through France. He asked to work under him and soon proved himself to be more talented and faster than his master. One day when he had to shoe a horse, he cut off its hooves and then returned them to their rightful position. Eloi observed him and the following day attempted to do the same thing. He cut off the first hoof and the horse began to bleed. Eloi was desperate and prepared to use the knife on himself, but the "apprentice" suddenly appeared and healed the hoof. Eloi took down his sign and changed the inscription to "You are the master and I am the apprentice." Jesus said to him, "Happy is the humble man," and Eloi recognized him and fell to his feet. Jesus added, "You are pardoned, but henceforth you shall know that I am the Master of all."

Miracle de saint François de Paule (Un) *(A Miracle of Saint Francis of Paola)*
See **Saint François de Paule guérissant Jean Caratello**.

Theodor van Thulden

Miracles de sainte Marie pénitente (Les) *(The Miracles of the Repentant Mary)*
(Christ. Trad.) This strange story is told in the *Golden Legend*. Through Mary Magdalene's, prayers a woman who had been barren for many years conceived. The woman's husband was overjoyed and wished to go to Rome to hear Saint Peter. On the boat, his wife gave birth and died. The sailors intended to throw her body into the sea, but the husband pleaded with them to allow him to disembark on an island with his dead wife, the child and Mary Magdalene. Curiously enough, he abandoned them and, despite his distress, continued his journey. He returned two years later to find the child, cared for by Mary Magdalene, in good health and on his arrival the mother appeared to awaken from a dream.

Philippe de Champaigne

Miracle des ardents *(The Miracle of the Burning-sickness)*
(Christ. Trad.) The "burning-sickness" was a type of gangrene and terrible epidemics of this illness were mainly due to malnutrition. The Parisians relied on the relics of their protectress, Saint Geneviève, which they had placed in a chapel built in honor of Saint Geneviève-des-Ardents. This painting celebrates the staying of the epidemic through the intervention of the saint in 1129.

Gabriel-François Doyen

Miracle du saint Voult *(The Miracle of Saint Voult)*

Cologne, 15th century

(Christ. Trad.) A musician came to play the viol before the image of Christ in Lucca, Toscany. This Byzantine crucifix is known as the Saint-Voult (Sainte-Face). The crucified Jesus rewarded the musician with one of his golden slippers.

Mise au tombeau *(The Entombment)*

Paris or Burgundy, 15th century
Cologne, 16th century
Jaime Huguet
Bartolomeo Schedone
Jan Tengnagel
Titian
Simon Vouet

(N.T.) Joseph of Arimathaea obtained permission from Pontius Pilate to bury Jesus' body (see **Descente de croix**). He bought a shroud and helped the small group of disciples and the holy women wrap the body. As the dead could not be buried on the Sabbath, he provided his own tomb.

Same subject: **Christ porté au tombeau**, attributed to Julio Cesare Amidano. **Ensevelissement du Christ**, Quentin Varin. **Christ mort au tombeau**, Perugino.

Mise au tombeau, Titian.

Moïse changeant en serpent la verge d'Aaron *(Moses Changing the Rod into a Serpent)*

Nicolas Poussin

(O.T.) God ordered Moses to lead the Israelites out of Egypt, where they were prisoners (see **Buisson ardent**). He went before Pharaoh with his brother Aaron whom he had told to bring a rod with him. Pharaoh demanded proof of their authority and Moses told his brother to throw the rod to the ground. As it fell, it was transformed into a serpent. Pharaoh's magicians threw their rods to the ground and they were also turned into serpents. Moses'serpent swallowed them.

Moïse enfant foulant aux pieds la couronne de Pharaon *(The Infant Moses Trampling Pharaoh's Crown)*

Nicolas Poussin
Otto Wagenfeldt

(Christ. Trad.) Moses was found by Pharaoh's daughter, Thermutis (see **Moïse sauvé des eaux**). She had no children and loved him as her own son. One day she suggested to her father that Moses inherit his dynasty. The Pharaoh received the boy with joy and placed his crown on the child's head, but Moses threw it to the ground and trampled on it. The court magician then predicted that the child would overthrow the Pharaoh. An officer raised his dagger and attempted to seize Moses, but Thermutis' servants acted quickly; one stopped his arm and the other fled with the child. The Pharaoh attributed the incident to the child's innocence.

Same subject: **Moïse foulant aux pieds la couronne de Pharaon**, French, 18th century.

Moïse enterrant sous le sable l'Égyptien qu'il avait tué *(Moses Burying the Egyptian in the Sand)*

Pierre Patel the Elder

(O.T.) The young Moses killed an Egyptian, whom he discovered attacking a Hebrew, and buried his body in the sand. The next day he saw two Hebrews fighting and asked one of them, "Why do you strike your fellow?" The man asked him what right he had to judge their quarrel and added, "Do you mean to kill me as you killed the Egyptian?" Moses was alarmed for he was convinced that there had been no witnesses to the murder. He fled to the land of Midian where he later married Jethro's daughter.

Moïse enterrant sous le sable l'Égyptien qu'il avait tué, Pierre Patel the Elder.

Moïse et le serpent d'airain *(Moses and the Brazen Serpent)*

Jean-Charles Frontier

(O.T.) Moses led the Israelites out of Egypt, where they were prisoners, but the journey to the Promised Land, Canaan, was long and full of trials. The Hebrews were hungry and thirsty and often complained that they should have stayed in Egypt. One day, shortly before they arrived in Canaan, God, who was irritated by their constant complaining, sent serpents to bite them. Many died and they asked Moses to come to their aid. He prayed to God who told him to forge a brazen serpent and place it on the end of a pole. All who looked up to it would be healed. (This was the model for the crosier or pastoral staff. The brazen serpent prefigured Christ on the cross to whom one must look up in order to be saved.)

Moïse foulant aux pieds la couronne de Pharaon *(Moses Trampling Pharaoh's Crown)*

French, 18th century

See **Moïse enfant foulant aux pieds la couronne de Pharaon.**

Moïse frappant le rocher *(Moses Striking the Rock)*
See **Frappement du rocher**.

Valerio Castello

Moïse sauvé des eaux *(The Finding of the Infant Moses)*
(O.T.) The Hebrews were prisoners in Egypt where they labored for the Pharaoh. The Pharaoh, probably Ramses II, fearing the Hebrews' increasing numbers, ordered their newborn males to be drowned. Moses' mother, Josabeth, hid him for the first three months and then, no longer able to conceal him, placed him in a papyrus basket among the reeds on the banks of the Nile. The child's elder sister, Myriam, remained behind. Pharaoh's own daughter, Thermutis, discovered the child and took him to her father's palace. Informed by Myriam, Josabeth went to the palace to offer her services as nurse. Thus, the infant Moses was raised by his mother in the court of the Pharaoh.

Niccolò dell'Abate
Thomas Blanchet
Charles de La Fosse
Nicolas de Largrillière
Nicolas Poussin

Montée au Calvaire *(The Road to Calvary)*
See **Portement de croix**.

Brunswick Monogrammist
Nicolas de Largrillière
Giuseppe Balzacès

Mort d'Adonis (La) *(The Death of Adonis)*
(Myth.) This story is an ancient Greek fable from Syria. Adonis was the son of Myrrha, who tricked her own father, Cinyras, into laying with her. Cinyras discovered the treachery and pursued her, intending to kill her. She wandered for months and prayed to the gods who took pity on her and transformed her into a tree (the myrrh tree). Her nurse Lucina stood near the tree and when it split open, received the young Adonis as he emerged. The child grew to be so handsome that two goddesses, Proserpine and Venus, fought over him. He spent four months in the underworld with Proserpine and eight months on earth with Venus, thus personifying

Jean-Baptiste Regnault
Lambert Sustris

the mystery of vegetation. He was mortally wounded by a boar and an anemone was formed from each drop of his blood. The goddesses shed tears and a rose sprang from each tear.

Same subject: **Vénus pleurant Adonis transformé en anémone**, Constantin Netscher.

Mort d'Alceste *(The Death of Alcestis)*   Pierre Peyron
See **Alceste se dévouant à la mort**.

Mort d'Atala (La) *(The Death of Atala)*   Anne-Louis Girodet
See **Atala portée au tombeau**.

Mort de Caton d'Utique *(Death of Cato of Utica)*   Giovanni Battista Langetti

(Hist.) Cato, a Roman statesman (95-46 B.C.), was a Stoic with a reputation for honesty and incorruptibility. He fought Caesar and was an ally of Pompey. After Pompey's defeat at Pharsala, Cato was determined not to fall into Caesar's hands and also wished to avoid witnessing the fall of the Republic. Cato was so determined that he took his time. He invited his friends to dinner, treated them with affection, discussed philosophy, read Plato, and tearfully implored his sons and friends to return his sword, which they had hidden. He also asked for news of his officers whom he had aided to escape by boat and then locked himself away and stabbed himself. A doctor attempted to save him, but he tore out the stitches and ripped off the bandages.

Mort de Cléopâtre (La) *(The Death of Cleopatra)*   Louis Lagrenée
Alessandro Turchi

(Hist.) Cleopatra, the irresistible queen of Egypt, seduced Julius Caesar; he helped her to consolidate her power and took her to Rome. After his death, she seduced his successor, Marc Antony, and they both traveled through Greece and Asia with sumptuous retinues. Marc Antony neglected his obligations to Rome, and Octavius (future Emperor Augustus) declared war on them. Following Octavius' victory, Marc Antony committed suicide. Unable to bear Marc Antony's death and her defeat, Cleopatra took her own life. Legend has it that she allowed an asp to bite her.

Same subject: **Suicide de Cléopâtre mordue par un aspic**, Giampietrino.

Mort de Démosthène (La) *(The Death of Demosthenes)*

Félix Boisselier

(Hist.) The speeches of this eminent orator (384-322 B.C.) fired the Athenians' revolt against the invasions of Philip and, later, Alexander of Macedonia. Demosthenes was pursued by their suc-

La Mort de Didon, Peter Paul Rubens.

cessor, General Antipater, and took refuge in the temple of Neptune on the Island of Kalauria. When summoned by Antipater's soldiers, he poisoned himself.

Mort de Didon (La) *(The Death of Dido)* Peter Paul Rubens
(Myth., Lit.) Aeneas, the hero of the *Aeneid*, was shipwrecked on the shore of Africa and was well received by Dido, queen of Carthage. She fell in love with him through Venus'intervention. Aeneas stayed with her a year and even participated in plans for reconstruction of the city. The gods became impatient since his destiny was to found a new city in Italy, and Mercury was sent to entreat him to set sail. Dido begged him to stay, but could not weaken his resolve. Finally, she fell silent and had a pyre erected at the summit of the city. Aeneas saw the flames from his ship, but it was not until he descended into the underworld and met Dido's ghost, that he understood what had happened. He attempted to reconcile her, but she drew away in anger.

Mort d'Élisabeth reine d'Angleterre Paul Delaroche
(The Death of Elizabeth I, Queen of England)
(Hist.) Elizabeth I ruled from 1558 to 1603 and during her reign England enjoyed unprecedented grandeur. Here she is supported by her ladies-in-waiting. The Lord Chancellor, the Lord Admiral and the bishop of Canterbury are in the background while the secretary of state, Lord Cecil, kneels before her asking for the name of her successor. She is said to have replied that having ruled like a king, she should be followed by one.

Mort de Géricault *(The Death of Géricault)* Ary Scheffer
(Hist.) The painter Théodore Géricault died on January 26, 1824, at the age of thirty-two, as a re-

sult of a wound sustained two years earlier when he fell from his horse. Two of his friends are present: Colonel Bro de Comène, behind the bed, and the painter Joseph Dedreux-Dorcy, seated on the chair.

Mort de la femme de Darius (La) *(The Death of the Wife of Darius)*

Louis Lagrenée

(Hist., Lit.) King Darius of Persia was conquered by Alexander the Great and escaped, but his wife and daughters were taken captive. The death of Darius'wife was a terrible blow for Alexander the Great who had treated his prisoners with royal respect and generosity (see **La Famille de Darius aux pieds d'Alexandre**). He feared that Darius would unjustly accuse him of her death.

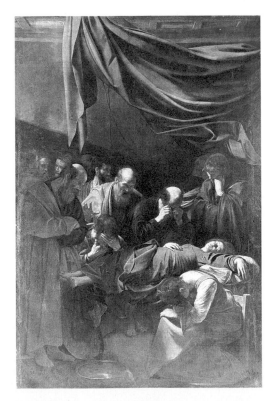

Mort de la Vierge, Caravaggio.

Mort de la Vierge *(The Death of the Virgin)*

Austrian, 15th century
Boccaccino Boccaccio
Caravaggio

(Christ. Trad.) According to some texts, after Jesus' death, the Virgin Mary went to Ephesus where she lived with Mary, the wife of Clopas, and Mary Magdalene. The angel Gabriel announced her death (second Annunciation, which can be distinguished from the first by Mary's age). She requested the presence of Saint John, who was immediately borne to her on a cloud. The other disciples, scattered throughout the world, were also miraculously informed of her imminent death and rushed to her bedside. Three days later, Mary was carried to heaven by angels (see **Assomption**). Catholic and orthodox dogma differ here: for the Catholics, Mary died and was resurrected like her son; for the orthodox, she only appeared to be dead and was carried to heaven sleeping (dormition).

Mort de Méléagre (La) *(The Death of Meleager)*

Charles Le Brun

(Myth.) When Meleager was seven days old the Fates informed his mother that he would not die until the log burning in the hearth was consumed. His mother snatched the log from the flames and locked it in a chest. After the Calydonian boar hunt (see **Chasse de Méléagre et d'Atalante**), Meleager offered the animal's hide and pelt to Atalanta. His uncles protested and were killed by Meleager in the ensuing dispute. Althaea, indignant at the murder of her brothers, fetched the log and burned it, thus causing Meleager's death. She subsequently regretted her act and hanged herself.

Mort d'Ophélie (La) *(The Death of Ophelia)*

Eugène Delacroix

(Lit.) Ophelia is Hamlet's fiancée in the Shakespearian tragedy bearing his name. She waits for him and does not understand his internal conflicts (see **Hamlet et Ophélie**). Suffering from madness, real or feigned, he rejects her.

Confused, she walks along the banks of a river and hangs garlands of flowers in the trees. A branch breaks and she falls in the water and drowns.

Mort de Roland *(The Death of Roland)*, also known as **Paysage. Mort de Roland** *(Landscape. The Death of Roland)*
(Hist., Lit.) Roland was a knight, presented in French epics as the nephew of Emperor Charlemagne. During a expedition in the Pyrenees against the Saracens, he commanded the rearguard. He had a small horn that he was to sound if he required assistance. Attacked treacherously at the Pass of Roncevalles, he waited too long before calling for help and his friends arrived to find him dead on the battlefield. Before dying, he attempted to break his sword, Durendal, against a rock, but split the rock instead.

Achille-Etna Michallon

Mort de saint Ambroise *(The Death of Saint Ambrose)*
(Christ. Trad.) On his deathbed, Saint Ambrose, bishop of Milan in the 4th century, saw Christ coming toward him, smiling. He died reciting prayers. At his funeral, some saw him ascend to heaven and others a star above his coffin. Numerous miracles followed his death.

Bon Boullongne

Mort de saint Antoine (La) *(The Death of Saint Antony)*
(Christ. Trad.) According to the *Golden Legend*, Saint Antony died simply in a monastery at the age of 150, after calling together and embracing his brethren. The date indicated is 340 A.D., under the reign of Constantine, which means that Saint Antony was in fact eighty nine. On the right, the painter has depicted Saint Paul the hermit who died praying just after Saint Antony left him (see **Saint Antoine et saint Paul ermite nourris par un corbeau**).

Claude Vignon

La Mort de saint Antoine, Claude Vignon.

Mort de saint Bonaventure *(The Death of Saint Bonaventure)*
See **Saint Bonaventure au concile de Lyon.**

Francisco de Zurbarán

Mort de saint Bruno *(The Death of Saint Bruno)*
(Christ. Trad.) Saint Bruno, the founder of the Carthusian monks, died in Calabria, in the cave he used as his cell, after summoning the community and confessing publicly (see **Scènes de la vie de saint Bruno**).

Vincente Carducho

Mort de Saphire (La) *(The Death of Sapphira)*
(N.T.) Ananias, Sapphira's husband, sold all his possessions to give the money to the community, as was the practice with the first Christians.

Sébastien Le Clerc the Younger
Nicolas Poussin

When he gave the money to Saint Peter he did not reveal that he had set aside a portion of the money for his personal needs. However, Saint Peter guessed what he had done and reproached him, saying "You have not lied to men but to God." At these words, Ananias fell down dead. His wife arrived several hours later and repeated the lie. She too was struck down.

La Mort de Sardanapale,
Eugène Delacroix.

Mort de Sardanapale (La) *(The Death of Sardanapalus)*

Eugène Delacroix

(Lit.) This painting was inspired by a poem by Lord Byron. Sardanapalus, an Assyrian ruler, is said to have died on the throne in 836. According to legend he led a voluptuous life. He was weakened by internal plots and external forces (40,000 soldiers from Persia, Media and Babylon, whom he fought three times). He resisted two year's of siege, but a wall that collapsed under the weight of the flooding Tiber provided an opening for the enemy. Sardanapalus prepared his suicide by ordering an immense pyre to be built in the court of his palace. His body and the bodies of his wives, eunuchs and horses, whom he had massacred before him, were to be burned along with his treasures.

Mort de Sénèque *(The Death of Seneca)*

Luca Giordano
Claude Vignon

(Hist.) Seneca, a Roman philosopher and playwright, was the tutor of young Nero. He was compromised by his involvement in political matters and Nero ordered him to commit suicide. He sat in a bath of warm water and slashed his wrists. He was sixty-one at the time of his death.

Mort de Virginie (La) *(The Death of Virginia)*

Guillaume Guillon

(Hist.) Virginia was a the daughter of a Roman centurion. Although she was engaged to another man, she was desired by the powerful Appius Claudius (5th century B.C.). Unable to seduce her, he had one of his dependents claim her as a former slave. Her father seized a knife and killed her to save her honor. Her death incited a rebellion in the army and led to the fall of the government.

Mort et apparitions de saint Jérôme *(Predella with Scenes of the Life of Saint Jerome)*

Sano di Pietro

(Christ. Trad.) According to legend, Saint Jerome died at the age of ninety-eight years and six months in a monastery that he had founded and where his sepulchre had been dug shortly before his death (420). He took his last com-

Mort et apparitions de saint Jérôme, Sano di Pietro.

munion in the presence of his disciples and the lion (see **Saint Jérôme et le lion**). After his death he appeared:

— to Saint Augustine accompanied by Saint John the Baptist. Saint John was carrying three crowns and Saint Augustine only two, symbolizing that he lacked the crown of a martyr.

— to the bishop of Bourges, Sulpicius Severus (6th century), who saw him carried up to heaven by Christ himself.

Mystère de la Passion, de la Cruxifixion, de la Résurrection de de l'Ascension du Christ

Antonio Campi

See entries under **Passion**, **Crucifixion**, **Résurrection**, and **Ascension**.

Nabuchodonosor fait crever les yeux à Sédécias, roi de Jérusalem, et massacrer ses enfants *(Nebuchadnezzar Has the Eyes of Zedekiah, King of Jerusalem, Put Out and His Children Massacred)*

Gabriel de Saint-Aubin

(Hist.) This event took place in the 6th century B.C. while Judah was ruled by Chaldea. Zedekiah, the king of Judah, imprisoned the prophet Jeremiah, who advised him not to rebel against Nebuchadnezzar, king of the Chaldeans. Nevertheless, Nebuchadnezzar was stronger and defeated Zedekiah. Nebuchadnezzar ordered Zedekiah's children to be massacred and his eyes to be put out. His final vision before being blinded was that of his sons being slain. Here he is shown bound in fetters to be taken to Babylon.

Naissance de l'Amour *(The Birth of Love)*

Eustache Le Sueur

(Myth.) There are several conflicting legends concerning the origins of Love or Cupid: the most recent say that he was the son of Venus and Mercury or Mars.

La Naissance de la Vierge, Bartolomé Esteban Murillo.

Naissance de la Vierge (La) *(The Birth of the Virgin)*

Annibale Carracci
Giovanni di Pietro
Master of the Life of the Virgin
Bartolomé Esteban Murillo
Carlo Saraceni

(Christ. Trad.) Mary was the miraculous daughter of Anne and Joachim, who had lost hope of having a child (see **Rencontre d'Anne et de Joachim à la Porte Dorée**). Her family was wealthy, which explains the affluent setting and the servants.

Same subject: **Nativité de la Vierge**, Pietro da Cortona, Nicolas Dipre.

Naissance de saint Jean-Baptiste *(The Birth of Saint John the Baptist)* See **Nativité de saint Jean-Baptiste**.

Lambert Sustris and his studio

Naissance d'Henri IV *(The Birth of Henry IV)*

Eugène Devéria

(Hist., Lit.) Henry IV was born in the castle of Pau on December 13,1553. This painting was inspired by a short story written by Abel Hugo, the son of Victor Hugo. An old guard donned his armor and helmet and took up his sword to celebrate the illustrious birth. He was accompanied by his grandson, Enriot, who carried a basket of garlic and aged wine. He made his way through the enthusiastic crowd and entered the chamber of the young mother, Jeanne d'Albret. Jeanne's father, Henry II of Navarre, raised his grandson in his arms and displayed him, saying that it was a son. The old guard presented him with his gifts. Henry II rubbed the lips of the newborn boy with garlic and had him drink a few drops of the wine from Jurançon. He asked the people to name the boy and all cried out in unison, "Henry, like his grandfather." Thus the child was named Henry III of Navarre before becoming Henry IV of France.

Naissance de Minerve *(The Birth of Minerva)*

Bon Boullongne the Younger

(Myth.) Minerva was the daughter of Jupiter and the goddess Metis, herself the daughter of the Ocean and Thetis. Before the child was born, Jupiter was warned that if Metis bore him a child, it would usurp his power. He swallowed both mother and child. At the end of the gestation, he asked Vulcan to split open his head and Minerva sprang forth, fully armed, shouting a war cry that shook heaven and earth.

Napoléon sur le champ de bataille d'Eylau *(Napoleon on the Battlefield at Eylau on February 9, 1807)*

Antoine-Jean Gros

(Hist.) The battle of Eylau, in Poland, was fought against the Russian general Bennigsen on February 8, 1807. There was heavy snow and the fighting claimed many lives. The victory was undecided, but Napoleon I finally won thanks to his military genius and the last-minute arrival of Marshal Ney, believed to have been lost. Bennigsen retreated. Close to 40,000 soldiers fell on the battlefield, 10,000 of them French.

Napoléon III à la bataille de Solferino *(Napoleon III at the Battle of Solferino)*

Ernest Meissonier

(Hist.) This battle between the French and the Austrians (1859) was undecided. It remained memorable because of the 40,000 men who died there.

Narcisse contemplant son reflet dans l'eau *(Narcissus Contemplating His Reflection in the Water)*

François Le Moyne

(Myth.) Narcissus was a handsome young man who scorned love. He disheartened many young women who fell in love with him (see **Écho et Narcisse**). A soothsayer predicted that he would live forever unless he looked upon his own face. Mirrors were kept from him, but one day he caught sight of his reflection in a pool and fell in love with it. Unable to reach his reflection, he pined away and died. Narcissi grew on the spot where he died. Another legend says that he had lost his beloved twin sister and believed his reflection to be her face, hence his constant contemplation of his own likeness.

Nativité (La) *(The Nativity)*

Cologne, 14th century
Italian, 14th century
Rhine, 15th century
Studio of Annibale Carracci
Bernardo Daddi
Nicolas Dipre

(N.T.) Mary and Joseph, who lived in Nazareth, went to Bethlehem for the census decreed by the Roman emperor Augustus. Mary was expecting a child and the time of the birth was approaching. Finding no room in the inn, she gave birth in a stable (the manger was a small feed trough: the ox and the ass were added in later renditions).

Same subject: **Nativité avec l'adoration des bergers**, Charles de La Fosse, Giulio Romano. **Nativité de Jésus**, Bernardino Luini. **Paysage avec la Nativité**, Cornelis van Poelenburgh.

Master of the Louvre Nativity
Master of the Life of the Virgin
Giovanni Battista Ortolano
Charles Poerson
Guido da Siena
Lo Spagna

Nativité avec l'adoration des bergers
(Nativity with the Adoration of the Shepherds)
See **Nativité** and **Adoration des bergers**.

Giulio Romano
Charles de La Fosse

Nativité de la Vierge (La) *(The Nativity of the Virgin)*
See **Naissance de la Vierge**.

Pietro da Cortona
Nicolas Dipre

Nativité de saint Jean-Baptiste (La) *(The Birth of Saint John the Baptist)*
(N.T.) Zacharias and Elizabeth, an elderly couple, had been barren for years when an angel appeared and announced to them the birth of a son. Zacharias, who was sceptical, became mute and did not regain his powers of speech until after the birth. Their son, John the Baptist, announced the coming of Christ. While the birth of the Virgin is generally depicted in an ornate setting, that of John the Baptist is generally situated in much more austere surroundings.

Same subject: **Naissance de saint Jean-Baptiste**, Lambert Sustris and his studio.

Luca Signorelli

Naufrage de Don Juan (Le) *(The Shipwreck of Don Juan)*
(Lit.) This painting is based on Lord Byron's epic poem *Don Juan*. The hero set sail in fine weather, but a sudden storm wrecked the ship. Don Juan remained perfectly calm; he prevented the sailors from panicking and becoming drunk, and climbed into a boat with several of them. This was the only boat whose occupants survived. They drifted for several days. Having exhausted

Eugène Delacroix

La Nef des fous,
Hieronymus Bosch.

their supplies, they lived on cadavers; the first was Don Juan's dog, which he ate with great remorse. They finally landed in a wild country.

Nef des fous (La) *(The Ship of Fools)*
(Lit.) The German satirical poem *Das Narrenschiff* by Sebastian Brandt, published in 1494 and translated into numerous languages, presents small illustrated portraits of various types of madness. In this painting the party of fools

Hieronymus Bosch

sails an unguided boat, drifting toward the fools' paradise. The men and women on board represent vices — gluttony and drunkenness — rather than madness. The mask hanging from the tree represents the lies or hypocrisy that hide vice.

Néoptolème et Ulysse enlèvent à Philoctète les flèches d'Hercule (Neoptolemus and Ulysses Stealing Hercules' Arrows from Philoctetes)

François-Xavier Fabre

(Myth.) Before dying, Hercules presented his bow and arrows to Philoctetes. On his way to Troy, Philoctetes was bitten by a snake or injured himself with one of Hercules' arrows. On Ulysses'advice he was abandoned on the island of Lemnos. Ten years passed. Achilles, Hector and Ajax were dead. The Greeks, despairing at Troy's strength, captured the Trojan soothsayer, Helenus, and forced him to pronounce an oracle. He revealed that Troy would be captured if Achilles's son, Neoptolemus (Pyrrhus), joined the fight and the Greeks were armed with Hercules'arrows. Ulysses and Neoptolemus set off for Lemnos and obtained the arrows from Philoctetes, either by persuasion or trickery. Philoctetes left with them, wounded Paris and then went to Italy where he founded two cities.

Neptune et Amymonè (Neptune and Amymone)

Carle van Loo

(Myth.) Amymone was one of the daughters of King Danaus of Argus. The country was suffering from drought inflicted as vengeance by Neptune. The god of the sea was jealous because the country had been attributed to Juno and not himself. Danaus sent his daughters to find water. The weary Amymone fell asleep in the countryside and a satyr attempted to rape her. She called on Neptune who chased the satyr with his trident. As Amymone and Neptune were celebrating their newfound love, his trident pierced a rock from which a triple source flowed.

Les Noces de Cana,
Veronese.

Noces de Cana (Les) *(The Marriage at Cana)*
(N.T.) Jesus was invited to a wedding feast. When the wine ran out, he ordered six stone jars destined for purification to be filled with water. They were brought to the steward who tasted the water and discovered that it had miraculously been transformed into excellent wine. This was Jesus' first public miracle.

Andalusia, 17th century
Flanders, 16th century
Leandro Bassano
Gerard David
Juan de Valdes Leal
Veronese

Noces de Thétis et de Pélée (Les) *(The Marriage of Thetis and Peleus)*
(Myth.) Thetis, a sea nymph, was loved and courted by both Jupiter and Neptune. After an oracle foretold that Thetis' son would be greater than his father (he was the greatest of heroes, Achilles), the gods both agreed that Thetis should be married to a mortal. Thetis attempted to escape this marriage through a series of metamorphoses, but finally submitted. The marriage of Thetis and Peleus was an occasion for great celebration among the gods. Eris, the goddess of Strife, was not invited, but appeared and threw down an apple marked "For the fairest." Juno, Minerva and Venus all fought for the apple. To solve the dispute, Jupiter ordered Mercury to take them to the shepherd Paris who would be the judge (see **Jugement de Pâris**).

Northern Italy, 15th century
Hendrick de Clerck
Bartolommeo di Giovanni

Noli me tangere
See **Jésus apparaît à la Madeleine**.

Fra Bartolommeo
Lorenzo di Credi

Nourriture de Bacchus (La) *(The Nurture of Bacchus)*
See **Enfance de Bacchus**.

Nicolas Poussin

Œdipe explique l'énigme, Jean Auguste Ingres.

Œdipe et Antigone *(Oedipus and Antigone)*

Johann Peter Krafft

(Myth., Lit.) Oedipus unwittingly fulfilled the oracle of his birth: he killed his father Laius, king of Thebes, and after being proclaimed king of Thebes, married Queen Jocasta, his mother (see **Œdipe explique l'enigme**). He vowed that Laius'murderer would be banished. Discovering himself to be the murderer, he put out his eyes. Jocasta hanged herself and Oedipus was banished for his crime. He lived a nomadic life, accompanied by his daughter and guide, Antigone, and finally died in Attica where he had been welcomed by Theseus.

Œdipe et le Sphinx *(Oedipus and the Sphinx)*

Jean Auguste Ingres

See **Œdipe explique l'enigme**.

Œdipe explique l'énigme or **Œdipe et le Sphinx** *(Oedipus Explains the Riddle of the Sphinx)*

Jean Auguste Ingres

(Myth., Lit.) Following an oracle's prediction that he would kill his father and marry his mother, Oedipus was exposed to wild beasts. He was saved by shepherds who raised him. As an adult, while on his way to Thebes, he killed a man. The victim was, in fact, his father Laius, king of the city. He continued on his way and met the Sphinx who asked all travelers to solve a riddle and devoured those who could not. She asked him, "What creature goes on four feet in the morning, on two at noonday, on three in the evening?" Oedipus answered easily, "Man, in childhood he creeps on hands and feet; in manhood he walks erect; in old age he helps himself with a staff." The frustrated Sphinx threw herself from the cliff and was killed, thus releasing Thebes from her curse. On his arrival in Thebes, Oedipus was proclaimed king and married the king's widow, Jocasta, not realizing that he was marrying his mother and thus fulfilling the oracle of his birth.

Œuvres de la Miséricorde (Les) *(The Works of Mercy)*

David Teniers the Younger
Simon de Vos

(Christ. Trad.) According to theologians, the seven works of mercy concerning the material needs of one's neighbor are:
— providing food or drink for those in need
— providing clothing for those in need
— visiting and relieving the sick
— ransoming prisoners
— visiting prisoners
— sheltering the poor and travelers
— burying the dead.

Oies du frère Philippe (Les) *(The Geese of Brother Philip)*

Pierre Subleyras

(Lit.) This painting is based on a tale by La Fontaine in which a man, embittered by his wife's death, goes to live in the woods with his newborn son. As the child grows older, his father teaches him about the trees and the birds, but never speaks to him of women. Late in life, he is obliged to take his son to the city to make provisions for him after his death. The young man is amazed by all that he discovers there, but particularly by the sight of a woman. He asks his father what it is and his father replies, "a goose." "What a pretty bird," exclaims the son and asks to take it back to the woods with him promising to allow it to graze.

Olinde et Sophronie sur le bûcher *(Olindo and Sophronia on the Pyre)*

After Eugène Delacroix

See **Clorinde intervenant pour sauver Olinde et Sophronie**.

Olympos et Marsyas *(Olympus and Marsyas)*

Nicolas Poussin

(Myth.) The famous flautist Olympus is considered either to be the father of Marsyas (as here) or his son. He was, in any case, very close to him and on Marsyas death (see **Apollon et Marsyas**), buried him and mourned.

L'Ombre de Samuel
apparaissant à Saül chez
la pythonisse d'Endor,
Salvator Rosa.

Ombre de Samuel apparaissant à Saül chez la pythonisse d'Endor, also known as **Apparition de l'Ombre de Samuel à Saül chez la pythonisse d'Endor** *(The Spirit of Samuel Called up before Saul by the Witch of Endor)*

Salvatore Rosa

(O.T.) King Saul was preparing to battle the army of Philistines who were a constant threat to the Israelites. Saul was frightened by God's silence and ordered his servants to bring him a necromancer. He commanded her to call up the spirit of the dead prophet Samuel who had anointed him king. She saw an old man wrapped in a cloak and described him to Saul. Recognizing the prophet, he fell before him, but received no comfort. Instead, Samuel reproached him for straying from the path of righteousness and announced his imminent death. Saul was defeated and succeeded by David.

Ombres de Francesca de Rimini et de Paolo Malatesta apparaissant à Dante et à Virgile (Les) *(Francesca and Paolo)*   Ary Scheffer
See **Francesca et Paolo**.

Ombres des héros français reçus par Ossain dans l'Élysée aérien *(The Souls of French Heroes Received by Ossian)*   Anne-Louis Girodet
See **Apothéose des héros français morts pour la patrie dans la guerre de la Liberté**.

Onction de Béthanie *(The Anointing at Bethany)*   Dirck Barendsz
See **Madeleine aux pieds du Christ**.

Onction de Salomon (L') *(The Anointing of Solomon)*   After Cornelis de Vos
(O.T.) Solomon, David's son and successor, was crowned in 970 B.C. and ruled for thirty-nine years. Here he is anointed with holy oil while the crown and scepter are prepared for him.

Orphée charmant les animaux *(Orpheus Charming the Animals)*   Roelant Savery
See **Orphée et Eurydice dans un paysage**.

Orphée descendu aux Enfers pour demander Eurydice *(Orpheus Descending to the Underworld to Claim Eurydice)*   Jean Restout
(Myth.) After the death of the beautiful Eurydice (see **Orphée et Eurydice dans un paysage**), Orpheus charmed the monsters of the underworld with his lyre and descended to plead with the rulers, Pluto and Proserpine, for the return of his beloved. His request was granted — he could return to earth with Eurydice, but under one condition: he must not look behind him until

he reached the limits of Hell. However, Orpheus could not resist and turned back to look at Eurydice's spirit, which withered before his eyes. This time she was lost forever.

Same subject: **Orphée devant Pluton et Proserpine**, François Perrier.

Orphée devant Pluton et Proserpine
(Orpheus Before Pluto and Proserpine)
See **Orphée descendu aux enfers...**

François Perrier

Orphée et Eurydice dans un paysage
(Orpheus and Eurydice), also known as **Eurydice mordue par le serpent**

Nicolas Poussin

(Myth.) Orpheus married the nymph Eurydice. While walking in the field with her fellow nymphs, she moved away from him and was mortally wounded by a snake. Orpheus pleaded with the gods of the underworld to allow him to descend to the world of the dead and return with Eurydice. After charming the infernal monsters with his lyre and almost accomplishing his mission, he lost her forever (see **Orphée descendu aux Enfers pour demander Eurydice**).

or
227

Orphée jouant du violon à l'entrée des Enfers
(Orpheus Playing the Violin at the Entrance to the Underworld)
See **Orphée et Eurydice dans un paysage** and **Orphée descendu aux Enfers pour demander Eurydice**.

Cornelis van Poelenburgh

Ossian unit Oïna-Morul et Thormod
(Ossian Reuniting Oïna-Morul and Thormod)

Augustin Franquelin

(Lit.) Ossian, a legendary hero, received young Oïna-Morul as a prize, but on learning that she was secretly in love with the defeated warrior Thormod, reunited them.

Othello et Desdémone *(Othello and Desdemona)* — Jules-Robert Auguste

(Lit.) Othello, the Moor, the main character in Shakespeare's play by the same title, is a general in the Venetian army. Invited to the home of Senator Brabantio, Desdemona's father, he spends evening after evening recounting his heroic exploits and wins Desdemona's affection. She marries him, despite the resistance of her father, displeased at the thought of her marrying a Moor. Manipulated by wicked Iago, Othello is seized by terrible jealousy and kills the innocent Desdemona.

Same subject: **Othello et Desdémone à Venise**, Théodore Chassériau.

Othello et Desdémone à Venise. Othello racontant à Desdémone l'histoire de sa vie *(Othello and Desdemona in Venise)* — Théodore Chassériau

See **Othello et Desdémone**.

Pan et Syrinx, Michel Dorigny.

Pan et Syrinx *(Pan and Syrinx)*

Paul Bril
Michel Dorigny
Pierre Mignard
After Peter Paul Rubens

(Myth.) Syrinx was a hamadryad, or woodland nymph. The god Pan fell in love with her and pursued her, but just as he was about to seize her she was transformed into a cluster of reeds on the riverbank. The sound of the wind stirring the stems inspired Pan for his famous flute, the syrinx. The instrument was made of reeds of varying lengths held together with wax.

Pape Nicolas V se fait ouvrir le caveau de saint François (Le) *(Pope Nicholas V Ordering the Opening of Saint Francis'Tomb)*

Laurent de la Hyre

(Christ. Trad.) Nicholas V visited Assyria in 1449. Arriving at the basilica, he was seized by "holy curiosity" and descended to the underground vault where Saint Francis of Assisi was buried. Under his orders, the tomb was opened for him to pay homage to the saint who was discovered standing upright, unsupported. Although Saint Francis had been dead for one hundred years, his body was miraculously preserved. The pope raised the saint's robe and saw the stigmata, still vividly marked, on his feet (see **Saint François d'Assise recevant les stigmates**).

Paphnuce libérant Thaïs *(Paphnutius Releasing Thais)*

Philippe de Champaigne

(Christ. Trad.) Thais was an Egyptian courtesan in the 4th century. Determined to save her from a life of debauchery, the monk Paphnutius presented himself at her home as a client. After her conversion, she made a public bonfire of her clothes and jewelry. To atone for her former life, she entered a convent where she remained in her cell for three years. Paphnutius came to open her cell at the end of her penitence.

Parabole de l'enfant prodigue (La) *(The Prodigal son)*

Frans Francken the Younger

(N.T.) Jesus told the parable of the prodigal son

to his disciples: a man divided his possessions between his two sons; one of them stayed in his father's home working, while the other left home and squandered his wealth in a life of indulgence. The prodigal son returned home, half starved, and begged his father's forgiveness. His father received him joyously and prepared the famous fatted calf. The father said to the jealous brother, " Son, you are always with me, and all that is mine is yours. It was fitting to make merry and be glad, for this your brother was dead, and is alive; he was lost, and is found. "

Parabole des aveugles *(The Parable of the Blind)*

Copy by Pieter Brueghel the Younger of a painting by Pieter Brueghel the Elder

(N.T.) The Gospel according to Matthew describes the healing of two blind men. Jesus compared the Pharisees to the blind saying, " They are blind guides. And if a blind man leads a blind man, both will fall into a pit. "

Paradis (Le) *(Paradise)*

Tintoretto

(Christ. Trad.) This is an image of heavenly paradise after the Last Judgment. In the center, Christ is crowning the Virgin (see **Couronnement de la Vierge**). The two figures are surrounded by the twelve apostles and below them, on several successive levels of clouds, are the Fathers of the Church, saints, martyrs, the blessed, popes and bishops, accompanied by angels.

Paradis terrestre (Le) *(The Earthly Paradise)*, also known as **Printemps (Le)** *(Spring)*

Nicolas Poussin

(O.T.) Chapter one of the Book of Genesis describes God's creation of heaven and earth, the planets, the sea and the first man and woman. Chapter two recounts another, probably earlier, version in which God formed Adam from clay and planted a magnificent garden, the Garden of Eden. Here Adam and his wife had everything they desired but were forbidden to touch the

Tree of Knowledge. Eve, tempted by the devil in the form of a snake, picked the fruit of this tree and shared it with Adam. God had them chased out of the garden.

Same subject: **Adam et Ève chassés du paradis terrestre**, Giuseppe Cesari.

Paradis terrestre (Le) *(The Earthly Paradise)*

Jan Brueghel the Elder
Paul de Vos

(O.T.) The Book of Genesis describes how God planted the Garden of Eden "in the east" for Adam and Eve, who were subsequently banished for their disobedience. It is often represented (particularly by prophets and in the Psalms) as a garden of luxurious vegetation where all species of wild beasts coexisted in perfect harmony.

Parement de Narbonne *(The Narbonne Altar-Frontal)*

French, 14th century

See **Crucifixion, Flagellation du Christ, Portement de croix, Mise au tombeau, Descente aux limbes, Jésus apparaît à la Madeleine.**

Pâris et Hélène *(Paris and Helen)*

Jacques-Louis David

(Myth., Lit.) The Trojan prince Paris abducted Helen, wife of Menelaus (see **Enlèvement d'Hélène**), and took her to Troy. During the siege to recapture Helen and avenge Menelaus, Paris, although he was not a coward, preferred to stay with his lover, rather than join the fighting. Helen was torn between her passion for the young prince and longing for her homeland and her husband whom she continued to esteem.

Pâris et Œnone *(Paris and Oenone)*, also known as **Paysage avec Pâris et Œnone**

Claude Gellée, called
Claude Lorrain

(Myth.) Before abducting Helen, the young Trojan Paris lived with the nymph Oenone who warned him of the dangers of the expedition. The abduction of Helen did, in fact, provoke the war that ended in the destruction of Troy. While fighting the Greeks, Paris was wounded and the unforgiving Oenone, although invested with miraculous powers of healing, refused to heal him. After his death, she took her own life.

Parnasse (Le) *(Parnassus)*, also known as **Mars et Vénus** *(Mars and Venus)*

Andrea Mantegna

(Myth.) Parnassus, a mountain in Plocis, Greece, was the symbolic home of Apollo and the Muses. Here Mars and Venus are embracing, while Cupid sends a poisoned arrow in the direction of Vulcan's forge. In the foreground the nine Muses are dancing to the sound of Apollo's lyre. Apollo is seated on the left and Mercury is leaning on the winged horse Pegasus to the right.

Pas de Suse forcé par Louis XIII (Le) *(The Suse Pass Captured by Louis XIII)*

Claude Gellée, called Claude Lorrain

(Hist.) The Suse Pass, which controlled the route to the Alps, was captured several times by French troops. It was taken by force in 1629 when the armies of Louis XIII drove back the Swiss and the Austrians.

Passage du Granique (Le) *(The Crossing of the Granicus)*

Charles Le Brun

(Hist.) Granicus was the ancient name for the Kocabas, a small coastal river in Asia Minor where Alexander the Great won his first victory over King Darius of Persia. By crossing the river in 334 B.C., Alexander dominated the straits of Bosporus and Dardanelles (the Hellespont), and controlled the passage between the Black Sea and the Mediterranean.

Passage du Rhin *(The Crossing of the Rhine)*

Adam Frans van der Meulen

(Hist.) This episode from the war between France and Holland occurred on June 12, 1762.

Louis XIV is on horseback, surrounded by his generals, while the cavalry, protected by the batteries, crosses the river. Over 100,000 men crossed the Rhine. Louis XIV advanced to less than fifteen kilometers from Amsterdam and forced the Dutch to negotiate with him.

Same subject: **Passage du Rhin par l'armée de Louis XIV à Tolhuis**, Joseph Parrocel.

Passage du Rhin par l'armée de Louis XIV à Tolhuis *(The Crossing of the Rhine by the Army of Louis XIV)*
Joseph Parrocel

See **Passage du Rhin**.

Passion
Frans Francken the Younger

(N.T.) The Passion, a major element in all four Gospels, is the description of Christ's suffering and death. It includes: the agony in the garden,

Passion, Frans Francken the Younger.

pa

233

the arrest, the judgment, the flagellation, the crowning with thorns, the road to Calvary with the carrying of the cross, the crucifixion, the deploration, the entombment and the descent into limbo. It is followed by the resurrection.

Paysage. Mort de Roland *(Landscape. Death of Roland)*
See **Mort de Roland**.

Achille-Etna Michallon

Paysage. Thésée poursuivant les Centaures *(Landscape. Theseus Chasing the Centaurs)*
See **Combat des Lapithes et des Centaures**.

Achille-Etna Michallon

Paysage avec Absalon percé d'une lance par Joab *(Landscape with Absalom Pierced by Job's Lance)*
See **Absalon percé d'une lance par Joab**.

Giovanni Battista Viola

Paysage avec Hercule combattant Acheloüs changé en taureau *(Landscape with Hercules and Achelous)*
See **Hercule et Acheloüs**.

Domenichino

Paysage avec Hercule tirant Cacus de sa caverne *(Landscape with Hercules and Cacus)*
See **Hercule assommant Cacus**.

Domenichino

Paysage avec Jacob, Rachel et Léa *(Landscape with Jacob, Rachel and Leah)*
See **Jacob reprochant à Laban de lui avoir donné pour femme Lia au lieu de Rachel** and **Jacob venant trouver les filles de Laban**.

Guercino

Paysage avec la Fuite en Égypte *(Landscape with the Flight into Egypt)*
See **Fuite en Égypte**.

Domenichino

Paysage avec la Nativité *(Landscape with the Nativity)*
See **Nativité**.

Cornelis van Poelenburgh

Paysage avec la prédication de saint Jean-Baptiste *(Landscape with John the Baptist)*
See **Saint Jean baptisant le peuple**.

Claes-Dircksz van der Heck

Paysage avec le repos pendant la fuite en Égypte *(Landscape with the Rest on the Flight into Egypt)*
See **Fuite en Égypte**.

Henri Mauperché
Pierre Patel the Elder

Paysage avec les pèlerins d'Emmaüs *(Landscape with the Pilgrims at Emmaus)*
See **Pèlerins d'Emmaüs**.

Paul Bril

Paysage avec Pâris et Œnone *(Landscape with Paris and Oenone)*
See **Pâris et Œnone**.

Claude Gellée,
called Claude Lorrain

Paysage avec Rachel, Jacob et Léa *(Landscape with Rachel, Jacob and Leah)*
See **Jacob venant trouver les filles de Laban**.

Nicolaes Berchem

Paysage historique: Psyché et le dieu Pan *(Historical Landscape: Psyche and Pan)*
See **Psyché et le dieu Pan**.

Joseph Bidauld

Pêche miraculeuse (La) *(The Miraculous Drought of Fish)*

Jean Jouvenet
Théodore Chassériau

(N.T.) This was one of Jesus' earlier miracles. While preaching on the shores of the Sea of Galilee, Jesus climbed into an empty fishing boat belonging to Peter. After he finished preaching, Jesus instructed Peter to cast out their nets. Peter replied that they had been fishing all night, but had caught nothing. However, trusting Jesus, they cast out their nets and hauled them in so full that James and John had to come to their aid. Jesus said to Peter, "Do not be afraid; henceforth you will be catching men." The three men subsequently became disciples of Jesus.

Peintre Sodoma porté à l'hôpital (Le), also known as Sodoma porté à l'hôpital *(Sodoma Carried to the Hospital)*

Marius Granet

(Hist.) Although he had a considerable reputation and many commissions, the Sienese painter Giovanni Antonio Bazzi, called Sodoma, ended his days in misery. Here he is shown in the hospital of Sienna during his final stay. His palette, his sword and coat are next to him. He died in 1549.

Pèlerinage à l'île de Cythère (Le), also known as Embarquement pour Cythère (L') *(The Embarkation for Cythera)*

Jean-Antoine Watteau

(Myth.) The island of Cythera, at the far south of the Ionian islands, was sacred to Venus. It symbolized idyllic life and was a privileged location dedicated to pleasure and love. The "pilgrims" are departing on an amorous journey.

Pèlerins d'Emmaüs (Les) *(The Pilgrims at Emmaus or The Supper at Emmaus)*

Italian, 16th century
Francesco Bassano
Matthieu Le Nain
Rembrandt
Titian

(N.T.) After his death, Jesus appeared to two of his disciples on the road from Jerusalem to Emmaus. One of them was Cleopas and the other,

La Pêche miraculeuse,
Jean Jouvenet.

*Le Pèlerinage à l'île de
Cythère*, Jean-Antoine
Watteau.

although not named, may have been Luke. They
did not recognize Jesus and, taking him to be a
pilgrim, spoke to him of Jesus' crucifixion, expressing their confusion and disappointment.
They invited him to stay with them at the inn in
Emmaus, where he blessed the bread and broke
it. As they witnessed this act, their eyes were
opened and they recognized him.
Same subject: **Cène à Emmaüs**, Giovanni Capassini. **Jésus et les disciples d'Emmaüs**, Dirck Barendsz. **Paysage avec les pèlerins d'Emmaüs**,
Paul Bril. **Repas d'Emmaüs**, Dirck van Sant-
voort.

Veronese

Pénitence de saint Jérôme *(The Penitence of Saint Jerome)*

See **Saint Jérôme dans le désert**.

Sano di Pietro

Pentecôte (La) *(Pentecost)*

(N.T.) On the day of the Jewish feast of Pentecost, seven weeks after Jesus' death, the apostles were gathered in a room (according to tradition, the Virgin Mary was also with them). A driving wind filled the room and tongues of fire appeared and rested on their heads. "And they were all filled with the Holy Spirit and began to speak in other tongues, as the Spirit gave them utterance."

Same subject: **Descente du Saint-Esprit**, Charles Le Brun.

Italian, 16th century
Louis-Simon Tiersonnier
Jean Restout

Persée délivrant Andromède *(Perseus and Andromeda)*

(Myth.) Andromeda, daugher of Cepheus and Cassiope, boasted that she was as beautiful as the Nereids, daughters of the Ocean. Displeased, they asked their father to send a monster to devastate her homeland. An oracle was consulted and foretold that the curse would be lifted if the young woman were sacrificed to the monster. She was chained to a rock by the Nereids, but Perseus, hero of numerous exploits, returning from an expedition against the

Nicolas Bertin
Antoine Coypel
Veronese

Persée délivrant Andromède, Antoine Coypel.

terrible Medusa, came to her rescue. He saved her after having obtained her parents'promise that she would become his wife.

Same subject: **Andromède**, Théodore Chassériau. **Persée secourant Andromède**, Joachim Wtewael.

Persée secourant Andromède *(Perseus and Andromeda)*

Joachim Wtewael

See **Persée délivrant Andromède**.

Peste à Rome sous le pape Nicolas V *(The Plague in Rome during the Office of Pope Nicholas V)*

Philippe Larivière

(Hist.) This outbreak of the plague occurred in the three centuries of endemic recurrence of the epidemic, between the Black Plague in the Middle Ages, which claimed three quarters of the population of Europe, and the terrible plague of Venice in 1575 during which Titian died (see **Honneurs funèbres rendus à Titien mort à Venise pendant la peste**).

Peste d'Asdod *(The Plague at Ashdod)*, also known as **Les Philistins frappés de la peste**

Nicolas Poussin

(O.T.) Once again the Israelites were at war with their neighbors, the Philistines. The Philistines had just stolen the Ark of the Covenant and taken it to the town of Ashdod. As punishment for their sacrilege, God struck them with the plague (plague being a general term covering all epidemics), finally forcing them to return the Ark.

Petite Bacchanale (La) *(The Nurture of Bacchus)*

Nicolas Poussin

See **Enfance de Bacchus**.

Phaéton conduisant le char du soleil *(Phaeton Driving Helios' Chariot)*

Nicolas Bertin

(Myth.) Phaeton was an adolescent when his

Phaéton conduisant le char du soleil, Nicolas Bertin.

mother, Clymene, told him that his father was Helios, the sun god. His father swore by the Styx to grant his wish as proof of his paternal love. The impetuous young man asked to drive Helios' chariot. His father tried in vain to dissuade him, but was bound by his promise, and could only warn him of the dangers. Phaeton soon lost control of the powerful horses, brushed the earth, burning it, and soared up high, leaving the earth to freeze. Jupiter intervened, striking him with lightning that hurtled him into the river Eridanus. His sisters, the Heliads, wept so profusely that they were changed into poplars.

Same subject: **Phaéton demande à Apollon la conduite du char du soleil**, Eustache Le Sueur.

ph
240

Phaéton demande à Apollon la conduite du char du soleil *(Phaeton Asks To Drive Helios' Chariot)*   Eustache Le Sueur
See **Phaéton conduisant le char du soleil**.

Phèdre et Hippolyte *(Phaedra and Hippolytus)*   Pierre-Narcisse Guérin
(Myth., Lit.) Phaedra, the wife of Theseus, fell in love with her handsome son-in-law Hippolytus, who rejected her advances. She took revenge by accusing him of violating her. Theseus cursed his son who was given no opportunity to explain. He died and Phaedra, unable to stand his death, took her own life.

Philippœmen reconnu par ses hôtes de Mégare *(Philopoemen, General of the Achaens, Is Recognized by His Hosts at Megara)*

(Hist., Lit.) General Philopoemen, whose story is recounted by Plutarch, was famous for his exploits. One day he was announced in Megara and a native woman had a sumptous meal prepared for him. He went to her house dressed so simply that she did not recognize him. Taking him to be a servant, she asked him to help her. The general willingly complied and started to break wood for the fire. When the woman's husband arrived, he was surprised to discover the general chopping wood, but the general replied, "It is fitting that I pay a penalty for my poor state of attire."

Peter Paul Rubens

Philistins frappés de la peste (Les) *(The Philistines Stricken with the Plague)* See **Peste d'Asdod**.

Nicolas Poussin

Pietà

(Christ. Trad.) At the end of the Middle Ages, artists began to separate two figures from the Lamentation of Jesus' death by his followers: the Virgin Mary and the dead Christ, whom she holds on her knees (in attempts at realistic portrayal, Jesus is stretched out next to her and only his head rests on her knees). (See **Déploration**).

Same subject: **Pietà avec saint François et sainte Marie-Madeleine**, Annibale Carracci. **Pietà de Saint-Germain-des-Prés**, Master of Saint-Germain-des-Prés. **Pietà de Villeneuve-lès-Avignon**, Enguerrand Quarton. **Pitié de Notre-Seigneur**, called **Grande Pietà ronde**, Jean Malouel. **Pitié de Notre-Seigneur** called **Petite Pietà ronde**, Dijon, 14th century. **Christ mort sur les genoux de la Vierge**, Charles Le Brun.

Spanish, 15th century
Florence, 16th century
Rhine, 15th century
Louis Bréa
Eugène Delacroix
Quentin Metsys
Rosso Fiorentino
Andrea Solario
Cosimo Tura

Pietà avec saint François et sainte Marie-Madeleine *(Pietà with Saint Francis and Mary Magdalene)*

Annibale Carracci

Pietà de Saint-Germain-des-Prés
(Pietà of Saint-Germain-des-Prés)

Master of Saint-Germain-des-Prés

Pietà de Villeneuve-lès-Avignon
(Pietà of Villeneuve-lès-Avignon)
See **Pietà**.

Enguerrand Quarton

Pilate présentant le Christ à la foule des Juifs *(Pilate Presenting Christ to the Crowd)*
See **Ecce Homo**.

Giovanni Battista Tiepolo

Pilate se lavant les mains *(Pilate Washing His Hands)*
(N.T.) (See **Ecce Homo**.) After handing Jesus over to the Jewish authorities who wished to put him to death, Pilate washed his hands in public saying, "I am innocent of this righteous man's blood; see to it yourselves."

Mathias Stomer

Pirates africains enlevant une jeune femme *(African Pirates Abducting a Young Woman)*
(Lit.) This painting was based on a ballad by Victor Hugo, a joyous pirate song with the refrain: "We were eighty oarsmen." These men landed near a convent, caught sight of a nun sleeping under a tree and abducted her despite her cries. The poem ends with the line, "The nun became a sultaness."

Eugène Delacroix

Pitié de Notre-Seigneur *(Lamentation for Christ)*, also known as **Grande Pietà ronde**

Jean Malouel

Pitié de Notre-Seigneur *(Lamentation for Christ)*, also known as **Petite Pietà ronde**
See **Pietà**.

Dijon, 14th century

Plaisirs de l'Age d'or (Les) *(The Pleasures of the Golden Age)*

Hendrik van Limborch

(Myth.) The classical poets divided the ages of the world into four distinct periods: the Golden, the Silver, the Bronze and the Iron ages. Under the reign of Saturn, the Golden Age was an era of youth, innocence, happiness, prosperity without toil, justice, peace and equality of men. A perpetual springtime made the earth a garden of delight. This ideal atmosphere was successively lost in the following ages (see **Age d'argent**).

Plan de la chartreuse de Paris porté par deux anges (Le) *(The Plan of the Charterhouse of Paris Carried by Two Angels)*

Eustache Le Sueur

See **Saint Bruno examine un dessin des thermes de Dioclétien**.

Poète et la Sirène (Le) *(The Poet and the Siren)*

Théodore Chassériau

See **Héro et Léandre**.

Polyxène sacrifiée aux Mânes d'Achille *(Polyxena Sacrificed to the Manes of Achilles)*

Giambattista Pittoni

(Myth.) Polyxena, the youngest daughter of Priam and Hecuba, is not mentioned in Homer's *Iliad*. Later legends recount her romance with Achilles. There are also several versions of her death. In one she was sacrificed on Achilles' tomb, either to ensure safe passage of the Greek ships after the fall of Troy (like the sacrifice of Iphigenia for their arrival in Troy), or because Achilles' ghost appeared to his son Neoptolemus (Pyrrhus) and demanded the sacrifice. She met her death with nobility, preventing the soldiers from restraining her and willingly baring her throat to the knife.

Portement de croix (Le) *(The Carrying of the Cross)*

(N.T.) Jesus was condemned to be crucified (see **Christ devant Caïphe** and **Ecce Homo**) and led by soldiers to Golgotha or Calvary (see **Calvaire**). According to the Gospels of Matthew, Mark and Luke, the soldiers compelled Simon the Cyrenian to carry Christ's cross. According to John, Jesus carried his own cross. He is depicted bending or falling beneath the weight of the cross.

Same subject: **Christ portant sa croix**, Spanish (?), 17th century. **Jésus-Christ montant au Calvaire**, Francesco Bassano. **Jésus portant sa croix**, Charles Le Brun, Eustache Le Sueur. **Jésus sur le chemin du Calvaire**, Pierre Mignard. **Jésus succombant sous le poids de la croix**, Veronese and his studio. **Jésus-Christ conduit au Calvaire tombe sous le poids de la croix**, Étienne-Barthélemy Garnier. **Montée au Calvaire**, Brunswick Monogrammist.

Cologne, 15th century
French, 14th century
Rhine, 15th century
Biagio d'Antonio
Niccolo da Foligno
Jacquemart de Hesdin
Nicolas de Largillière
Lorenzo Lotto
Master of Delft
Master of Delft
Simone Martini

Prédelle *(Predella)*
See **Crucifixion**, **Banquet d'Hérode**, **Décollation de saint Jean-Baptiste**, **Rencontre entre saint Jacques le Majeur et Hermogène** and **Martyre de saint Jacques le Majeur**.

Lorenzo Monaco

Prédelle des Miracles de saint Jérôme *(Predella of the Miracles of Saint Jerome)*
See **Saint Jérôme ressuscite le cardinal Andrea** and **Saint Jérôme soutenant deux jeunes pendus**.

Perugino

Prédelle du Couronnement de la Vierge *(Predella of the Coronation of the Virgin)*
See **Christ mort**, **Saint François recevant les stigmates** and **Saint Jérôme dans le désert**.

Lo Spagna

Le Portement de croix,
Rhine, 15th century.

Prédication de saint Barthélemy *(The Ministry of Saint Bartholomew)*
(Christ. Trad.) Before being beheaded, Saint Bartholomew (1st century) was flaycd alive. Here he is shown preaching before an elegant assembly, while he covers himself with his stripped skin. This representation led to his being considered the patron saint of tailors.

Pietro di Giovanni d'Ambrogio

Prédication de saint Bernardin de Sienne *(The Ministry of Saint Bernardine of Siena)*
(Christ. Trad.) This Italian monk (1380-1444), member of the Order of the Franciscan Observants, was one of the most popular medieval preachers. He was known as "the people's preacher."

Domenico Beccafumi

Prédication de saint Étienne à Jérusalem *(The Ministry of Saint Stephen in Jerusalem)*
(N.T.) After Jesus' death, the apostles chose seven deacons to administer the Church. One of

Vittore Carpaccio

Prédication de saint Étienne à Jérusalem, Vittore Carpaccio.

these men was Saint Stephen who, as a Greek-speaking Christian, addressed the Greeks. He preached and performed miracles in Jerusalem. The Jews constantly debated with him but were unable to convert him. Their hostility resulted in his stoning (see **Martyre de saint Étienne**).

pr

246

Prédication de saint Géry *(Saint Gery Preaching)*, also known as **Instruction pastorale (L')**
(Hist.) Saint Desiderius, called Didier or Dizier in certain regions of France, was bishop in Cahors in the 6th century.

Master of the View of Saint Gudule

Prédication de saint Jean-Baptiste (La) *(Saint John the Baptist Preaching)*
See **Saint Jean baptisant le peuple**.

Flanders, 16th century
Filippo Napoletano
Giovanni Battista Gaulli
Eugène Roger

Prédication de saint Paul à Ephèse (La) *(Saint Paul Preaching in Ephesus)*
(Christ. Trad.) Saint Paul gathered the disciples interested in his doctrine in Ephesus where he taught for two years. Converted pagan priests brought their books to be burned. The magical treaties destroyed were valued at 5,000 pieces of silver.

Eustache Le Sueur

Premier chapitre de l'ordre du Saint-Esprit tenu par Henri IV dans l'église du couvent des Grands-Augustins à Paris *(First Chapter of the Order of the Holy Spirit Held by Henry IV in the Church of the Paris Convent of the Grands-Augustins)*

Jean-François de Troy

(Hist.) Henry III founded the Order of the Holy Spirit in 1578 to remedy the discredit into which the Order of Saint Michael had fallen. The new order rapidly acquired considerable prestige. Here Henry IV is depicted seated, wearing a plumed hat. The duke of Montpensier kneels before him and to his right are Henry of Orléans (the first by this name) and four important officials. This chapter was held on January 8, 1595.

Premier des trois combats de Fribourg (Le) *(The First of Three Battles in Freiburg)*

Franz Josef Cassanova

(Hist.) This battle took place on August 3, 1644, during the Thirty Years' War. Germany was divided by civil war between the Catholics and the Protestants; Austria intervened, followed by several other European countries. France, supported by Germany, declared war on Austria. Turenne of France and Louis II of Condé scored brilliant victories, including this one in Freiburg im Breisgau. The war was ended by the Peace of Westphalia.

Préparatifs du combat de Pâris et de Ménélas *(Paris and Menelaus Preparing for Combat)*, also known as **Serment de Priam et d'Agamemnon (Le)** *(The Oath of Priam and Agamemnon)*

Louis Lagrenée

(Myth., Lit.) The abduction of Helen, Menelaus' wife, and the theft of treasures by the Trojan prince, Paris, were the cause of or the pretext for the Trojan War.

War raged, but Paris appeared unconcerned. Reproached by his brother, Hector, he offered to meet Menelaus in single-handed combat. The winner would have the right to Helen and the treasures, and the war would be over. The two champions prepared their arms and made sacrifices to the gods. The Greek king, Agamemnon, and the Trojan king, Priam, swore to respect the treaty, but intervention by the gods confused the issue and little was resolved.

La Présentation au Temple, Gentile da Fabriano.

Présentation au Temple (La) *(The Presentation in the Temple)*

(N.T.) Jesus was born in a cave or stable in Bethlehem. At the age of forty days, as was the custom, his parents took him to the Temple. Ritual sacrifices of two doves or young pigeons were made for the purification of Mary.

The priest Simeon, an old man, visited by divine inspiration, came to the Temple before them and received them. The Holy Spirit had revealed to him that he would not die before he had seen the Messiah. Taking the child in his arms, he said, "Lord, now lettest thou thy servant depart in peace, according to thy word," and proclaimed Jesus to be the Messiah.

The aged prophetess Anna (not to be confused with Saint Anne, traditionally mother of the Virgin) was also present, celebrating the arrival of the Savior.

Same subject: **Présentation de Jésus au Temple**, Master of the Life of the Virgin.

Cologne, 14th century
Flanders, 16th century
Bartolo di Fredi
Il Bergognone
Louis de Boullongne
Sébastien Bourdon
Gentile da Fabriano
Guido da Siena
Master of Saint Severin
Hyacinthe Rigaud
Simon Vouet

Présentation de Jésus au Temple (La) *(The Presentation in the Temple)*
See **Présentation au Temple**.

Master of the Life of the Virgin

Présentation de la Vierge au Temple (La) *(The Presentation of the Virgin in the Temple)*

Nicolas Dipre
Master of the Life of the Virgin

(Christ. Trad.) The presentation of the Virgin in the Temple is different from the presentation of Jesus in the Temple. The rite including Jesus was part of the tradition concerning Jewish males. For Mary the event was the result of a vow pronounced by her mother, Saint Anne. She prayed to be cured of her barrenness and promised to dedicate her daughter to service in the Temple. At the age of three or four, Mary was taken to the Temple. She left her mother's arms and climbed the fifteen steps to the Temple (symbols of the fifteen psalms of degrees) by herself.

Same subject: **Vierge montant les degrés du Temple**, Master of the Life of the Virgin.

Printemps (Le) *(Spring)* or **Paradis terrestre (Le)** *(The Earthly Paradise)*
See **Paradis terrestre**.

Nicolas Poussin

Prise de Constantinople par les croisés, also known as **Entrée des croisés à Constantinople (L')** *(The Entry of the Crusaders into Constantinople)*

Eugène Delacroix

(Hist.) This is the fourth crusade, undertaken by Pope Innocent III in 1202-1204, and commanded by Baudoin, count of Flanders. The crusaders left for the Holy Land with the support of a powerful Venetian fleet; they stopped in Constantinople which they pillaged twice. Here they are shown disembarking before the terrified population.

Prise de la frégate anglaise *The Ceylon* par la frégate française *La Vénus* au large de l'île de France *(Capture of the English Ship, The Ceylon, by the French Ship, La Vénus)*

Tendre

(Hist.) This battle took place on September 17,

Prise de la frégate anglaise The Ceylon *par la frégate française* La Vénus, Tendre.

1810, during the Peninsular War between Napoleon I and the coalition of Great Britain and Austria. During the allied blockade of goods destined for France, Napoleon instituted the Continental System in an attempt to prevent Britain from trading. He hoped to force an armistice through an economic crisis. To improve his position at sea he also aimed at new conquests near Africa. L'île de France is today known as Mauritius Island.

Prise de Villefranche-sur-Mer *(The Capturing of Villefranche-sur-Mer)*

Hippolyte Lecomte

(Hist.) This victory occurred during the French Revolutionary Wars led by the Legislative Assembly against the enemies of France in league with the royalist forces. Villefranche-sur-Mer was captured on September 29, 1792.

Prise d'habit de saint Bruno et de saint Hugues *(Saint Bruno and Saint Hugh Receiving the Habit)*

Master of Saint Bruno

(Christ. Trad.) On the left, Saint Bruno is depicted receiving the habit from the bishop of Grenoble, Saint Hugh. On the right, he in turn conveys the habit to Saint Hugh, who had decided to join the Carthusians.

Also see: **Scènes de la vie de saint Bruno.**

Prisonnier de Chillon (Le) *(The Prisoner of Chillon)*

Eugène Delacroix

(Hist., Lit.) The prisoner who recounts his tale in Lord Byron's poem *"The Prisoner of Chillon "* is François de Bonivard (1493-1570). He fought for the Republic of Geneva against the duke of Savoy. In 1530, the duke imprisoned him in the castle of Chillon where he remained six years without being questioned. On his release he was overjoyed to discover that Geneva had become a republic. This painting represents an imaginary scene. While sharing a cell with his brother, François witnessed his death by starvation, but was unable to come to his aid because of the chains restraining him.

Procession de saint Grégoire au château Saint-Ange *(The Procession of Saint Gregory to Saint'Angelo)*

Giovanni di Paolo

(Christ. Trad.) Saint Gregory, a pope, despite his desire to lead a recluse life, intervened during the plague which ravaged Rome (6th century). At Easter, he ordered this procession, preceded by a portrait of the Virgin attributed to Saint Luke.

pr

251

Procession de saint Grégoire au château Saint-Ange, Giovanni di Paolo.

The image immediately stopped the spread of the plague and cleansed the air; angels were heard singing and the archangel Michael appeared on the castle of Saint'Angelo where he wiped a bloody sword and returned it to its sheath, thus ending the epidemic.

Prométhée *(Prometheus)*

Théodore Caruelle d'Aligny

(Myth., Lit.) Prometheus formed man from clay and then stole the gods' fire from Jupiter to give him life. As punishment for this unpardonable crime, Jupiter had Prometheus chained to a rock in Caucasus where an eagle pecked at his liver each day. The liver was regenerated and the torture repeated daily. Hercules put an end to his suffering (see **Hercule délivrant Prométhée**).

Same subject: **Prométhée attaché sur le Caucase**, Jean-Charles Frontier.

Proserpine cueillant des fleurs avec ses compagnes dans la prairie d'Enna *(Proserpine Gathering Flowers)*

Nicolaas Verkolje

See **Enlèvement de Proserpine**.

Psyché et l'Amour *(Psyche and Cupid)*

French, 19th century

See **Amour et Psyché**.

Psyché et le dieu Pan *(Psyche and Pan)*, also known as **Paysage historique; Psyché et le dieu Pan**

Joseph Bidauld

(Myth.) Psyche had driven Cupid away (see **Amour et Psyché**). Abandoned and suffering terribly, she threw herself in a river. She was enclosed in a wave and carried to the bank. Pan found her and consoled her.

Psyché recevant des baisers de l'Amour *(Psyche Receiving the First Kiss of Love)*

François Gérard

See **Amour et Psyché**.

Psyché reçue dans l'Olympe *(Psyche Received on Olympus)*
Polidoro da Caravaggio

(Myth.) After the drama which separated her from her lover, Cupid (see **Amour et Psyché**), Psyche erred throughout the world. Venus, jealous of her beauty, challenged her and finally put her to sleep with a flask of magic water. Cupid could not forget Psyche, woke her with an arrow and asked Jupiter for permission to marry her and take her to Olympus. His request was granted and Venus and Psyche were reconciled. Psyche was made a goddess.

Psyché surprend l'Amour endormi *(Psyche Discovers Cupid Sleeping)*
Louis Lagrenée

See **Amour et Psyché**.

Ptolémée Philadelphe donnant la liberté aux Juifs *(Ptolemy II Liberating the Jews)*
Noël Coypel

(Hist.) Ptolemy II was the second ruler of the Ptolemaic dynasty (3rd century B.C.). He had the Pentateuch, the first five books of the Old Testament, translated into Greek (the Septuagint). This painting shows him liberating the Jews in recognition for the translation. It is said that he paid 20,000 drachma to the owner of each slave and that many of the masters demanded the same sum, or more, for the slaves' children.

Purification de la Vierge (La) *(The Purification of the Virgin)*
Guido Reni

(N.T.) Forty days after Jesus' birth, the Virgin Mary underwent ritual purification in the Temple where she sacrificed two doves and presented her son (see **Présentation au Temple**).

Pygmalion et Galatée *(Pygmalion and Galatea)*
Octave Tassaert

(Myth.) Pygmalion, a celebrated sculptor of Cyprus, was disgusted by the debauchery of the women on the island where the temple of Venus was found. He decided to live a chaste life and to dedicate himself to his work. One of his statues was of such perfection that the artist fell in love with his creation. During the festival of Venus he made an offering to the gods and prayed for a wife "like the ivory maiden." Although he had not dared to ask for the staute to become real, Venus guessed his true desire and granted his wish. (This Galatea should not be confused with the nymph Galatea in the painting **Acis et Galatée se dérobant aux regards de Polyphème**.)

Pyrame et Thisbé *(Pyramus and Thisbe)*

Leonaert Bramer

(Myth., Lit.) This tale is taken from Ovid's *Metamorphoses*. Pyramus and Thisbe, two young Babylonians, were in love, but their parents opposed their meeting. They communicated through a crack in the wall separating their homes and arranged to meet below a certain mulberry tree. Thisbe, who arrived first, caught sight of a lion and fled dropping her veil. The lion whose jaws were dripping with blood tore the veil and left the scene. Pyramus arrived to discover the blood-smeared, torn veil. Believing his beloved dead, he stabbed himself with his sword. Thisbe returned and upon discovering Pryamus' body, took her life with the sword. The white fruit of the mulberry tree was stained with the lovers'blood.

Quatre Évangélistes (Les) *(The Four Evangelists)*

Jacob Jordaens

(N.T.) The youngest of the Evangelists, Saint John, is dressed in white. Saint Mark and Saint Luke are standing to his left and Saint Matthew to his right. The painter imagines that they consulted one another before writing their Gospels, but this is historically impossible.

Les Quatre Évangélistes, Jacob Jordaens.

Racine lisant *Athalie* devant Louis XIV et Mme de Maintenon *(Racine Reading* Athalie *To Louis XIV and Mme de Maintenon)*

Julie Philipaut

(Hist.) The marquise de Maintenon, Louis XIV's mistress, whom he secretly married late in life, founded a school in Saint-Cyr for young girls from noble, but poor families. She commissioned several plays from the French dramatist Racine. The first play he wrote for her was *Esther*. He then proposed *Athalie*, which was to be his final play. Judging that the young women had performed *Esther* too passionately, the marquise merely had them read *Athalie* in public.

Radeau de la Méduse (Le) *(The Raft of the Medusa)*

Théodore Géricault

(Hist.) The *Medusa* was a French ship sent by the French Restoration government (1815) to claim Senegal, which had been returned to France by peace treaties. Due to the incompetence of the captain, the *Medusa* sank five hundred kilometers off the African coast on July 2, 1816. One hundred and forty-nine passengers took refuge on a raft. After twelve days adrift at sea, the raft was finally sighted by the brig *Argus*. Fifteen dying men were recovered, the rest having drowned or been eaten by the survivors.

Ravissement de saint Paul *(The Ecstatic Vision of Saint Paul)*

Domenichino
Nicolas Poussin

(N.T.) Saint Paul describes his ecstatic vision in his second Letter to the Corinthians. "I know a man in Christ who fourteen years ago was caught up to the third heaven — whether in the body or out of the body I do not know, God knows... and he heard things that cannot be told, which man may not utter."

Rébecca au puits *(Rebecca at the Well)*
See **Éliézer et Rébecca**.

Gian Domenico Tiepolo

Ravissement de saint Paul, Nicolas Poussin.

Rébecca enlevée par le templier *(Rebecca Abducted by the Templar)*
See **Enlèvement de Rébecca.**

Eugène Delacroix

Rébecca recevant des mains d'Éliézer les présents d'Abraham *(Rebecca Receiving Abraham's Presents)*
See **Éliézer et Rébecca.**

François Boucher

Réception de Christophe Colomb par la cour d'Espagne à Barcelone *(Christopher Columbus Received by the Spanish Court)*
(Hist.) The Italian navigator Christopher Columbus believed that the earth was round and that India could be reached by traveling westward. He was granted the necessary backing by the Spanish queen, Isabella of Castile, and set sail in 1492. He arrived on a small island which

Joseph-Nicolas Robert-Fleury

he believed to be India and called it San Salvador. Although he had not yet discovered the American continent, he was triumphantly received by King Ferdinand V and Queen Isabella I when he returned from his first voyage in 1493.

Réception de l'ambassadeur Domenico Trevisano au Caire *(The Reception of the Ambassador Domenico Trevisano in Cairo)*, also known as **Audience d'une ambassade vénitienne dans une ville orientale** *(Audience of a Venetian Ambassador in an Eastern City)*

Venice, 16th century, previously attributed to Gentile Bellini

(Hist.) This painting depicts a diplomatic incident caused by the arrest, in May 1511, of Venetian consuls and merchants in Damascus and Alexandria. The men were arrested by order of the Egyptian sultan, Aboul Feth Quansou Ghoury. The Venetian Senate, informed of this violation of its rights, decided to send a special ambassador to the sultan. The ambassador, chosen from the nobility of the Republic, was Domenico Trevisano. He left the following year with his attendants, and was most certainly accompanied by a painter, as this scene corresponds exactly to descriptions given by members of the mission.

Règne de Comus *(The Reign of Comus)*

Lorenzo Costa

(Myth.) Comus, one of the lesser gods, was admitted to Olympus with Momus in order to amuse the greater gods. He ruled over feasting, drinking and love.

Remords d'Oreste (Les) *(Orestes' Remorse)*

Philippe-Auguste Hennequin

(Myth., Lit.) Orestes, son of King Agamemnon and Queen Clytemnestra, was only a child when his mother and her lover, Aegisthus, murdered Agamemnon on his return from the Trojan War. He was rescued and raised in exile by his uncle,

Réception de l'ambassadeur Domenico Trevisano au Caire, Venice, 16th century.

Strophius. As an adult he was ordered by Apollo to avenge his father's death. He killed Aegisthus and then, encouraged by his sister Electra, also took his mother's life. He defended the murder of Aegisthus, saying that the usurper deserved to be punished, but the killing of his mother unleased the Furies which followed him everywhere and drove him mad. He was finally judged and acquitted by a tribune presided over by Minerva.

Renaud et Armide *(Rinaldo and Armida)*

François Boucher

(Lit.) The story of Rinaldo and Armida is recounted in Tasso's *Jerusalem Delivered*. The action takes place during the first crusade, commanded by Godfrey of Bouillon. Armida, a sorceress, was an ally of the Egyptian king. She used her magical powers against the Christian knights and, like Circe, turned them into swine. When the pious knight Rinaldo went to rescue his unfortunate companions, she retained him on an enchanted island, whose charms captivated him. Caught in her own trap, Armida fell in love with him. After Rinaldo was released from her spell and abandoned her, she killed herself. Also see: **Carlo et Ubaldo allant délivrer Rinaldo** and **Évanouissement d'Armide au départ de Renaud**.

Same subject: **Renaud et l'enchanteresse Armide**, Anthony van Dyck. **Renaud présentant un miroir à Armide**, Domenichino.

Renaud et l'enchanteresse Armide Renaud présentant un miroir à Armide
See **Renaud et Armide**.

Anthony van Dyck
Domenichino

Rencontre à la Porte Dorée (La). Annonce à sainte Anne (L') *(The Meeting at the Golden Gate. Annunciation to Saint Anne)*
See **Rencontre d'Anne et de Joachim à la Porte Dorée**.

Wilhelm Ziegler

Rencontre d'Abraham et de Melchisédech (La) *(The Meeting of Abraham and Melchizadek)*
See **Abraham et Melchisédech**.

Giovanni Castiglione

Rencontre d'Anne et de Joachim à la Porte Dorée *(The Meeting of Anne and Joachim at the Golden Gate)*
(Christ. Trad.) After twenty years of marriage, Joachim, a rich and virtuous man, and his wife Anne were childless. Anne despaired and Joachim was rejected by the community. One day when he went to the temple to make a sacrifice, he was driven out. Embittered, he went to the mountains with his flocks and refused to return. Anne, overcome with anxiety, prayed and an angel appeared to her promising that she

Nicolas Dipre

Rencontre d'Anne et de Joachim à la Porte Dorée, Nicolas Dipre.

would give birth. At the same time the angel appeared to Joachim and told him that he would have a child and should return home. Anne had been told to wait for him at the Golden Gate (one of the gates to Jerusalem). After a long wait, she saw her husband coming toward her to share her joy. Their miraculous child was Mary, mother of Jesus.

Same subject: **Rencontre à la Porte Dorée. Annonce à sainte Anne**, Wilhelm Ziegler.

Rencontre d'Antoine et de Cléopâtre (La) *(Marc Antony and Cleopatra)*
See **Débarquement de Cléopâtre à Tarse**.

Sébastien Bourdon
Gérard de Lairesse

Rencontre de saint Jacques le Majeur de d'Hermogène et Martyre de saint Jacques le Majeur *(The Meeting Between Saint James the Greater and Hermogenes)*

Lorenzo Monaco

(Christ. Trad.) A Pharisaic magician named Hermogenes sent one of his disciples to Saint James to convince him of the fallacy of his doctrine. The disciple, Philetus, returned converted. Hiding his anger, Hermogenes sent Philetus to James once again, but first cast a spell on him. Philetus was unable to move. James freed him from the spell by covering him with his cloak. Hermogenes, increasingly irritated, ordered demons to bring him the two men in chains. The demons failed miserably and begged James to take pity on them. He then asked them to tie up Hermogenes and bring him. This mission proved to be much simpler. James then taught Hermogenes a lesson in clemency by freeing him without seeking revenge, and Hermogenes was converted. Also see: **Martyre de saint Jacques le Majeur**.

Reniement de saint Pierre *(The Denial of Saint Peter)*

French?, 17th century
David Teniers the Younger

(N.T.) Peter, one of Jesus' first disciples, was a

simple, impulsive, passionate man, capable of both intense energy and weakness. During preparations for the Last Supper, Peter asked Jesus to purify him and protested violently when Jesus said to him "this very night, before the cock crows twice, you will deny me three times." Peter was one of the disciples who fell asleep while Jesus was praying in the Garden of Olives. He attacked one of the guards who arrested Jesus and cut off his ear. Then he followed at a distance and was accused of being one of Jesus' disciples. Three times he denied it and then as the cock crowed he remembered his master's prophecy and wept bitterly at his betrayal. After Jesus' death and resurrection, Peter became a pillar of the Church and his faith was unfailing to his death (see **Martyre de saint Pierre**).

Same subject: **Larmes de saint Pierre**, Guercino. **Saint Pierre repentant**, Gérard Seghers.

Repas chez Simon (Le) *(The Meal in the House of Simon)*
See **Madeleine aux pieds du Christ**.

Pierre Subleyras
Juan de Valdes Leal.

Repas d'Emmaüs (Le) *(The Supper at Emmaus)*
See **Pèlerins d'Emmaüs**.

Dirck van Stanvoort

Repas d'Esther et d'Assuérus (Le) *(The Banquet of Esther and Ahasuerus)*
(O.T.) Determined to risk everything to save her people (see **Évanouissement d'Esther**), Esther overcame her fears and invited her husband, King Ahasuerus, to dine with her. The minister Haman was one of the guests. Ahasuerus was so charmed that he returned the next day. In the meantime, troubled by Esther's allusions, he made enquiries and recognized both Haman's treachery and the devotion of Esther's cousin Mordecai (see **Triomphe de Mardochée**).

Jean-François de Troy

Ahasuerus could not revoke the decree calling for the massacre of the Jews, but he repealed the decree forbidding them to bear arms, and they were able to defend themselves.

Repas de Sancho (Le) *(Sancho's Supper)*

Studio of Antoine Coypel

(Lit.) Sancho Panza, Don Quixote's squire, was as down-to-earth as his master was visionary. By the second part of Cervantes' book, some of the master's noble ideals had rubbed off on his servant. All who knew Don Quixote were familiar with his obsessive wish to reestablish the world of chivalry, justice and love. A duke and duchess in a neighboring village invited them to stay so that they could amuse themselves at their guests' expense. They flattered Sancho and offered him the governorship of an "island," which was in fact only a village. After being solemnly enthroned, Sancho was served a sumptuous meal. However, before he could taste a single dish, a "doctor" whisked them away claiming concern for the "governor's" health. Sancho reversed the situation by losing his temper and threatening to strike the so-called doctor.

re

263

Repentir de David (Le) *(David Repents)*

Domenichino

See **Bethsabée au bain**.

Repentir de saint Joseph *(Joseph Repents)*   Alessandro Tiarini

(Christ. Trad.) The Virgin Mary conceived of the Holy Ghost, but her husband Joseph had doubts. Here he is depicted asking her to forgive him for having doubted her.

Repos de Diane (Le) *(The Repose of Diana)*   Jacob Jordaens

(Myth.) Diana, surrounded by her companions the nymphs, smiles at an old satyr who is presenting her with a basket of fruit. Satyrs, unlike men, were admitted into her presence while she was resting.

Repos de la Sainte Famille pendant la fuite en Égypte *(The Rest on the Flight into Egypt)*   Orazio Gentileschi

(Christ. Trad.) Joseph and Mary fled to Egypt with Jesus shortly after his birth (see **Fuite en Égypte**). According to legend, they rested on the third day of the voyage. The weary Virgin dismounted from the ass and sat under a tree. Some paintings show the angels bringing them fruit.

Same subject: **Repos de la Sainte Famille**, Simone Cantarini, Laurent de la Hyre. **Repos en Égypte**, Michel Corneille the Younger. **Repos pendant la fuite en Égypte**, Ippolito Andreasi, Giovan Francesco Caroto, Giaquinto Corrado, Jean Honoré Fragonard, Francesco Vanni. **Repos de la Sainte Famille en Égypte**, Michel Corneille the Younger, Pierre Patel the Elder.

Repos de Vénus and Vulcain *(Venus and Vulcan Resting)*   Francesco Albani

See **Vénus et Vulcain**.

Repos en Égypte
Repos pendant la fuite en Égypte   Michel Corneille the Younger
    Giovan Francesco Caroto
See **Repos de la Sainte Famille pendant la fuite**   Ippolito Andreasi
en Égypte.   Giaquinto Corrado

Same subject: Jean Honoré Fragonard, Francesco Vanni.

Représentation mythologique d'un couple *(Daphnis et Chloé?)* *(Mythological Representation of a Couple (Daphnis and Chloe?))*
See **Daphnis et Chloé**.

Bordone Paris

Réprobation de Caïn après la mort d'Abel (La) *(The Punishment of Cain after the Death of Abel)*
(O.T.) Cain, the eldest son of Adam and Eve, was a farmer and his brother, Abel, a shepherd. Both of them offered sacrifices to the Lord. Cain offered a sheaf of corn and Abel a lamb. God preferred Abel's offering (an idea which probably originated from the fact that the nomadic shepherds of the day considered themselves superior to the settled farmers). When his brother's offering was accepted, but not his own, Cain called Abel into the fields and killed him. He was condemned to wander the earth. He protested against his punishment saying that he would be a fugitive whom anyone could kill. God put a mark on him to protect him.

Noël Coypel

re
265

Résurrection (La) *(The Resurrection)*
(N.T.) Jesus announced his death and resurrection to his disciples. His resurrection is recounted by the Evangelists in two ways. On the first day of the week following the crucifixion, Jesus' tomb was discovered to be empty, despite the fact that it had been sealed with a heavy stone and was guarded by soldiers (see **Apparition de Jésus aux trois Marie**, **Jésus apparaît à la Madeleine**). In the following period, Jesus appeared several times to the Virgin and the disciples (see **Pèlerins d'Emmaüs**, **Pentecôte**, **Incrédulité de saint Thomas**). Paintings of the resurrection show Jesus rising from the tomb, surrounded by angels, while the soldiers appear to be asleep or paralysed.
Same subject: **Résurrection du Christ**, Giovanni Baglione, Bartolomeo di Tommaso da Foligno, Annibale Carracci.

Flanders, 16th century
Provence, 15th century
Simon Julien
Hans Memling

La Résurrection, Hans Memling.

Résurrection de la fille de Jaïre *(The Raising of Jairus'Daughter)*

Veronese

(N.T.) While Jesus was preaching to the crowd, Jairus, a ruler of the synagogue, came to him and asked him to revive his daughter, who had just died. Jesus accompanied him with only three of his disciples. He said, " The child is not dead but sleeping," but no one believed him. He then told the child to rise and ordered that food be brought for her and she was healed.

Résurrection de Lazare (La) *(The Raising of Lazarus)*

Bon Boullongne
Master of Coetivy
Guercino
Jean Jouvenet
School of Bonifacio da Pitati
Peter Paul Rubens
Geertgen tot Sint Jans

(N.T.) Martha and Mary of Bethany and their brother, Lazarus, were all friends of Jesus. When Jesus arrived in Bethany, Lazarus had been dead for four days and had already been placed in his tomb. Martha ran ahead to meet

Jesus and was followed by Mary. When Jesus called to Lazarus, he rose alive from the tomb, his hands and feet still tied with linen bands and his face wrapped in a cloth.

Retable de la Déploration du Christ *(Retable of the Lamention for Christ)*
See **Déploration du Christ**.

Joos van Cleve

Retable de saint Denis *(Retable of Saint Denis)*
See **Crucifixion** and **Martyre de saint Denis**.

Henri Bellechose

Retable de Thouzon *(Retable of Thouzon)*
See **Saint André**.

Provence, 15th century

Retable des Sept Joies de Marie, also known as **Retable des Sept Joies de la Vierge** *(Retable of the Seven Joys of the Virgin)*
See **Sept Joies de Marie**.

Master of the Holy Kindred

Retable du Parlement de Paris *(Retable of the Parlement of Paris)*
See **Crucifixion**.

Paris, 15th century

Retour de l'enfant prodigue (Le) *(The Return of the Prodigal Son)*
See **Parabole de l'enfant prodigue**.

Lionello Spada

Retour de Marcus Sextus *(The Return of Marcus Sextus)*
(Imag.) Having escaped the exile imposed by Sulla (2nd-1st centuries B.C.), Marcus Sextus returned home to find his daughter weeping beside the body of his dead wife. This character was invented by the painter, but is most probably an allusion to the return of the emigrés after the 1789 Revolution.

Pierre-Narcisse Guérin

Retour de Marie Stuart en Écosse Charles Thévenin
(Mary Stuart Returns to Scotland)
(Hist.) Mary Stuart, or Mary Queen of Scots,
(1542-1567) was the daughter of James V of Scotland and Mary of Guise. She was sent to France
by her mother, where she was raised and later
married to the French dauphin, Francis II. She
became queen of France for a very short period,
but returned to Scotland after Francis II's
death. Her father had died and her mother was
Regent. Mary was popular for a short time, but
then faced many enemies.

Retour de Tobie (Le) *(The Return of* Eustache Le Sueur
Tobias)
See **Archange Raphaël quittant la famille de
Tobie**.

Le Rêve de Pâris, Pieter
Coecke van Aelst.

Rêve (Le) *(The Dream)*, also known as *Voltaire composant "La Pucelle" (Voltaire Writing "La Pucelle")*
(Imag.) Voltaire, seated at his desk, contemplates medallions bearing the effigies of Charles VII, the king's mistress, Agnès Sorel, Joan of Arc (Jeanne la Pucelle or Joan the Maid) and Dunois, the knight who accompanied her on her battles. Voltaire appears to find inspiration in these portraits. A small faun presents him with the inkpot. The cup of coffee is an allusion to Voltaire's favorite beverage.

Gabriel de Saint-Aubin

Rêve de Pâris (Le) *(The Dream of Paris)*
(Myth.) The Judgment of Paris (see **Jugement de Pâris**) is depicted as a dream in this painting. While sleeping, Paris sees the three goddesses coming toward him, fighting over the apple. Jupiter had ordered Mercury to lead them to Paris, the son of Priam. His judgment was the cause of the Trojan War and eventually resulted in the destruction of Troy. Jupiter had little sympathy for Priam's family as his father, Laomedon, had cheated the gods (see **Hercule et Hésione**). It is therefore hardly surprising that he allowed Paris to make this disastrous choice.

Pieter Coecke van Aelst

Robe ensanglantée de Joseph apportée par Jacob (La) *(Jacob Bringing Joseph's Bloody Coat to His Father)*
See **Joseph et ses frères**.

François-Joseph Heim

Roger délivrant Angélique *(Ruggiero Frees Angelica)*
(Lit.) Angelica, one of the heroines of Ariosto's epic poem, *Orlando Furioso*, was queen of Cathay, in China. She was taken to France by Roland when he returned from the Crusades. He wished to marry her, but she refused him and her other suitors and fled into the forest. She was discovered by a hermit who cast a spell on

Jean Auguste Ingres
Louis-Édouard Rioult

her. Meanwhile, on a nearby island, because of a dispute between a king and the god of the sea, an enormous orc (a sea monster) devoured the inhabitants. An oracle commanded the sacrifice of a beautiful young maiden. Two sailors, who discovered Angelica sleeping on the shore, abducted her and attached her to a rock. Ruggiero, returning from other adventures on a hippogrif (a winged monster), killed the orc and rescued Angelica. The story did not, however, have the traditional happy ending. She did not fall into his arms, but rejected him for another man (see **Angélique et Médor**).

Same subject: **Angélique**, Léon Riesener.

Roi Jean à la bataille de Poitiers (Le)
(King John at the Battle of Poitiers)
See **Bataille de Poitiers**.

Eugène Delacroix

ro

270

Roi païen envoie des ambassadeurs demander pour son fils la main de sainte Ursule (Le) *(The Pagan King Sending His Ambassadors to Request Saint Ursula's Hand For His Son)*
See **Légende de sainte Ursule**.

Master of the Legend of Saint Ursula

Romance du saule (La) *(The Song of Willow)*
See **Coucher de Desdémone**.

Théodore Chassériau

Roméo et Juliette *(Romeo and Juliet)*
(Lit.) In Shakespeare's play *Romeo and Juliet*, the two young lovers belong to feuding families, the Montagues and the Capulets. The lovers are secretly married by a hermit, but Juliet's family wants her to marry another man. The hermit devises a plan and prepares a potion that will make Juliet appear to be dead for two days. Romeo, who has been banished for having killed Juliet's cousin, is to be informed of the plan and to wait

Théodore Chassériau

for Juliet to regain consciousness in her tomb and then flee with her. The message does not reach Romeo in time and, hearing of her death, he rushes to the tomb, discovers her lifeless body and poisons himself. Juliet awakes to find him dead and stabs herself. The tragic event reconciles the two families.

Romulus et Rémus *(Romulus and Remus)*

Émile Champmartin

(Myth.) According to one of the numerous legends of Romulus and Remus, they were the twin sons of the vestal virgin Rhea. The vestal virgins, priestesses of Vesta, the goddess of the Hearth, were sworn to chastity. Rhea defended herself by claiming that she had been raped by Mars, but the boys were snatched from her to be thrown into the Tiber. According to one legend, they were rescued and raised by a she-wolf (symbol of Mars), according to another, they were found by a shepherd: the stories are also combined (see **Romulus et Rémus recueillis par Faustulus**).

Romulus founded the city of Rome and became its first king after killing his brother.

Romulus et Rémus recueillis par Faustulus or Faustulus recueillant Romulus et Rémus *(Romulus and Remus Brought Back by Faustulus)*

Pietro da Cortona

(Myth.) Faustulus, a shepherd, discovered Romulus and Remus on the banks of the Tiber before they were thrown into the river (see **Romulus et Rémus**). Pretending that his wife had just lost a son and would be happy to care for the young children, Faustulus took them from the servant who had been ordered to drown them. According to another legend, he found them in a forest, suckling a she-wolf. Faustulus was later killed when he intervened in a dispute between Romulus and Remus.

Romulus vainqueur d'Acron *(Romulus Conqueror of Acron)*

Jean Auguste Ingres

(Hist.) King Acron of Cenina, a small town in Latium, was killed by Romulus, the first (legendary) king of Rome, who invaded his territory.

Ruth et Booz *(Ruth and Boaz),* also known as **Été (L')** *(Summer)*

Émile Champmartin

(O.T.) After the death of her husband, Ruth and her mother-in-law, Naomi, left Moab to escape famine. They went to Naomi's native land, Bethlehem, but eventually returned to Moab. Crossing the fields of a rich Israelite, Boaz, they asked for and received his permission to glean corn. One evening, Ruth went and lay down at the feet of Boaz. He awoke at midnight to find her there and she declared her devotion to him. He was flattered to be preferred to a younger man and, knowing her to be a virtuous woman, decided to take her as his wife. Their grandson was King David.

Sabines arrêtant le combat entre les Romains et les Sabins (Les) *(The Sabine Women)* Jacques-Louis David

(Hist.) Abducted several years earlier by the Romans, who needed women to ensure their descendants (see **Enlèvement des Sabines**), the Sabines threw themselves into the midst of the fighting between their Roman husbands and their Sabine brothers commanded by King Tatius. Their intervention resulted in peace. The woman in the foreground is Hersilia, Romulus' wife. They had two sons, Prima and Aolius. After her death she was immortalized under the name of Harta.

Same subject: **Hersilie séparant Romulus et Tatius**, Guercino.

Sacerdoce de la Vierge *(The Calling of the Virgin)* Amiens, 15th century

(Christ. Trad.) The cult surrounding Mary in the Middle Ages was such that she was often assigned the functions and attributes of Christ. It is through the Virgin Mary that Christ was incarnated. It is Mary who transmitted the priesthood from her ancestor Levi to Jesus, whom she holds by the hand. She is dressed in priest's garments and, like a priest, offers her son as victim for the sacrifice. At the altar where the sacrifices of Abel, Abraham and Melchizadek were made, she gives the priest the "vesture," which is at the same time a garment, the calling and the incarnation.

Sacre de Napoléon *(Consecration of the Emperor Napoleon I)* Jacques-Louis David

(Hist.) Emperor Napoleon I was consecrated on December 2, 1804, in the Cathedral of Notre Dame. Empress Josephine was crowned on the same day. Witnesses said that Napoleon seized the crown to place it on his own head and then crowned the Empress himself. He wanted his court to be as glorious as that of the kings.

Sacrifice d'Abraham (Le) *(The Sacrifice of Abraham)*

(O.T.) Abraham and Sarah had a son late in life (see **Abraham et les trois anges**). Abraham was ordered by God to sacrifice his only son. Being a simple and faithful man, he intended to obey and took his son to the mountains. As he was about to kill Isaac, his hand was stayed by an angel. God was satisfied with his obedience and no longer demanded the sacrifice.

Same subject: **Sacrifice d'Isaac par Abraham**, Peter Paul Rubens. **Abraham s'apprête à sacrifier Isaac**, Antonio Burini.⸓

French, 18th century
Brunswick Monogrammist
Annibale Carracci
Pieter Lastman

Sacrifice d'Iphigénie (Le) *(The Sacrifice of Iphigenia)*

(Myth.) The Greeks, commanded by Agamemnon, king of Kings, prepared their vessels to attack Troy, but there was no wind in the sails. This was a sign of Diana's anger against Agamemnon. The soothsayer Calchas said that Agamemnon should sacrifice his daughter Iphigenia to appease the goddess. Agamemnon hesitated, but was finally convinced by Menelaus and Ulysses. He had Iphigenia sent to him under the pretext of wanting to betroth her to Achilles. As Iphigenia was about to be sacrificed, Diana took pity on her and replaced her with a doe. The goddess took her to Tauris where she made her a priestess.

Betholet Flemalle
François Le Moyne

Sacrifice d'Isaac par Abraham (Le) *(Abraham Sacrificing Isaac)*
See **Sacrifice d'Abraham**.

Peter Paul Rubens

Sacrifice de Gédéon *(The Sacrifice of Gideon)*

(O.T.) In the 12th century B.C. the Israelites were was oppressed by the Midianites. An angel appeared to judge Gideon and said to him, " Go in this might of yours and deliver Israel from the hand of Midian." Gideon demanded proof that it

François Boucher

Le Sacrifice d'Iphigénie,
Betholet Flemalle.

was an angel of God who was addressing him.
The angel ordered him to place meat and unleav-
ened bread on a rock and pour broth over them.
Then the angel touched them with the tip of his
staff and a fire sprang from the rock and
consumed them. Gideon went on to conquer the
Midianites.

Sacrifice de la fille de Jephté (Le)
(The Sacrifice of Jephthah's Daughter)

After Antoine Coypel

(O.T.) The warrior Jephthah was one of the
judges of Israel (12th century B.C.). Just before
going to battle against the Ammonites, he made
an oath saying "whoever comes forth from the
doors of my house to meet me, when I return
victorious from the Ammonites, shall be the
Lord's, and I will offer him up for a burned offering." On his return, he was met by his only
daughter who rushed to meet him playing tim-
bals and dancing. Jephthah despaired, but his
daughter encouraged him to keep his promise,
asking only for two months to go into the mountains with her companions and lament her virginity. She was sacrificed on her return.

Sacrifice de Manué (Le) *(The Sacrifice of Manoah)*
Carle Vanloo

Manoah and his wife had no children. A man announced that Manoah's wife would give birth to a son (he was to be the Israelite hero Samson). On hearing the news, Manoah sacrificed a kid and cereal, which were immediately consumed. The man ascended in the flames and Manoah and his wife realized that the messenger had been an angel of the Lord.

Saint André, retable de Thouzon *(Saint Andrew, Retable of Thouzon)*
Provence, 15th century

(Christ. Trad.) **Saint André fait éteindre un incendie par son disciple** *(Saint Andrew's Disciple Extinguishing the Fire)*
Saint Andrew was one of Jesus' disciples. He preached the Gospel and miraculously delivered Saint Matthew from prison, thus incurring the hostility of the Romans. While a young Roman noble, whom he had converted, was in Saint Andrew's house, the young man's parents set the house on fire. The saint gave the young man a small bottle of water with which he miraculously put out the fire.

sa

276

Saint André chasse les démons de la ville de Nicée *(Saint Andrew Chasing the Demons Away from Nicaea)*
Nicaea was surrounded by demons who tore to pieces anyone who left the town. Saint Andrew ordered the demons to be like little dogs and retire to where no one could see them. They immediately disappeared, only to show up in the neighboring town where they devoured a young man. Informed of the incident, Saint Andrew rushed to revive the victim.

Saint Anselme écrivant sous l'inspiration de la Vierge *(Saint Anselm Inspired by the Virgin)*
Giuseppe Maria Crespi

(Christ. Trad.) Saint Anslem of Aosta, who was

Saint Antoine et le miracle de la mule, Beccafumi.

the archbishop of Canterbury in the 11th century, defended the doctrine of the immaculate conception (See **Immaculée Conception**). Together with Saint Bernard, he was one of those called "chaplains of the Virgin." Here the Virgin inspires him, while an angel holds the bishop's crozier and mitre.

Saint Antoine de Padoue guérissant un jeune homme *(Saint Antony of Padua Healing a Young Man)*
Sebastiano Ricci

(Christ. Trad.) Interpreting the Gospels too literally, a young man cut off his foot to punish himself for kicking his mother. Saint Antony miraculously restored the foot.

Saint Antoine et le miracle de la mule *(Saint Antony and the Miracle of the Mule)*
Domenico Beccafumi

(Christ. Trad.) A Jew denied the presence of Christ in the Eucharist. Saint Antony showed him a mule who refused feed, but knelt before the consecrated host. Astounded, the man admitted his error.

Saint Antoine et saint Paul ermite nourris par un corbeau *(Saint Antony and Saint Paul the Hermit Fed by a Raven)*
Flanders, 17th century

(Christ. Trad.) Saint Antony retreated to the desert and believed himself to be the only hermit in the region. When he learned that a Christian named Paul was living in a cabin in the neighboring forest, he went to see him. Paul refused to open his door, but Saint Antony said that he would rather die on the spot than leave. Paul finally opened his door. The two men embraced and entered a lengthy discussion. At mealtime, a raven brought food for both men. Antony was surprised, but not Paul, for the raven brought him food every day. As Antony left, he saw two angels carry off Paul's soul. He rushed back to the cabin to discover that Paul had died praying. He was still kneeling and appeared to be alive. Antony worried about how to dig him a grave, but two lions appeared and accomplished the task.

Saint Basile dictant sa doctrine (Saint Basil Dictating His Doctrine)

Francisco de Herrera

(Hist.) Saint Basil, one of the Fathers of the Catholic Church in the 4th century, defended the orthodox doctrine against Arianism, which he considered to be a heresy. He left behind several theological works.

Saint Benoît ressucite un enfant (Saint Benedict Reviving a Child)

Louis de Silvestre

(Christ. Trad.) Saint Benedict, who lived in the 6th century, founded the Benedictine Order. One day when he was on his way to work in the fields, the monks' gardener brought his dead child to the monastery. Saint Benedict rushed to the child's side, knelt down and bent over the body. Like Eli and Elisha in the Old Testament, he placed his cheek against the child's cheek and prayed, thus reviving the child.

Saint Bernard de Clairvaux rend visite au R.P général Guigues Ier (Saint Bernard of Clairvaux)

Vincente Carducho

(Christ. Trad.) Saint Bernard, born near Dijon in

Saint Bonaventure au concile de Lyon,
Francisco de Zurbarán.

1090, entered the Abbey of Cîteaux at the age of twenty-three and founded the Monastery at Clairvaux in Champagne two years later. Guido de Castro had established the statutes of the Carthusian Order; here he receives Saint Bernard as prior of the Grande Chartreuse.

Saint Bonaventure au concile de Lyon *(Saint Bonaventure at the Council of Lyons)*

Francisco de Zurbarán

(Christ. Trad.) Saint Bonaventure joined the Franciscan Order at the age of twenty-one. He became general of the Franciscans in 1257 and reformed the order. He acquired such a reputation for perfection and wisdom that after the death of Pope Clement IV, the cardinals asked him to choose the new pope, who was Gregory X. In 1274 Saint Bonaventure was sent as a legate to the Council of Lyons and died at the age of fifty-three during the council (see **Exposition du corps de saint Bonaventure**).

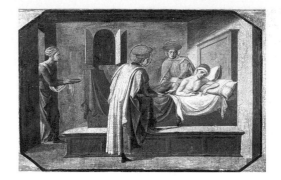

Saint Côme et saint Damien soignant un malade, Francesco di Pesellino.

Saint Bonaventure enfant guéri par saint François *(Saint Bonaventure Healed by Saint Francis)*, also known as **Guérison de saint Bonaventure enfant par saint François**

Francisco de Herrera

(Christ. Trad.) Saint Bonaventure was born a fragile child. At the age of twelve he fell so seriously ill that even his father, a doctor, despaired of healing him. His mother was particularly devoted to Saint Francis of Assisi who had just been canonized. She prayed and the child was immediately healed. For this reason he later joined the Franciscan order.

Saint Bonaventure recevant la communion des mains d'un ange *(Saint Bonaventure Receiving Communion From an Angel)*

Francisco de Herrera

(Christ. Trad.) In his younger years, Saint Bonaventure hesitated to celebrate communion for he considered himself unworthy to receive the body of Christ. One day as he was attending the sacrament and meditating on the Passion, an angel appeared, took the host from the celebrant and placed it between his lips.

Saint Bruno examine un dessin des thermes de Dioclétien, emplacement de la future chartreuse de Rome *(Saint Bruno Examining the Future Site of the Roman Charterhouse)*

Eustache Le Sueur

(Hist.) Saint Bruno established his first monastery at the Grande Chartreuse in the mountains near Grenoble, thus giving the name *chartreuse*, "charterhouse", to all Carthusian monasteries. He built other charterhouses in Rome, Paris and Pavia (see **Scènes de la vie de saint Bruno**).

Saint Côme et saint Damien soignant un malade *(Saints Cosmas and Damian Healing a Sick Man)*

Francesco di Pesellino

(Christ. Trad.) These two brothers, born and martyred on the same day, studied medicine and were granted the power of healing men and animals by God (see **Martyre de saint Côme et saint Damien**).

Saint Denis communie en prison *(Saint Denis Celebrating Communion in Prison)*

Henri Bellechose

(Christ. Trad.) Saint Denis was the first bishop of Paris in the 3rd century. He arrived in Paris (Lutetia) from Rome to preach the Gospel and was imprisoned and martyred (see **Martyre de saint Denis**).

Saint Dominique *(Saint Dominic)*
See **Histoire de saint Dominique**.

Fra Angelico

Saint Étienne conduit au martyre *(Saint Stephen on His Way to be Martyred)*
See **Martyre de saint Étienne**.

René Houasse

Saint François d'Assise recevant les stigmates *(Saint Francis of Assisi Receiving the Stigmata)*

Giotto di Bondone
Perugino
Frans Pourbus the Younger

(Christ. Trad.) One day while praying, Saint Francis saw a crucified seraph who turned toward him and marked his body with the stigmata. These are the five wounds of Jesus' crucifixion; the marks left in his hands and feet by the nails, and the wound in his side from the soldier's lance (see **Crucifixion**). Saint Francis hid the stigmata, but they were discovered on his body after his death.

Same subject: **Saint François recevant les stigmates**, Domenico Beccafumi, Lo Spagna.

Saint François d'Assise réconforté par les anges après sa stigmatisation *(Saint Francis of Assisi Comforted by Angels)*

Gérard Seghers

See **Saint François d'Assise recevant les stigmates**.

Saint François de Paule guérissant Jean Caratello *(Saint Francis of Paola Healing Giovanni Caratello)*

Theodoor van Thulden

(Christ. Trad.) Giovanni Caratello, who lived in the town of Paola, suffered from atrophy of the leg for fifteen years. No remedy could be found to end his suffering. Saint Francis of Paola made the sign of the cross above his leg and placed a medicinal plant and wild mint on it. The leg was instantly healed.

Saint François de Paule prophétisant un fils à Louise de Savoie *(Saint Francis of Paola Prophesying the Birth of a Son to Louise of Savoy)*

Theodoor van Thulden

(Hist.) Louise of Savoy (1476-1531) was the mother of Francis of Angoulême, who succeeded Louis XII under the name of Francis I. Francis of Paola (1416-1508), founder of the Minims (the "least brethren") had spent twenty years in a cave on the coast. His reputation as a holy man

Saint François d'Assise recevant les stigmates, Giotto di Bondone.

was widespread, and he was consulted several times by the French court. In 1482, Louis XI summoned him to his royal residence, Plessis-lez-Tours, where Saint Francis remained for the rest of his life.

Saint François recevant les stigmates

(Saint Francis Receiving the Stigmata)
See **Saint François d'Assise recevant les stigmates**.

Lo Spagna
Domenico Beccafumi

Saint François-Xavier rappelant à la vie la fille d'un habitant de Cangox-ima *(Saint Francis Xavier Reviving the Daughter of an Inhabitant of Kagoshima)* (Christ. Trad.) In this painting, Saint Francis Xavier, a 16th century Jesuit, and his companion (with his back to the artist) Saint Juan Fernandez are praying on either side of a young girl's bed. The scene took place in Japan during Saint Francis Xavier's evangelizing mission, but there are no written accounts of this miracle.

Nicolas Poussin

Saint Georges combattant le dragon
Saint Georges luttant avec le dragon
(Saint George Fighting the Dragon)
See **Saint Georges terrassant le dragon**.

Eugène Delacroix
Raphaël

Saint Georges terrassant le dragon
(Saint George Fighting the Dragon)
(Christ. Trad.) A dragon devastated Libya, breathing death on all who passed. The population defended itself through a daily offering of two ewes, but was forced to sacrifice children when there were no ewes. When it was his daughter's turn to be sacrificed, the king offered his riches and half of his kingdom to anyone who would save her. The people demanded her sacrifice and, dressed as a bride, she was sent crying before the dragon. Saint George suddenly appeared, but she told him to flee saying that there was no point in his being devoured with her. Saint George spurred on his horse, made the sign of the cross and threw the monster to the ground. He asked the princess to put her girdle around the beast's neck and the dragon was then led docilely to the town. The inhabitants preferred to see it killed and Saint George consented in exchange for their conversion to Christianity. (Also see **Scènes de la Légende de saint Georges**.)
Same subject: **Combat de saint Georges contre le dragon**, Rhine, 15th century.

Champagne or Burgundy, 16th century
Raphaël

Saint Gervais et saint Protais, amenés devant Astasius, refusent de sacrifier à Jupiter *(Saint Gervase and Saint Protase, Brought Before Astasius For Refusing to Sacrifice to Jupiter)*

Eustache Le Sueur

(Christ. Trad.) The brothers saints Gervase and Protase were the sons of Saint Vitalis and the blessed Valery. They gave their possessions to the poor and lived in an oratory with Saint Nazarius. Soldiers led them to Milan before Astasius who was preparing to leave for war. Pagans claimed that he would not be victorious unless he sacrificed Gervase and Protase. Astasius ordered them to sacrifice to idols, but they refused and were beheaded and martyred.

Saint Hyacinthe sauvant la statue de la Vierge des ennemis du nom chrétien *(Saint Hyacinth Saving the Statue of the Virgin Mary From Enemies of the Christians)*

Nicolas Colombel

(Christ. Trad.) Saint Hyacinth, a Polish monk who lived in the 13th century, saved the statue of the Virgin Mary during the pillage of Kiev (which belonged to Poland) by the Mongols. He performed miraculous healings through the intervention of the statue.

Saint Jacques le Majeur, conduit au supplice, guérit un paralytique et embrasse son accusateur *(Saint James the Greater Healing a Paralytic and Embracing His Accuser)*
(Christ. Trad.) The apostle James the Greater was condemned to death by Herod Agrippa. On his way to his execution, he met a paralytic and healed him. His accuser asked to be pardoned and Saint James complied.

Noël Coypel

Saint Jean baptisant le peuple *(Saint John Baptizing the People)*
(N.T.) John the Baptist's mission was to announce the coming of the Messiah and to preach penitence. He lived in the desert on wild honey and locusts. He is usually represented dressed in a garment made of camel skin bound with a leather girdle. He baptized in the Jordan waters all who came to him (see **Baptême du Christ**).
Same subject: **Prédication de saint Jean-Baptiste**, Flanders, 16th century, Abraham Bloemaert, Giovanni Battista Gaulli, Pier Francesco Mola, Filippo Napoletano, Joachim Wtewael. **Saint Jean prêchant**, Henri de Favanne. **Paysage avec la prédication de saint Jean-Baptiste**, Claes-Dircksz van der Heck. **Saint Jean-Baptiste dans le désert**, French, 18th century.

Nicolas Poussin

Saint Jean Évangéliste et la coupe empoisonnée *(Saint John the Evangelist with the Poisoned Cup)*
(Christ. Trad.) After the death of Emperor Domitian, persecutor of the Christians, John was allowed to return to Ephesus where there was a cult of Diana. To test him, Diana's high priest told him to drink from a poisoned cup, which had killed two sinners. John made the sign of the

Alonso Cano

Saint Jean baptisant le peuple, Nicolas Poussin.

cross and the poison left the cup in the form of a small two-headed dragon. John drank from the cup, but was unharmed.

Saint Jean prêchant *(Saint John Preaching)*

See **Saint Jean baptisant le peuple**.

Henri de Favanne

Saint Jérôme dans le désert *(Saint Jerome in the Desert)*

(Christ. Trad.) After a miraculous dream (see **Songe de saint Jérôme**), Jerome entered the Church where he was soon named cardinal and then pope (end of the 4th century). He became unpopular through his criticism of the monks' corruption. He went to study with the bishop of Constantinople and then retreated to the Chalcidian desert in Syria. He remained there for four years, leading a celibate life of meditation. He suffered from heat, hunger, thirst, scorpions and erotic hallucinations, which forced him to spend his nights praying. The demon tempted him in the form of a naked woman.

Same subject: **Saint Jérôme méditant dans le désert**, Lorenzo Lotto. **Saint Jérôme en prière dans un paysage**, Dossi Battista. **Saint Jérôme en prière dans une grotte**, Pieter Slingelandt. **Pénitence de saint Jérôme**, Sano di Pietro.

Joachim Patenier
Jacopo del Sellajo
Lo Spagna

Saint Jérôme en prière dans un paysage
Saint Jérôme en prière dans une grotte *(Saint Jerome Praying)*
See **Saint Jérôme dans le désert**.

Dossi Battista
Pieter Slingelandt

Saint Jérôme et le lion *(Saint Jerome and the Lion)*

Sano di Pietro

(Christ. Trad.) After retreating to the desert (see **Saint Jérôme dans le désert**), Saint Jerome, one of the Latin Fathers of the Church, went to Bethlehem where he wrote his treatises and founded several monasteries. One day he encountered a limping lion in one of the monasteries. The frightened monks ran away, but Saint Jerome approached the lion and, seeing that it was wounded, called back the monks. He asked the monks to wash the wounded paw (a symbolic gesture as the monks washed the feet of their visitors) and removed the thorn. The lion, now tamed, remained in the monastery and became invaluable. It accompanied the donkey which carried sacks of grain to the mill, or fetched wood. One day, when the donkey was stolen, the monks accused the lion of eating it. In the end the lion found the caravan of camel traders who had stolen the donkey. He frightened them and brought them to the monastery where they returned the donkey and, as a sign of their repentance, promised an annual offering to the monastery.

Saint Jérôme méditant dans le désert *(Saint Jerome in the Desert)*
See **Saint Jérôme dans le désert**.

Lorenzo Lotto

Saint Jérôme ressuscite le cardinal Andrea *(Saint Jerome Reviving Cardinal Andrea)*

Perugino

(Christ. Trad.) The death of Cardinal Andrea in Rome was witnessed by many people. During the funeral procession, in the presence of the pope and the entire population who came to honor his memory, moans were heard in the tomb of the cardinal (although he is dressed as a bishop here). The cardinal emerged alive from his tomb and, later, told the pope that he had ascended to heaven and had been severely judged for his weakness and gluttony, but that through the intervention of Saint Jerome, he had been brought back to life to be redeemed by him.

Saint Jérôme soutenant deux jeunes pendus, Perugino.

Saint Jérôme soutenant deux jeunes pendus *(Saint Jerome Supporting Two Men on the Gallows)*

Perugino

(Christ. Trad.) Two young Romans had set off on a pilgrimage to Saint Jerome's tomb. On their way back, they were unjustly accused of a crime that had been committed in the area. Attempts were made to torture them, but the weapons broke and the flame would not burn. The judge ordered them to be hung for eight days, and said that if they remained alive after this period, he would believe in their innocence. Almost immediately after they were hung, Saint Jerome appeared and supported them for eight days (according to legend, by the soles of their feet). They were then pardoned and received triumphantly by the people.

Saint Joseph charpentier *(Saint Joseph the Carpenter)*

Georges de La Tour

(Christ. Trad.) Saint Joseph, Jesus' foster father, was a carpenter. Here he is bending over to drill a hole in a piece of wood which, added to another piece of wood, evokes the cross on which Jesus was crucified.

Saint Joseph et les prétendants *(Saint Joseph and the Suitors)*

Master of the Life of the Virgin

See **Mariage de la Vierge**.

Saint Louis roi de France distribuant les aumônes *(Saint Louis King of France Distributing Alms)*

Luis Tristan

(Hist.) Louis IX, or Saint Louis, son of Louis VIII, ruled first under the regency of his mother Blanche of Castile, and then alone from 1226 until his death in 1270. His reputation for piety, justice and charity spread throughout Europe.

Saint Macaire de Gand secourant les pestiférés *(Saint Macarius of Gand Tending the Plague-Stricken)*

Jacob van Oost the Younger

(Christ. Trad.) The saint depicted in this painting did not actually exist. In the 9th century, monks from the Abbey of Saint-Bavon created his legend from fragments of other legends. According to their account, he was the bishop of Antioch, but renounced his functions out of humility and set out on a pilgrimage to Jerusalem. He was thrown into prison and crucified on the ground, with a burning stone on his breast, but the nails came out of his hands and feet, and the prison door opened. After his miraculous release, he returned to Europe where he came to the aid of the pest-stricken in Gand, Belgium. He himself was afflicted with the epidemic and prophesied that the plague would end on his death. His prediction came true.

Saint Martin donnant la moitié de son manteau *(Saint Martin Dividing His Cloak)*

Fra Angelico

(Christ. Trad.) Before his conversion, Saint Martin was a Roman soldier. Arriving with his legion at the gates of Amiens, he caught sight of a poor man unsuitably dressed for the cold winter and gave him half of his cloak. (Why only half and not the entire cloak as with Saint Francis of Assisi? Because as a soldier he had only paid for half of the garment; the other half belonged to the army).

Same subject: **Saint Martin partageant son manteau**, Master of the Rebel Angels. **Charité de saint Martin**, Touraine, 16th century.

Saint Matthieu inspiré par l'Ange, Rembrandt.

Saint Martin partageant son manteau *(Saint Martin Dividing His Cloak)*
See **Saint Martin donnant la moitié de son manteau**.

Master of the Rebel Angels

Saint Matthieu et l'Ange *(Saint Matthew and the Angel)*
See **Saint Matthieu inspiré par l'Ange**.

Rembrandt

Saint Matthieu inspiré par l'Ange *(Saint Matthew Inspired by an Angel)*, also known as **Saint Matthieu et l'Ange** *(Saint Matthew and the Angel)*
(Christ. Trad.) Saint Matthew was a tax-collector before he was called by Jesus to become one of the first disciples. The Gospel according to Matthew was written around 40 A.D. The angel who appears to be providing him with inspiration is his attribute.

Rembrandt

Saint Michel *(Saint Michael)*
See **Saint Michel terrassant le démon**.

Raphaël

Saint Michel terrassant le démon *(Saint Michel Victorious)*
(Christ. Trad.) When the angels rebelled against God, the dragon, their leader Lucifer, was expelled from heaven by archangel Michael. The other rebel angels were thrown down after him. Michael imprisoned them in a dark, damp place where they will remain until the Last Judgment (see **Chute des anges rebelles**).
Same subject: **Saint Michel**, Raphaël.

Raphaël

Saint Nicolas *(Saint Nicholas)*
(Christ. Trad.) Saint Nicholas, bishop of Myra, in Asia Minor, in the 4th century, was one of the most popular saints of the Middle Ages. The famous legend of Saint Nicholas restoring three children to life was probably the result of an image of the saint with three soldiers in which the saint's size was exaggerated.

Joseph Garcin

Saint Nicholas offrant une dot à des jeunes filles *(The Charity of Saint Nicholas)*

Ambrogio Lorenzetti

(Christ. Trad.) Saint Nicholas was bishop of Myra in the 4th century. Famed for his generosity, he was said to have aided a nobleman whose poverty forced him to sell his three daughters as prostitutes. When he heard of their misfortune, Nicholas went to the poor man's house and, for three nights in a row, thrust bags of gold into the window as a dowry for the young women.

Saint Paul à Malte *(Saint Paul on the Island of Malta)*

Martin de Vos

(N.T.) Saint Paul preached in many Greek towns and was imprisoned and threatened with death several times. During his fourth voyage, he was shipwrecked with the crew and fellow travelers on the island of Malta. They were welcomed by the inhabitants who prepared a great fire to provide warmth for the castaways. Paul gathered sticks which he threw into the fire. A viper, hidden in the woodpile, came out and bit his hand. The Maltese saw this as a sign that he was a murderer fleeing justice. However, to their surprise, Paul tossed off the snake into the fire and was unharmed. They changed their minds and decided that he must be a god.

Saint Paul recevant les adieux des prêtres éphésiens *(The Ephesian Priests Bidding Farewell to Saint Paul)*

Louis Galloche

(N.T.) Saint Paul lived in Ephesus for two years (see **Prédication de saint Paul à Éphèse**), but was driven away by the hostility of the inhabitants.

Saint Philippe baptisant l'eunuque de la reine Candace *(Saint Philip Baptizing Queen Candace's Eunuch)*

Nicolas Bertin

(N.T.) Candace was not a proper name, but rather the title given to all ancient Egyptian queens. The queen's eunuch, who was also her treasurer, went to Jerusalem to worship. On his way back he read the prophet Isaiah. He met Philip the Deacon and asked him to help him understand the Scriptures. Saint Philip converted him by speaking to him of Jesus Christ. When they came to some water, the eunuch stopped the chariot and asked to be baptized.

Same subject: **Baptême de l'eunuque éthiopien par le diacre Philippe**, Herman Nauwincx, Lambert Sustris and his studio.

Saint Pierre délivré de prison *(Saint Peter Delivered From Prison)*

Pieter Neefs the Elder

(Christ. Trad.) After Jesus' death, Saint Peter, the first of the disciples, became the undisputed leader of the apostles. After the death of Herod the Great, his son Herod Antipas, and then his grandson Herod Agrippa, ruled. Herod Agrippa persecuted the Christians to gain favor with the Jews of Judea. He imprisoned Saint Peter but, by law, had to wait until after Passover to put him to death. During the night an angel broke the prisoner's chains and set him free to go and preach. Herod decided to execute the jailors, but they were spared as Herod died before he could carry out his plan.

Saint Pierre guérissant les malades avec son ombre *(Saint Peter Healing the Sick With His Shadow)*

Laurent de la Hyre

(N.T.) After Jesus' death, the apostles preached the Gospels and performed miraculous acts of healing. They stood around Saint Peter under the portico of the Temple of Solomon where crowds of sick and lame came to see him. Families brought their sick on beds and pallets and placed them around Peter so that they would at least be touched by his shadow. Those who were covered by his shadow were healed.

Saint Pierre repentant *(Saint Peter Repenting)*

Gérard Seghers

See **Reniement de saint Pierre**.

Saint Pierre ressuscitant Tabithe Pierre-Jacques Cazes
(Saint Peter Raising Tabitha)
(N.T.) Tabitha was a pious and charitable woman who fell ill and died. Peter, who was in the vicinity, was sent for by his disciples. He told the widows who were mourning over Tabitha's body to leave the room and then knelt down and prayed. Finally he said, "Tabitha, rise." She opened her eyes and held out her hand to him. He called back her friends and neighbors who watched as she rose from her deathbed.

Saint Sébastien *(Saint Sebastian)* Giovanni Antonio Boltraffio
Same subject by Camille Corot, Perugino, Andrea Mantegna.

Saint Sébastien martyr dans un Guido Reni
paysage *(Landscape with The Martyrdom of Saint Sebastian)*

Saint Sébastien soigné **sa**
par Irène, Georges de La   295
Tour.

Saint Sébastien secouru par les anges *(Saint Sebastian Healed by Angels)*
See **Martyre de saint Sébastien**.

Anthony van Dyck

Saint Sébastien soigné par Irène *(Saint Sebastian Tended By Saint Irene)*
(Christ. Trad.) According to legend, after Saint Sebastian had been left for dead *(see* **Martyre de saint Sébastien**), a Roman widow named Irene nursed him back to health. Irene became the patron saint of nurses.

Georges de La Tour

Saint Thomas de Villeneuve distribuant les aumônes *(Saint Thomas of Villanueva Distributing Alms)*
(Hist.) This Spanish prelate (1488-1555) studied in Salamanca and then joined the Augustinian friars. His preaching earned him the title of "The New Apostle of Spain." He refused the honor several times, but was finally forced to accept by Charles V who named him archbishop of Valencia. He is represented here in bishop's robes.

Mateo Cerezo

Saint Victor renversant les idoles *(Saint Victor Overturning the Idoles)*
(Christ. Trad.) Victor was a young Roman soldier who was converted to Christianity. Here he is led, hands bound, before the tribunal to sacrifice to the gods. The sacrifice had been prepared, but Victor overturned the idols. He was immediately seized and martyred in 290.

Jean-Baptiste Deshays

Sainte Anne trinitaire *(The Virgin and Child with Saint Anne)*
(N.T., Christ. Trad.) See **Annonciation**. The Virgin and Child with Saint Anne is a common representation which shows Saint Anne holding her daughter Mary in her arms (or in her lap) together with Mary's son, Jesus, as if both children were her own.

Bartholomaüs Zeitblom

Same subject: **Anna Selbdritt**, Alsace, 15th century.

Sainte Conversation. Sainte Famille avec sainte Catherine, saint Sébastien et un donateur *(The Holy Family with Saint Catherine, Saint Sebastian and a Donor)*
See **Sainte Famille**.

Sebastiano del Piombo

Sainte Famille (La) *(The Holy Family)*
(Christ. Trad.) The portrait of the Holy Family always includes the Virgin Mary and the Infant Jesus; it may also include Saint Joseph and Saint John the Baptist, slightly older than Jesus. Saint Anne, the Virgin's mother, is often depicted. A variation is the *Sacra Conversazione* in which the mother and child may be accompanied by several adoring saints.

Italy, 16th century
Bagnacavallo
Bonifacio da Pitati
Bronzino
Felice Brusasorzi
Frans Floris (and his studio)
Giovanni Agostino da Lodi
Charles Le Brun
Bernardino Luini
Marco da Oggiono
Allessandro Mazzola
Bartolomé Esteban Murillo
Polidoro Lanzani
Nicolas Poussin
Raphaël
Rembrandt
Andrea del Sarto
Scarsellino
Godfried Schalcken
Bartolomeo Schedone
Bernardo Strozzi

La Sainte Famille,
Rembrandt.

Sainte Madeleine méditant dans la solitude *(Mary Magdalene Meditating in Solitude)*
Sainte Madeleine pénitente *(The Penitent Magdalene)*
See **Sainte Madeleine repentante renonce à toutes les vanités du monde.**

Adriaen van der Werff
Pieter Slingelandt

Sainte Madeleine repentante renonce à toutes les vanités du monde *(Mary Magdalene)*

Charles Le Brun

(Christ. Trad.) The Gospels recount several episodes involving a woman named Mary, Mary of Magdala (Mary Madgalene) or Mary of Bethany, the sister of Martha and Lazarus. However, it is not certain these names refer to the same woman. Mary Magdalene was a courtesan from whom Jesus exorcized seven devils. She was a model of religious fervor and was present at the crucifixion. Christ also appeared to her after his resurrection. According to legend, she retreated to the desert, but it appears that after the death of John the Baptist, whom she intended to marry, she reverted to a life of sin before she was converted a second time.

Same subject: **Sainte Madeleine méditant dans la solitude**, Adriaen van der Werff. **Sainte Madeleine pénitente**, Pieter Slingelandt. **Madeleine ou une pénitente dans le désert**, Jean-Marc Nattier. **Madeleine pénitente**, Guy François. **Madeleine à la veilleuse**, Georges de La Tour.

Sainte Ursule annonce à la cour de son père sa décision d'aller en pèlerinage à Rome avec onze mille vierges *(Saint Ursula Announces Her Pilgrimage to the Court of Her Father)*
See **Légende de sainte Ursule**.

Master of the Legend of Saint Ursula

Sainte Véronique *(Saint Veronica)*
(Christ. Trad.) According to the apocryphal Gospel of Nicodemus, Saint Veronica is the wo-

Paul Delaroche

man Jesus healed of an issue of blood. She is recognized in legend as the woman who wiped Jesus'face on the road to Calvary. His face made an imprint on the veil. A relic said to be the original "Veronica's veil" is preserved in Saint Peter's in Rome.

Salmacis et Hermaphrodite, Francesco Albani.

Saintes Femmes au tombeau *(The Holy Women at the Tomb)*

Giovanni Capassini
Lorenzo Monaco

(N.T.) Three days after Jesus' crucifixion, on the first day of the week, the three Maries went to his tomb with ointments. They found that the stone sealing the tomb had been rolled away and that the tomb was empty. Angels announced that Christ had risen and they were afraid.

Salmacis et Hermaphrodite *(Salmacis and Hermaphroditus)*

Francesco Albani

(Myth.) Hermaphroditus was the son of Mercury and Venus (his name was formed from his parents' Greek names, Hermes and Aphrodite). He was raised by nymphs on Mount Ida and was extremely handsome. He traveled to remote places and one day stopped at the edge of a magnificent lake. Salmacis, who lived in the lake, fell in love with him. He rejected her advances and she feigned resignation while, in fact, she hid herself and spied on him. When he entered the water, she embraced him despite his resistance. She prayed to the gods that their two bodies would never be separated and thereafter Hermaphroditus was both man and woman. As revenge, he begged his parents to grant that all who bathed in Lake Salmacis would become impotent.

Salomé recevant la tête de saint Jean-Baptiste *(Salome Receiving the Head of John the Baptist)*
See **Banquet d'Hérode** and **Décollation de saint Jean-Baptiste**.

Giuseppe Caletti
Lorenzo Lotto

Salomon au trésor du Temple *(Solomon in the Temple)*
(O.T.) The Bible describes in minute detail how Solomon built the famous Temple of Jerusalem. The temple was not particularly large, but was magnificently decorated. Solomon had almost the entire interior overlaid with gold and installed a golden altar with candelabra, lamps, vessels, chalices, knives, cups and braziers, all of solid gold. To these golden treasures, he added the silver vessels that had been consecrated by his father David.

Frans Francken the Younger

Salomon et la reine de Saba *(Solomon and the Queen of Sheba),* previously known as **Esther et Assuérus** *(Esther and Ahasuerus)*
(O.T.) King Solomon's reputation was so great that the queen of Sheba, a powerful ruler of Arabia, set out with all her attendants to visit him and satisfy her curiosity. Their meeting was magnificent and they exchanged sumptuous gifts.

Claude Vignon

Samson et Dalila,
Domenico Fiasella.

Salomon sacrifiant aux idoles *(Solomon's Idolatry)*
(O.T.) Toward the end of his life, the mighty and
wise King Solomon gathered a large harem of
foreign women. God warned him against the women, but they eventually persuaded him to worship idols.

A. Bélange
Sébastien Bourdon

Salutation angélique *(The Annunciation)*
(N.T.) The angel Gabriel entered Mary's house
saying, "Hail, full of grace, the Lord be with
you" and announced the birth of Jesus (see **Annonciation**).

Eustache Le Sueur
Rogier van der Weyden

Samson et Dalila *(Samson and Delilah)*
(O.T.) Samson was an athlete and a popular hero,
comparable to Hercules. His name means "like
the sun." He fought constant battles against the
Philistines, who unsuccessfully attacked his
people, the Israelites. He was captured by 3,000
men and bound with "new ropes," but through
God's intervention managed to escape and then
slew them with the jawbone of an ass that he
found on the ground. He became the lover of a
Philistine named Delilah who was charged with
discovering the secret of his strength. Samson
finally revealed that the secret was his hair and
she waited until he was sleeping and called a
man who shaved it off. She then delivered him to
her countrymen who put out his eyes, put him in
fetters and forced him to grind at the mill in the
prison of Gaza. His hair grew back and he took
revenge.
Same subject: **Dalila coupant les cheveux de
Samson**, Master H B.

Domenico Fiasella

**Sarah engage Abraham à prendre
Agar pour femme**
Sarah présentant Agar à Abraham
Sarah présente Agar à Abraham
(Sarah Presenting Hagar to Abraham)
See **Agar dans le désert**.

Cornelis van Poelenburgh
Philip van Dyck
Adriaen van der Werff

Satyre et le Paysan (Le) *(The Satyr and the Peasant)*   Sebastiano Ricci

(Lit.) This theme is taken from one of Aesop's fables. A peasant and a satyr were together in an inn on a winter's day. The man warmed his hands by blowing on them and the satyr asking why he was blowing on his hands. The man replied "to warm them." When they were served hot soup, the peasant blew on it. This time when questioned by the satyr, he said that he was blowing to cool the soup. The satyr quickly took his leave, saying that he wanted nothing more to do with a man whose mouth could breathe both hot and cold air.

Scène de la Saint-Barthélemy. Assassinat de Briou, gouverneur du prince de Conti, 24 août 1572 *(The Massacre of Saint Bartholomew's Day. Assassination of Briou)*   Joseph-Nicolas Robert-Fleury

See **Scène du massacre de la Saint-Barthélemy**.

Scène de l'Inquisition *(Scene From the Inquisition)*   Eugenio Lucas y Velazquez

(Hist.) The Inquisition, a tribunal of the Roman Catholic Church, was formed by the papacy to suppress heresy. On the basis of secret denunciation, those presumed to be guilty were arrested and attempts were made to force them to recant under the threat of being burned at the stake. In 1252, Pope Innocent IV authorized torture. The Inquisition at times also served political ends. In Spain, particularly when headed by Torquemada (1420-1498), the Inquisition was so cruel that it was denounced by the population and part of the clergy.

Scène du Déluge *(Scene From the Flood)*   Théodore Géricault

See **Déluge**.

Scène du massacre de la Saint-Bar-thélemy *(Scene From the Massacre of Saint Bartholomew's Day)*

Alexandre-Evariste Fragonard

(Hist.) France was divided between the Catholics and the Protestants. The military successes of Admiral Coligny, the French Protestant leader, and the fact that Henry IV, also a Protestant, became legal heir to the throne threatened the Catholics. Catherine de'Médici convinced King Charles IX to order the massacre of the Protestants, which began in Paris on the night of August 23-24, 1572 and claimed over 3,000 lives. Coligny was the first victim of the massacre.

Same subject: **Scène de la Saint-Barthélemy. Assassinat de Briou, gouverneur du prince de Conti, 24 août 1572**, Joseph-Nicolas Robert-Fleury.

Scènes de la légende de saint Georges *(Scenes From the Legend of Saint George)*

Bernardo Martorell

(Christ. Trad.) This retable includes the following panels:

Jugement de saint Georges *(The Judgment of Saint George)*.
Saint Georges traîné au supplice *(Saint George Dragged Through the City)*.
Flagellation de saint Georges *(The Flagellation of Saint George)*.
Décapitation de saint Georges *(The Saint Decapitated)*.

After slaying the dragon (see **Saint Georges terrassant le dragon**), Saint George abandoned his armor, distributed his possessions and became a simple Christian. He fell into the hands of the Roman proconsul in Persia, who tortured him for refusing to worship idols. All manners of torture were attempted, but each time, George made the sign of the cross and escaped. He also managed to convert many of his torturers. For this reason the proconsul finally decided to have him decapitated, after having him dragged through the city and scourged.

Scènes de la vie de la Vierge *(Scenes From the Life of the Virgin)*
See **Douze scènes de la vie de la Vierge**.

Master of the Life of the Virgin

Scènes de la vie de Saint Bruno *(Scenes From the Life of Saint Bruno)*

Eustache Le Sueur

(Christ. Trad.) This cycle of twenty-two paintings represents the life of Saint Bruno (1035-1101).

1. **Saint Bruno assiste au sermon de Raymond Diocrès** *(Saint Bruno Attends the Sermon of Raymond Diocrès).*
The young Bruno, before becoming a saint, listens attentively to the sermon of his tutor, Raymond Diocrès, at Notre Dame in Paris.

2. **Mort de Raymond Diocrès** *(The Death of Raymond Diocrès)*
The canon died piously in the midst of his followers, but the small devil is an evil omen.

3. **Raymond Diocrès répond après sa mort** *(Raymond Diocrès Replying After His Death)*
During the funeral, Raymond Diocrès sat up in his tomb. When questioned, he replied that he had been justly condemned by God.

4. **Saint Bruno en prière** *(Saint Bruno Praying)*
Bruno was marked by Raymond Diocrès' last words and, wishing to be saved, dedicated himself to prayer.

5. **Saint Bruno enseigne la théologie dans les écoles de Reims** *(Saint Bruno Teaching Theology in the Schools of Rheims)*
Saint Bruno was more of a preacher than a teacher and, above all, advocated penitence.

6. **Saint Bruno engage ses disciples et ses amis à quitter le monde** *(Saint Bruno Convincing His Disciples and His Friends to Leave the World)*
Saint Bruno announced that he intended to retreat and devote himself to prayer. Many of his friends decided to follow him. One of them is already bidding farewell to his father.

7. **Songe de Saint Bruno** *(Saint Bruno's Dream)*
In a dream, Bruno saw angels indicating the site of a future monastery, while the voice of the Lord called him to solitude.

Saint Bruno assiste au sermon de Raymond Diocrès, detail, Eustache Le Sueur.

8. **Saint Bruno et ses compagnons, avant de partir pour Grenoble, distribuent tous leurs biens aux pauvres** *(Saint Bruno and His Companions Distributing Their Possessions Among the Poor, Before Leaving for Grenoble)*

Saint Bruno wished to visit Bishop Hugh of Grenoble to obtain permission to build a monastery in his diocese. Bruno and his companions rid themselves of their possessions before leaving.

9. **Arrivée de saint Bruno à Grenoble chez saint Hugues** *(The Arrival of Saint Bruno in Grenoble)*

Arriving in Grenoble, Saint Bruno was received by Bishop Hugh.

10. **Voyage à la Chartreuse** *(Journey to the Grande Chartreuse)*

Saint Hugh was willing to grant permission for the monastery and took Saint Bruno to the Grande Chartreuse to see if the location was suitable.

11. Saint Bruno fait construire le monastère
(The Building of the Monastery)

The saint went to the arid desert to accelerate work and discuss the project with the architect.

12. Saint Bruno prend l'habit monastique
(Saint Bruno Receives the Habit)

After granting the land for the monastery, Saint Hugh also gave the monks the habit of their new order.

13. Le pape Victor III confirme l'institution des chartreux *(Pope Victor III Confirms the Institution of the Carthusians)*

The order, named after the site in the Grande Chartreuse, was dedicated to a combination of monastic life and the solitude of desert hermits. It was consecrated in 1084.

14. Saint Bruno donne l'habit à plusieurs personnes *(Several Monks Receiving the Habit from Saint Bruno)*

The reputation of the Grande Chartreuse spread rapidly and novices flocked there. There were also many pilgrims.

15. Saint Bruno reçoit un message du pape *(Saint Bruno Receives a Message From the Pope)*

Pope Urban II, who had been a pupil of Bruno's, called him to be his adviser. Bruno left reluctantly for Rome. Although he attempted to dissuade his brothers from following him, several accompanied him.

16. Arrivée de saint Bruno à Rome *(Saint Bruno Arriving in Rome)*

Saint Bruno was received with great demonstrations of esteem and affection. He and his companions were guests in the papal residence. Although they had total freedom, it was difficult for them to observe the rules of the monastery, particularly concerning silence. They asked to return to the Grande Chartreuse. Only Bruno remained behind in Rome.

17. Saint Bruno refuse l'archevêché de Reggio que lui offre Urbain II *(Saint Bruno Refuses the Archbishoric of Reggio)*

Saint Bruno's only desire was to return to solitude. In a letter he wrote, " Only those who have experienced it can know the benefit and delight

to be had from the quietness and solitude of a hermitage."

18. **Saint Bruno en prière dans son oratoire**
(Saint Bruno Praying in His Oratory)

Bruno obtained permission from the Pope to establish another charterhouse at La Torre in Calabria. The two men parted expressing their mutual esteem. Monks dig trenches around the praying Saint Bruno to cut their links with the world.

19. **Rencontre de saint Bruno et du comte Roger**
(The Meeting of Saint Bruno and Count Ruggiero)

Ruggiero was the count of Sicily in Calabria. He strayed from his companions and came on Saint Bruno meditating (lost painting).

20. **Apparition de saint Bruno au comte Roger** *(The Apparition of Saint Bruno to Count Ruggiero)*

During Count Ruggiero's siege of Capua, one of his officers, Sergius, was preparing to betray him. Saint Bruno appeared to Ruggiero in a dream and warned him of the plot.

21. **Mort de saint Bruno** *(The Death of Saint Bruno)*

At the end of September, 1101, eleven years after his arrival in the desert of Calabria, Bruno fell ill. He summoned his brethren, confessed publicly, proclaimed his faith and died peacefully on October 6.

22. **Saint Bruno est enlevé au ciel** *(Saint Bruno Carried to Heaven)*

Angels carry Saint Bruno up to Heaven.

Scènes de l'histoire de Virginie
(Scenes From the Story of Virginia)
See **Mort de Virginie**.

Filippino Lippi

Scènes des massacres de Scio (Les)
(Scenes of the Massacres of Scio), also known as **Massacres de Chio** *(The Massacre at Chios)*

Eugène Delacroix

(Hist.) This is an episode from the Greek uprising against the Turks. The island of Chios rebelled and was sacked, and its inhabitants were massacred by the Turks on April 11, 1822.

Séparation de saint Pierre et de saint Paul allant au martyre *(Saint Peter and Saint Paul Separated on Their Way to be Martyred)*

Michel Dumas

(Christ. Trad.) Emperor Nero persecuted Peter and Paul. He summoned them and, angered by their preaching, had them condemned. Peter was crucified like a slave, whereas Paul, a Roman citizen, was beheaded. For this reason, they were separated before their execution. Saint Denis, who witnessed their separation, recounts

Scènes des massacres de Scio, Eugène Delacroix.

that after their death they were seen entering the gates of the city, holding hands and dressed in brilliant garments, as if clothed in light and crowned with truth and splendor.

Sept Joies de Marie (Les) *(The Seven Joys of the Virgin Mary)*

Master of the Holy Kindred

For details on these paintings refer to the entry under the French title.

(Christ. Trad.) The Seven Joys of Mary include: the annunciation (**Annonciation**), the visitation (**Visitation**), the adoration of the Magi (**Adoration des mages**), the presentation in the temple (**Présentation au temple**), Jesus discussing with the doctors (**Jésus discutant avec les docteurs**), the assumption (**Assomption**) and the crowning (**Couronnement**).

(The Seven Sorrows include the prophesy of Simeon, the flight into Egypt (**Fuite en Égypte**), Jesus lost in Jerusalem, Judas' betrayal, the crucifixion (**Crucifixion**), the descent from the cross (**Déposition**) and the entombment (**Mise au tombeau**).

Sept œuvres de la Miséricorde *(The Seven Works of Mercy)*
See **Œuvres de la Miséricorde**.

David Teniers the Younger

Serment de Priam et d'Agamemnon (Le) *(The Oath of Priam and Agamemnon)*
See **Préparatifs du combat de Pâris et de Ménélas**.

Louis Lagrenée

Serment des Horaces (Le) *(The Oath of the Horatii)*
(Hist., Lit.) To avoid war between Rome and Alba (7th century B.C.), three champions were chosen from each side to battle in the name of their cities. The Horatii fought for Rome and the Curiatii for Alba. The father of the Horatii made his sons swear to conquer or die. Corneille's tragedy *Horace* emphasizes the suffering of the women, Sabina, sister of the Curiatii and wife of the eldest of the Horatii, and Camille, sister of the Horiatii and betrothed to one of the Curiatti, for whom victory also implied mourning.

Jacques-Louis David

Sibylle de Tibur (La) *(The Tiburtine Sibyl)*
(Myth., Christ. Trad.) The sibyls were priestesses of Apollo who foretold the future. The Tiburtine sibyl was famous for having shown Emperor Augustus a vision of the Virgin and Infant Jesus during a glorious victory.

Antoine Caron

Siège d'Audenarde *(The Siege of Audenarde)*
(Hist.) This siege took place in 1667, during the Dutch War led by Louis XIV against William of Orange. Louis XIV led the siege himself, accompanied by the Marshal of Turenne and several cavalrymen.

Adam Frans van der Meulen

Le Serment des Horaces, Jacques-Louis David.

Le Siège de La Rochelle par Louis XIII, Claude Gellée, called Claude Lorrain.

Siège d'Audenarde, 1745 *(The Siege of Audenarde, 1745)*

Attributed to Charles Parrocel

(Hist.) This is the same town as in the painting by van der Meulen, but not the same siege. In 1745, the town was captured and destroyed by the French.

Siège de La Rochelle par Louis XIII (Le) *(The Siege of La Rochelle by Louis XIII)*

Claude Gellée, called Claude Lorrain

(Hist.) During the Wars of Religion, La Rochelle, a fortified town, was granted to the Protestants by Henry IV. In 1627, Richelieu used the pretext of an agreement between the English and the inhabitants of La Rochelle to besiege the town. He built a dyke to prevent supplies arriving by sea. La Rochelle capitulated after fifteen months of resistance: the fortifications had been razed and the municipal franchise eliminated, leading to the city's decline.

Siège de la ville et du château de Dinant sur la Meuse *(Siege of the Town and Castle of Dinant on the Meuse)*

Adam Frans van der Meulen

(Hist.) Louis XIV laid siege and captured the town of Dinant, in Belgium, in May, 1675. The cavalryman in the foreground to the left may be the king himself.

Socrate arrachant Alcibiade au sein de la volupté *(Socrates Tearing Alcibiades Away From Carnal Pleasure)*

Jean-Baptiste Regnault

(Hist., Lit.) In his youth Alcibiades, an Athenian statesman and general, led a decadent life. Socrates became friends with him and had a strong influence on him. Alcibiades listened to him with great emotion and even shed tears, but Socrates did not manage to help him completely overcome his taste for luxury, the easy life and flattery.

Sodoma porté à l'hôpital *(Sodoma Carried to the Hospital)*

Marius Granet

See **Peintre Sodoma porté à l'hôpital**.

Solon soutenant la justice de ses lois contre les objections des Athéniens *(Solon Defending the Justice of His Laws)*

Noël Coypel

(Hist.) Solon (6th century B.C.) was an Athenian statesman, famous for having given Athens its laws and its first Constitution. It was on the basis of these laws and respect for democracy that Athens succeeded in defending itself against tyranny and remained a free people in the midst of a world governed by dictators. Solon was continually visited by citizens who presented their ideas and discussed alterations to the laws he had passed. He listened to them patiently.

Sommeil d'Antiope *(The Sleep of Antiope)*
Correggio

See **Vénus, Satyre et Cupidon**.

Sommeil de Diane (Le) *(The Sleep of Diana)*
Jan Thomas van Yperen

(Myth.) Diana, goddess of the hunt, could not tolerate being surprised while resting with her nymphs. Mortals who caught her in her intimacy were severely punished, but here she is surprised by a satyr whose curiosity she tolerates.

Sommeil d'Endymion. Effet de lune *(Endymion. Effect of the Moon),* also known as **Endymion**
Anne-Louis Girodet

(Myth.) Endymion was a beautiful young shepherd and the son or grandson of Jupiter. While sleeping he inspired Selene, the Moon, with a violent passion. She asked Jupiter to grant the young man's wish to remain eternally asleep and therefore eternally young.

Songe de Joseph (Le) *(Joseph's Dream)*
Pierre Subleyras

See **Songe de saint Joseph**.

Songe de saint Jérôme *(Saint Jerome's Dream)*
Sano di Pietro

(Christ. Trad.) Jerome was extremely involved in his studies of Latin, Greek and Hebrew. He also read Plato and Cicero and tended to neglect the Scriptures. Around the middle of Lent, he was weakened by a high fever that cooled so quickly that he was believed to be dead. While his brethren were preparing his funeral, he dreamed that he was before the tribunal of Christ. Christ reproached him for being more of a Ciceronian than a Christian and had him whipped by angels. Jerome cried out for mercy while the public at the tribunal interceded in his favor. He was pardoned, but promised not to read another secular book. He returned to earth and awoke healed of his fever, but with his cheeks covered in tears and his body still bearing the marks of the punishment he had received in his dream.

Same subject: **Songe de saint Jérôme**, Orazio Borgianni, also known as **Vision de saint Jérôme**.

Songe de saint Joseph (Le) *(Joseph's Dream)*

Philippe de Champaigne
Francesco Solimena

(N.T.) After the birth of Jesus, an angel warned Joseph in a dream that King Herod wished to kill the Child and told him to take Mary and the Child to Egypt.

Same subject: **Songe de Joseph**, Pierre Subleyras.

Souper à Emmaüs (Le) *(The Supper at Emmaus)*

Titian

See **Pèlerins d'Emmaüs**.

Suicide de Cléopâtre mordue par un aspic (Le) *(Cleopatra Bitten by an Asp)*

Giampietrino

See **Mort de Cléopâtre**.

Sujet grec moderne. Après le massacre de Samothrace *(Modern Greek Subject. After the Massacre of Samothrace)*

Auguste Vinchon

(Hist.) As with the massacre of Chio (see **Scènes des massacres de Scio**), this is an episode from the Greek uprising against the Turks in 1827.

Supplice de Marsyas (Le) *(The Punish-*
ment of Marsyas)
See **Apollon et Marsyas**.

Filippo Lauri

Suzanne au bain,
Tintoretto.

Suzanne au bain *(Susanna at Her Bath)*
(O.T.) Susanna was the beautiful, virtuous wife
of a wealthy man named Joakim. She was
secretly desired by two elders. They hid in her
garden to watch her bathe. As soon as her maids
left her alone, they revealed themselves and
threatened to accuse her of having been in the
company of a young man if she did not submit to
them. Susanna knew that adultery was pun-
ishable by death, but did not give in. She was
condemned, but the young judge Daniel, inspired by God, suggested that the two men be
separated for questioning. The elders told conflicting stories, thus proving Susanna's innocence, and were condemned to death.
Same subject: **Chaste Suzanne**, Théodore Chassériau. **Suzanne et les vieillards**, Bartolomeo
Guidobono, Giambattista Pittoni, Jean-Baptiste
Santerre, follower of Sellaer, Veronese.

Follower of Jacopo
Palma the Younger
Tintoretto

Suzanne et les vieillards *(Susanna and*
the Elders)
See **Suzanne au bain**.

Veronese

Télémaque raconte ses aventures à Calypso *(Telemachus Recounting His Adventures to Calypso)*

Jean Raoux

(Myth., Lit.) In the *Adventures of Telemachus* by the French writer Fénelon, Telemachus, the son of Ulysses and Penelope, sets out to find his father who has not yet returned from the Trojan War. Like Ulysses, he is guided and protected by Minerva, who assumes the guise of an old man, Mentor. Following his father's trail, Telemachus encounters the same dangers and the same figures — evil or kind — such as the nymph Calypso.

Tentation de saint Antoine *(The Temptation of Saint Antony)*

Pieter Huys
Alessandro Magnasco
Sebastiano Ricci
David Teniers the Younger
Frederick Valckenborgh

(Christ. Trad.) At the age of twenty, Antony sold all his possessions, distributed the proceeds to the poor and founded several monasteries. The

Tentation de saint Antoine, David Teniers the Younger.

devil was displeased and tempted him, unsuccessfully, several times. Antony's style of life had a strong influence on his contemporaries and on the development of monastic life.

Jacques-Antoine Vallin
Louis-Joseph Watteau de Lille

Tentation de saint Hilarion *(The Temptation of Saint Hilarion)*
(Christ. Trad.) Hilarion, a desert hermit, (4th century) suffered from terrible temptations, as did Saints Antony and Jerome. In this painting the devils bring him a naked woman. He is depicted on his knees, leaning toward the cross to find the strength to resist the temptation. Saint Hilarion had great power over the devil; simply by making the sign of the cross, he forced a dragon to sacrifice himself on a pyre.

Octave Tassaert

Tentation du Christ (La) *(The Temptation of Christ)*
(N.T.) After his baptism (see **Baptême du Christ**), Christ went to the desert where was tempted three times by the devil. The temptations are described in detail in the Gospels. Here the devil tells him to throw himself from the temple and be borne by angels to prove his supernatural powers. Jesus refused saying, " It is said, 'You shall not tempt the Lord your God.' "

Ary Scheffer
François Verdier

Tentation du Christ au désert *(Christ Tempted in the Wilderness)*
(O.T.) See **Tentation du Christ**. This is the first temptation: the devil challenged Jesus to prove that he was the Son of God by turning stone into bread. Jesus replied " It is written, 'Man shall not live by bread alone.' "

Martin Freminet

Tête de saint Jean-Baptiste *(Head of Saint John the Baptist)*
See **Banquet d'Hérode**.

Andrea Solario

Thésée poursuivant les Centaures *(Theseus Pursuing the Centaurs)* also known as **Paysage. Thésée poursuivant les Centaures**

See **Combat des Lapithes et des Centaures**.

Achille-Etna Michallon

Thomyris faisant plonger la tête de Cyrus dans un vase de sang *(Tomyris Dipping Cyrus'Head in an Urn of Blood)* (Hist.) Tomyris was queen of the Scythians in the 6th century B.C. After Cyrus the Great, king of Persia, caused her son's death, she waged war on the Persians and captured Cyrus and part of his army. Brought before her, Cyrus spoke with pride and she ordered him to be beheaded. She then took his head and dipped it in an urn filled with blood.

Same subject: **Thomyris, reine des Sythes, fait plonger la tête de Cyrus dans un vase de sang,** Mattia Preti.

Pierre-Paul Rubens

th

318

Tobie et l'Ange, Salvator Rosa.

Timoclée captive amenée devant Alexandre *(Timoclea Brought Before Alexander)*, also known as **Alexandre et Timoclée** *(Alexander and Timoclea)*
See **Alexandre et Timoclée**.

Domenichino

Titus faisant distribuer des secours au peuple *(Titus Ordering Aid for the People)*
(Hist.) The reign of Emperor Titus in the 1st century A.D.(see **Titus pardonnant à des conjurés**) was a glorious era, despite the fact that Italy was subjected to a series of catastrophes: the great fire of Rome, epidemics and the eruption of Vesuvius. Titus was famous for his generosity and clemency.

François-Joseph Heim

Titus pardonnant à des conjurés *(Titus Pardoning Conspirators)*
(Hist.) Emperor Titus (1st century A.D.) was a benevolent ruler. He began his life in debauchery and violence, but after he became emperor thought only of the welfare of the Empire. There was not a single death sentence passed during his rule.

François-Joseph Heim

Tobie et l'Ange *(Tobias and the Angel)*
(O.T.) During his travels with his dog and the angel (see **L'Archange Raphaël quittant la famille de Tobie**), young Tobias, advised by the angel, caught a large fish. They ate the fish but set aside the heart, the liver and the gall. When Tobias arrived at Sara's home he burned the heart and the liver to exorcise the demon who possessed her and had made her strangle seven husbands. On his return, Tobias placed the fish gall on his father's eyes and cured his blindness. Same subject: **Ange et Tobie**, Alfred Moullion.

Salvator Rosa

Tobie et l'Archange Raphaël *(Tobias and the Archangel Raphael)*, also known

Eustache Le Sueur

as **Retour de Tobie (Le)** *(The Return of Tobias)*
See **Archange Raphaël quittant la famille de Tobie** and **Tobie et l'Ange**.

Tobit enterre les morts *(Tobit Burying the Dead)*

Giovanni Castiglione

(O.T.) Tobit is the father of Tobias. According to the book of Tobit, the Jews were exiled to Assyria (8th century B.C.) and persecuted by King Sennacherib of Nineveh. The king had the bodies of those he had executed thrown over the ramparts of the town and forbade their burial. Tobit, a pious Jew, ignored the decree and went out at night to provide his compatriots with a proper burial.

Toilette d'Esther (La) *(The Toilet of Esther)*, also known as **Esther se parant pour être présentée à Assuérus** *(Esther Preparing To be Presented to Ahasuerus)*

Théodore Chassériau
Jean-François de Troy

(O.T.) After dismissing his wife, Vashiti, the Persian king Ahasuerus (5th century B.C.) ordered all the provinces of his kingdom to send their most beautiful virgins to him so that he could chose a new wife. The young women arrived and were placed in the charge of the king's eunuch. They were given ointments to prepare themselves for their appearance before the king. Esther was one of the nine young women chosen to be presented to Ahasuerus. He was immediately seduced by her beauty and intelligence and chose her as his queen (also see **Évanouissement d'Esther**).

Tombeau de Maître André (Le) *(The Tomb of Master André)*

Claude Gillot

(Lit.) This painting is based on an Italian farce: Mazzetin and Scaramouche were fighting over a jar of wine and asked Harlequin to arbitrate the dispute. To help him decide, he ate a loaf of bread and a saveloy which he washed down with the wine from the jar.

La Tour de Babel, Lucas van Valckenborgh.

Tour de Babel (La) *(The Tower of Babel)*

Lucas van Valckenborgh

(O.T.) This episode takes place after Noah's death. His three sons gave birth to several generations all of which spoke the same language. The men decided to build a tower that would reach heaven and remain united, forming a single people. God, angered by their pride, decided to foil their plans. He confused their language so that they could no longer understand one another and they were scattered over the face of the earth. The Tower of Babel remained unfinished.

Trahison de Judas (La) *(Judas' Betrayal)*

Dirck Barendsz

(N.T.) Judas Iscariot, one of the twelve apostles, was destined to betray Jesus. Here he is seen on his first visit to the Jewish leaders who wished to see Jesus dead. He received thirty pieces of silver to deliver Jesus to them (this was the price for a foreign slave). The scene in the background was taken from the Gospels. In preparation for Passover, Jesus commanded two of his disciples to follow a man carrying a jar, saying that they would have supper in a room in the house he entered. During the Last Supper, Jesus alluded to the man who would betray him (see **Cène**). Judas kissed Jesus to identify him to the soldiers who had come to arrest him in the Garden of Olives (hence the expression "kiss of Judas"). After Jesus' arrest, Judas was stricken with remorse and hanged himself.

Trajan donnant des audiences publiques *(Trajan Granting Public Audience)*
Noël Coypel

(Hist.) Emperor Trajan of Rome (98-117) was a great administrator who respected popular institutions. He organized an emergency fund for the poor and a service of loans for farmers. He was obsessed with justice. It is said that on his way to an emergency military expedition, he descended from his horse to listen to the complaints of a poor woman and grant her justice. Here, like Solomon, he gives an audience to litigants, but without ceremony.

Translation des corps de saint Gervais et de saint Protais *(The Transfer of the Bodies of Saint Gervase and Saint Protase)*
Philippe de Champaigne

tr

322

(Christ. Trad.) Saint Ambrose discovered the bodies of these two saints three hundred years after their death; the bodies were perfectly preserved and gave off a delicate perfume. The saints lay beside one another on the same bed. As the procession passed, a blind man recovered

Le Triomphe de Flore,
Nicolas Poussin.

his sight and several sick people were cured. A possessed man, who was pushed back, is held by two men, one of whom is pointing to the martyrs' bodies. (See **Saint Gervais et saint Protais, amenés devant Astasius, refusent de sacrifier à Jupiter** and **Apparition de saint Gervais et de saint Protais à saint Ambroise**.)

Triomphe d'Alexandre (Le) *(The Triumph of Alexander)*
See **Entrée d'Alexandre dans Babylone**.

Charles Le Brun

Triomphe de Bacchus (Le) *(The Triumph of Bacchus)*
(Myth.) Bacchus is on his chariot drawn by panthers. The bacchantes, his priestesses, satyrs and putti honor him with bunches of grapes and gold and silver ewers filled with wine. The goat is a reminder that Bacchus was turned into a kid-goat after his birth (see **Enfance de Bacchus**).

Charles de La Fosse
Charles-Joseph Natoire

Triomphe de David (Le) *(The Triumph of David)*
See **David tenant la tête de Goliath**.

Matteo Rosselli
Giovanni Battista Tiepolo

Triomphe de Flore (Le) *(The Triumph of Flora)*
(Myth.) Flora is the goddess of vegetation, trees, flowers and spring. Here she is seated on a golden chariot with the permission of Venus who, crowned with roses and dancing with the putti, is leading the triumph herself.

Nicolas Poussin

Triomphe de Mardochée *(The Triumph of Mordecai)*
(O.T.) Haman, the minister of the Persian king Ahasuerus, was an enemy of the Jews and he convinced the king to pass a decree calling for their massacre. They were saved through the

Jean-François de Troy

intervention of Queen Esther (see **Évanouisse-ment d'Esther** and **Repas d'Esther et d'As-suérus**). Haman was a personal enemy of Mordecai, Esther's cousin, who held an important position in the court. Ahasuerus' began to suspect Haman of treachery and prepared a trap for him by asking how the most loyal subject in the kingdom should be rewarded. Convinced that he himself was this subject, Haman said that he should be given princely garments and led around the city on the king's horse. To his frustration, these honors were bestowed on Mordecai and Haman was hanged on the gallows he had prepared for his rival.

Triomphe de saint Thomas d'Aquin
(The Triumph of Saint Thomas Aquinas)

Benozzo Gozzoli

(Christ. Trad.) Saint Thomas Aquinas was a Dominican who taught at the Sorbonne in Paris in the 13th century. His main work *Summa theologica* earned him the title of *Doctor communis* (universal teacher). Here he is surrounded by Plato on his right and Aristotle on his left. Above them is Christ granting his blessing. Below them are the four Evangelists, Moses and Saint Paul. At Saint Thomas'feet is his Arab adversary, the philosopher Averroës, struck by the eloquence of the Christian theologian. A council is depicted in the background.

Triomphe de Titus et de Vespasien
(The Triumph of Titus and Vespasian)

Giulio Romano

(Hist.) The triumph was a grand procession in honor of a victorious general on his return to Rome. After Augustus, who ruled from 27 B.C. to 14 A.D., the ceremony was reserved exclusively for emperors. Vespasian (69-79) had won several victories in Africa and was besieging Jerusalem when he was chosen emperor. He entrusted the command to his son Titus, who completed the destruction of Jerusalem before himself becoming emperor in 79 A.D. after his father's death. Titus was known as a benevolent ruler.

Triomphe de Vénus vénérée par six amoureux légendaires *(The Triumph of Venus, Venerated by Six Legendary Lovers)*   Master of the Taking of Tarento

(Imag.) The six legendary lovers are Achilles, Tristan and Lancelot, knights of the Round Table, Samson, a biblical hero, Paris and his brother Troilus.

Triomphe du tsar Alexandre Ier (Le) *(The Triumph of Czar Alexander I)*, also known as **Paix (La)** *(Peace)*   Louis-Léopold Boilly

(Hist.) Alexander I ascended to the Russian throne in 1801. He immediately introduced liberal reforms and concluded peace treaties with England and Napoleonic France. (He later became a bitter enemy of Napoleon.)

Trois Grâces (Les) *(The Three Graces)*   Jean-Baptiste Regnault
See **Trois Grâces supportant l'Amour**.

Trois Grâces supportant l'Amour *(The Three Graces Carrying Cupid)*   François Boucher

(Myth.) The Graces were the goddesses of Beauty and perhaps originally of vegetation. They spread joy in the hearts of men and gods. On Olympus they danced to the sound of Apollo's lyre. Together with the Muses, they were the gods' attendants. Hesiod named them Aglaia, Thalia and Euphrosyne. At various times they have been associated with chastity, beauty and love, or generosity.

Same subject: **Trois Grâces**, Jean-Baptiste Regnault.

Trois Parques filent la destinée de la reine Marie de Médicis *(The Destiny of Marie de Médicis)*   Peter Paul Rubens
See **Marie de Médicis**, first painting.

Trois Scènes de la Passion *(Three Scenes From the Passion)*
See **Portement de croix**, **Crucifixion** and **Mise au tombeau**.

Cologne, 16th century

Trois Scènes de l'histoire d'Esther *(Three Scenes From the Story of Esther)*
See **Évanouissement d'Esther**, **Aman irrité de ce que Mardochée ne se lève pas pour l'adorer** and **Triomphe de Mardochée**.

Filippino Lippi

Trois Scènes de l'histoire de Virginie *(Three Scenes From the Story of Virginia)*
See **Mort de Virginie**.

Filippino Lippi

Turnus tué par Énée *(Turnus Killed by Aeneas)*
(Myth., Lit.) Turnus, king of the Rutulians, was a bitter enemy of the Trojans. He fought several times against Aeneas who finally killed him in single-handed combat. This is the final episode of the *Aeneid*.

Antoine Coypel

Ulysse remettant Chryséis à son père, Claude Gellée, called Claude Lorrain.

Ulysse reconnaissant Achille parmi les filles de Lycomède *(Ulysses Recognizes Achilles Among the Daughters of Lycomedes)*

Studio of Frans Francken the Younger

(Myth., Lit.) In Homer's *Iliad*, a prediction was made to Achilles that he would either go to the siege Troy, be victorious and die young; or not go and live for a long time. Achilles did not hesitate to join in the battle. Post-Homeric poets, however, say that Achilles allowed his mother Thetis to hide him with the daughters of King Lycomedes on the island of Scyros. He was dressed as a woman, called Pyrrha (Redhead) and remained there for nine years. When Ulysses was told by an oracle that Troy could only be captured with Achilles' help, he set out for Scyros. He took with him jewels and trinkets, which he offered to the daughters, but he had taken care to hide precious arms in the jewels. Achilles seized a sword thus revealing his true sex.

Ulysse remettant Chryséis à son père *(Ulysses Returns Chryseis to Her Father)*, also known as **Chryséis rendue à son père par Ulysse**

Claude Gellée, called Claude Lorrain

(Myth., Lit.) Abducted by Achilles during the Trojan War, Chryseis was later claimed by Agamemnon. Her father, Chryses, one of Apollo's priests, arrived with gifts in an attempt to buy her back. He was rudely dismissed. Apollo intervened and afflicted the Greek army with the plague. Following heated discussions, Agamemnon finally agreed to return Chryseis to her father, but demanded a prisoner who belonged to Achilles, Briseis, in exchange. This demand was the cause of Achilles'anger and his refusal to fight as described in the *Iliad*. Chryseis was eventually returned to her father on a ship commanded by wise Ulysses.

Vénus à sa toilette *(The Toilet of Venus)*

School of Fontainebleau
Vincent Sellaer

(Myth.) Venus, the goddess of love, was extremely beautiful. She is usually depicted during her amorous adventures or caring for her beauty. There is, however, another aspect to her personality: the violence with which she punishes those who lack respect or mortals of whose beauty she is envious, such as Psyche.

Same subject: **Toilette de Vénus**, François Boucher.

Vénus, Adonis et l'Amour *(Venus, Adonis and Cupid)*

Attributed to Dirck
de Quade van Ravesteyn

See **Mort d'Adonis**.

Vénus anadyomène *(Venus Anadyomene)*

Jean Auguste Ingres

(Myth.) *Venus Anadyomene* (from the Greek meaning " rising from the sea ") is the term used to describe paintings of the birth of Venus. The goddess of beauty was born of the foam of the sea produced by the genitals of Uranus (see **Jupiter foudroyant les Titans**). Venus appears on a scallop shell pushed by Zephyrus to Cyprus where she was received by the other gods.

Same subject: **Vénus marine**, Théodore Chassériau.

Vénus chasseresse apparaissant à Énée, Pietro da Cortona.

Vénus armant Énée *(Venus Arming Aeneas)*

Attributed to Juste d'Egmont

(Myth., Lit.) After many adventures, Aeneas, hero of the *Aeneid*, arrived in Latium where he was to fight King Turnus. His mother, Venus, asked her husband, Vulcan, for arms for him. The magnificent arms she gave to her son are said to be like those — also forged by Vulcan — that were given to Achilles in the *Iliad*.

Vénus avec Adonis partant à la chasse *(Venus and Adonis Departing For the Hunt)*
See **Mort d'Adonis**.

Giovanni Francesco Romanelli

Vénus blessée par Diomède *(Venus Injured by Diomedes)*

Antoine-François Callet

(Myth., Lit.) This is an episode from Homer's *Iliad*. Venus ventured into the midst of the fighting to protect her son Aeneas who was defending Troy against the Greek Diomedes. Diomedes injured her hand and she returned, crying, to Olympus. Minerva, the goddess of war, mocked her.

Vénus chasseresse apparaissant à Énée *(Venus as a Huntress Appears to Aeneas)*

Pietro da Cortona

(Myth.) Aeneas, hero of the *Aeneid*, fled the burning city of Troy and was shipwrecked on the coast of Africa. Tired, he stretched out on the beach with his companions, but could not fall asleep. At dawn he set off with only his faithful friend, Achates, armed with two javelins. In the forest, they met a virgin huntress who claimed to be looking for her sister. Aeneas did not recognize his mother, Venus, in this disguise but, suspecting that the huntress was in fact a goddess, complained to her of his ordeals. She gave him council, " and as she turned away her loveliness shone, a tint of rose glowed on her neck and a scent of Heaven breathed from the divine hair of her head. Her gown trailed down to her feet; her gait alone proved her a goddess." Too late, he recognized his mother.

Vénus chez Vulcain *(Venus and Vulcan)*   François Boucher

Vénus demandant à Vulcain des armes pour Énée *(Venus Requesting Arms for Aeneas from Vulcan)*   François Boucher

Vénus demande à Vulcain des armes pour Énée *(Venus Requesting Arms for Aeneas from Vulcan)*   Anthony van Dyck

See **Forges de Vulcain**.

Vénus désarmant l'Amour *(Venus Disarming Cupid)*   François Boucher

(Myth.) This subject depicts Venus and her son Cupid, but it is imaginary and does not correspond to a specific legend.

Vénus du Pardo *(The Pardo Venus)*, previously known as **Jupiter et Antiope** *(Jupiter and Antiope)*   Titian

(Myth.) Venus is lying on a tiger's skin while a satyr observes her and raises her veil. Titian described the painting, commissioned by the Spanish king, Philip II, for his Pardo palace, as "The naked woman, the landscape and the satyr." There is no legend that includes a naked woman, a satyr and a hunting scene. It was initially thought that the figures were Jupiter and Antiope, but the story concerning them took place indoors. It was also thought that the woman could be Diana because of the hunting scene, but the main figure appears almost certainly to be Venus and the erotic symbols associated with her (the satyr, the couple and the stag killed by the dogs) confirm this interpretation.

Vénus et Adonis *(Venus and Adonis)*   Francesco Albani
See **Mort d'Adonis**.

Vénus et les Grâces
surprises par un mortel,
Jacques Blanchard.

Vénus et les Grâces surprises par un mortel *(Venus and the Graces Surprised by a Mortal)*, previously known as **Cimon et Éphigène** *(Cimon and Iphigenia)*

Jacques Blanchard

(Myth.) This painting was renamed, as the story of Iphigenia describes her with a veil, sleeping in a clearing near a fountain, accompanied by two other women and a man. The man who surprises them is a stooped peasant with a stick. In this painting there is no stick and no male companion, but there is a cherub curled up against the breast of the main figure. It would appear to be a painting of Venus and the Three Graces, although this subject does not correspond to a particular myth.

Vénus et Vulcain *(Venus and Vulcan)*

François Boucher
Studio of Giulio Romano

(Myth.) Venus, goddess of beauty, was married to the divine blacksmith, Vulcan, who was deformed and lame. The *putti* playing around her are her constant companions.
Same subject: **Repos de Vénus et Vulcain**, Francesco Albani.

Vénus marine *(Venus Anadyomene)*
See **Vénus anadyomène**.

Théodore Chassériau

Vénus pleurant Adonis transformé en anémone *(Venus Weeping Over Adonis)*
See **Mort d'Adonis.**

Constantin Netscher

Vénus présente l'Amour à Jupiter *(Venus Presenting Cupid to Jupiter)*
See **Naissance de l'Amour.**

Eustache Le Sueur

Vénus, Satyre et Cupidon *(Venus, a Satyr and Cupid)*, previously called **Sommeil d'Antiope** *(The Sleep of Antiope)* or **Jupiter et Antiope** *(Jupiter and Antiope)*

Correggio

(Myth.) This painting was renamed. Representations of a naked woman are generally of Venus. Her son Cupid is lying on a lion's skin, a garment abandoned by Hercules when he was overcome by Omphale's charms (see **Hercule et Omphale**). The bow, quiver and torch also confirm that it is Venus and her son. The satyr is charged with watching over the sleeping Venus.

Vénus terrestre avec Éros et Vénus céleste avec Antéros et deux autres cupidons *(Earthly Venus with Eros and Heavenly Venus with Anteros and Two Other Putti)*, previously called **Allégorie de l'Amour** *(Allegory of Love)*

Sodoma

(Myth.) Anteros was the companion Venus found for her son Eros. She had noticed that when he was alone he reverted to childhood, but matured in the presence of a companion. This allegory emphasizes the importance of reciprocity in love.

Vénus versant le dictame sur la blessure d'Énée *(Venus Pouring Dictamus on Aeneas' Wound)*

Giovanni Romanelli

(Myth., Lit.) This is Aeneas' final combat before his victory and the end of the *Aeneid*. It is decided that he will meet the enemy leader, Turnus, in single-handed combat, but Aeneas'

Vertumne et Pomone,
François Boucher.

companions want to join him. As Aeneas attempts to restrain them, "bare-headed and
stretching out an unarmed hand," he is injured
by an arrow. Two of his companions carry him
back to the camp. Venus immediately picks dictamus, "whose stalk is tressed with luxuriant
leaves and whose flower is bright red" on
Mount Ida. She mixes it with ambrosia and a
doctor applies the mixture to Aeneas' wound
which is immediately healed. The doctor shouts,
"Quick! Bring our hero his arms!"

Vertumne et Pomone *(Vertumnus and
Pomona)*

(Myth., Lit.) Pomona was the goddess of gardens
and orchards. She was worshiped in a sacred
forest between Rome and Ostia. Chaste, she
spent her time tending gardens and rejected the
numerous tributes paid to her. Vertumnus fell
in love with her and assumed various disguises
in an attempt to approach her: harvester, fisher-
man, and finally an old woman with white hair.

François Boucher
Frans Francken the Younger
Attributed to Jan
van den Hoecke

The woman showed Pomona a vine wrapped around a tree and asked her how the vine could possibly survive if it were not supported by the tree. A long discussion on love followed. The god finally revealed himself in all his glory and Pomona was "smitten with a passion equal to his own."

Vestale Émilie rallumant le feu sacré (La) *(The Vestal Virgin Emily Relighting the Sacred Fire)*

Joseph Benoît Suvée

(Lit.) The vestal virgins were priestesses of Vesta, the Roman goddess of the Hearth. They were vowed to chastity and tended the sacred fire. The eldest of the vestal virgins entrusted the fire to a younger virgin who let the fire go out. This evil omen caused concern throughout the city. It was suspected that an impure virgin had approached the hearth. Suspicion fell on Emily. She ran to the altar in the presence of the other virgins, the high priest and the people, and invoked heaven and the gods to bear witness to her innocence. She threw her veil on to the cold ashes and flames immediately leapt up, proving her innocence.

Vie de saint Jérôme *(The Life of Saint Jerome)*

Sano di Pietro

See **Apparition à saint Jérôme**, **Pénitence de saint Jérôme**, **Saint Jérôme et le lion**, **Mort et apparition de saint Jérôme** and **Songe de saint Jérôme**.

Vierge apparaît à saint Luc et à saint Yves (La) *(The Virgin Appearing to Saint Luke and Saint Yves)*

Jacopo Chimenti

(Christ. Trad.) Saint Luke was the patron saint of physicians and painters who wrote about the Virgin and also painted her portrait. Saint Yves was the patron saint of lawyers. Here, through the intermediary of a young orphan, Saint Yves presents Jesus, sitting on Mary's lap, with the act for the founding of a school. Saint Yves (14th century) studied law in Paris and was shocked by those who took advantage of orphans by stealing their possessions.

Vierge de douleur au pied de la croix (La) *(The Virgin at the Foot of the Cross)*

Philippe de Champaigne

(N.T.) The Virgin Mary is represented mourning at the foot of the cross after the Crucifixion (*Mater Dolorosa*) or with the body of her son across her knees (see **Pietà**).

Vierge du Carmel apparaissant à saint Simon Stock *(The Virgin of Saint Simon Stock)*

Giovanni Battista Tiepolo

(Christ. Trad.) Simon Stock, born in England, was the sixth General of the Carmelite Order, founded in 1210. He prayed to the Virgin, the patron of the order. One day she appeared to him with a multitude of angels and held out the Carmelite scapular which she promised would save all who wore it. (The scapular is a double piece of material which falls from the shoulders and covers the chest and the back).

Vierge montant les degrés du Temple (La) *(The Virgin Climbing the Steps of the Temple)*

Master of the Life of the Virgin

See **Présentation de la Vierge au Temple**.

Vierge pleurant le Christ mort (La) *(Mater Dolorosa)*

Bernardino Gatti

See **Pietà**.

Virgile lisant l'Énéide devant Auguste *(Virgil Reading the Aeneid Before Augustus)*

Pieter Verhagen

(Hist.) In 42 B.C., after the battle of Philippi, the estate of the poet Virgil was confiscated by soldiers. Octavian — the future emperor Augustus — had it returned to him and was rewarded with Virgil's gratitude and lasting devotion. While writing the *Aeneid*, Virgil surpassed Augustus' desire to exalt the heroic virtues of their ancestors and revive the national religion. Augustus asked to read some of the passages before they were made public. Virgil read Cantos II, IV and VI to him. Octavia, Augustus' sister, fainted at the mention of the ghost of her son, Marcellus.

La Vision de Saint Bruno, Pier Francesco Mola.

Vision de Constantin (La) *(The Vision of Constantine)*

(Christ. Trad.) At the beginning of the 4th century A.D. the extensive Roman Empire was governed by four rulers, two entitled "Augustus" and two "Caesar." This was the first tetrarchy, or joint government by four rulers. In the next generation, the Caesars took the place of the two named "Augustus" and chose two other Caesars. Maxentius, son of an Augustus and Constantine, son of a Caesar, did not agree in this matter: each of them wished to be the sole ruler. Constantine attacked Rome, which was

Copy by Louis-Gabriel Blanchet of a painting by Giulio Romano occupied by his adversary, on October 27, 312. The armies met at the Milvian bridge. Constantine was victorious. The following day, he declared that he was a Christian and that he had won the battle through the intervention of Christ. Two historians of the period recounted this miracle differently. According to one, shortly before the battle, Constantine had a dream in which Christ ordered him to place on the shield of his men a heavenly sign formed by two Greek letters. This sign is found on coins from the period of Constantine's rule. According to the other historian, Constantine invoked the Christian God as he was about to enter battle. He saw a luminous cross in the sky with the inscription *"In hoc signo vinces"* ("by this sign shalt thou conquer"). Christ appeared to him the day after his victory and told him to create a new insignia in the form of the cross.

Same subject: **Bataille de Constantin contre Maxence**, Studio of Charles Le Brun.

Vision de saint Bruno (La) *(The Vision of Saint Bruno)*

Pier Francesco Mola

(Christ. Trad.) Saint Bruno retreated to the desert in Sèche-Fontaine, near Troyes, in Champagne. God appeared to him, and bid him to build a house to his glory, and seven stars showed him the route. It was on the basis of this vision that Saint Bruno built a monastery in the Grande Chartreuse, near Grenoble. The Carthusian Order combined the brotherhood of monastic life and the solitude of the hermetics (also see **Scènes de la vie de saint Bruno**).

Vision de saint François d'Assise (La) *(The Vision of Saint Francis of Assisi)*

Luis Tristan

See **Saint François d'Assise recevant les stigmates.**

Vision de saint Hubert (La) *(The Vision of Saint Hubert)*

Félix Cottrau

(Christ. Trad.) Hubert was a nobleman who lived

in the 7th century (he later became bishop of Liège). He loved hunting so much that he even went hunting on holy days. One Good Friday, in the forest of Ardenne, he saw a magnificent stag with a luminous crucifix between its antlers. This vision inspired his conversion.

Vision de saint Jérôme (La) *(The Vision of Saint Jerome)*

Guercino

(Christ. Trad.) While he was living in the desert (see **Saint Jérôme dans le désert**), Saint Jerome imagined that he was awakened by the trumpets of the Last Judgment.

Visitation (La) *(The Visitation)*

Orazio di Domenico Alfani
Rhine, 15th century
Domenico Ghirlandaio
Master of the Life
of the Virgin
Alessandro Moretto
Sebastiano del Piombo

(N.T.) After the annunciation, Mary, pregnant with Jesus, went to visit her much-older cousin Elizabeth, who was also expecting a child through the intervention of the Holy Ghost (see **Annonciation** and **Naissance de saint Jean-Baptiste**). When Mary entered and greeted her cousin, Elizabeth was filled with the Holy Spirit and felt her child kick in her womb. She greeted Mary, saying "Blessed are you among women, and blessed is the fruit of your womb."

Vivant Denon mettant dans leur tombeau les restes du Cid et de Chimène *(Vivant Denon Placing The Remains of El Cid and Jimena in Their Tomb)*

Adolphe Roehm

(Hist.) Vivant Denon, general director of French museums, was in charge of classifying works of art captured during the Napoleonic conquests. He was sent to Spain in 1808-1809 during the French occupation. The tomb of El Cid and Jimena in the monastery of San Pedro de Cardena was pillaged by the French. To remedy this profanation and gain public approval, General Thiébault, the governor of Castile, built a monument in El Cid's native town of Burgos to house the remains of the two heroes. El Cid's and Jimena's remains were transferred to Burgos where Denon placed them in the tomb.

La Visitation, Domenico Ghirlandaio.

Vocation de saint Matthieu (La) *(The Calling of Saint Matthew)*

Dirck Barendsz

(N.T.) Saint Matthew was a tax-collector in Galilee. When Jesus called him, he immediately followed and became one of the twelve disciples.

Voltaire composant "La Pucelle" *(Voltaire Writing "La Pucelle")*

Gabriel de Saint-Aubin

See **Rêve**.

Volumnie et Véturie devant Coriolan *(Volumnia and Veturia Before Coriolan)*

Eustache Le Sueur

(Hist.) After he was exiled from Rome (see **Adieux de Coriolan à sa femme**), Roman general Coriolan joined his enemies, the Voluscians, and led their siege against Rome. His mother, Volumnia, and his wife, Veturia, crossed the enemy lines to plead with him and convinced him to call off the attack.

Vulcain présentant à Vénus des armes pour Énée *(Vulcan Presenting Venus with Arms for Aeneas)*

François Boucher

See **Forges de Vulcain**.

**Zeuxis choisissant pour modèles les
plus belles filles de Crotone** *(Zeuxis
Chosing the Most Beautiful Young Women of Croton)*

François-André Vincent

(Hist.) Zeuxis was a famous Greek painter in the
5th century B.C. He was chosen to decorate the
Temple of Juno and proposed to paint a picture
of Helen. The Crotonians were eager for him to
use one of their most beautiful young women as
a model. However, after scrutinizing them he decided that no single individual had all the qualities he desired and so he combined the features
of five women in his portrait of Helen.

INDEX and GLOSSARY

This index contains the names of persons (in capital letters) and places (in lowercase) mentioned in the titles of the paintings. The numbers refer to the corresponding pages.

A short explanation is given for figures that recur in several paintings or for the writers who inspired the painters (with the corresponding page numbers if their names are included in painting titles). The main sources, if applicable, are cited at the end of each explanation.

AARON, 201, 202.

ABEL, 265.

ABRAHAM. The first patriarch in the Bible, progenitor of the Hebrews and founder of monotheism. His name means "of a great multitude" (Genesis), 11, 18, 274.

ABSALOM, 12.

Abydos, 119.

ACHELOUS, 133.

ACHILLES. Son of Thetis and Peleus, he was a demigod and king of the Myrmidons, people of Thessaly. Achilles was the greatest warrior of the Trojan War (Iliad), 12, 14, 102, 243, 327.

ACIS, 14.

ACRON, 272.

ACTAEON, 93.

ADAM. The first man, formed from clay, and given the breath of life by God. His name means "man," from the Hebrew word Adham (Genesis), 14, 15.

ADONIS, 204.

AEGISTHUS, 71.

AENEAS. Son of Venus and a Trojan prince. He fled Troy as it was burning and went to Latium where he founded the Roman dynasty (Aeneid), 90, 95, 104, 105, 122, 326, 329, 332.

AESCULAPIUS. Son of Apollo and god of medicine (Greek equivalent: Asclepius).

AGAMEMNON. Legendary king of Argos or Mycenae, brother of Menelaus and leader of the Greek forces against the Trojans (Iliad, Greek tragedies), 71, 247, 248.

AGLAUROS, 193.

AGNES (Saint), 35.

AGRICOL (Saint), 62.

AHASUERUS. (ruled 486-465 B.C.) King of Persia, he married Esther after repudiating his wife, Vashti. His name means "king" (Book of Esther), 262, 300, 320.

ALCESTIS, 21.

ALCIBIADES, 312.

ALEXANDER I (czar). (1777-1825), 323.

ALEXANDER SEVERUS, 24.

ALEXANDER, known as ALEXANDER THE GREAT (356-323 B.C.) king of Macedonia. He conquered Greece, Egypt and Persia and advanced his empire to Northern India, (Plutarch, The Parallel Lives), 22, 23, 110, 117.

ALEXANDER. See Paris.

AMALEKITES, 160.

AMBROSE (Saint), 36, 104, 210.

AMOR. See Cupid.

AMYMONE, 220.

ANANIAS, 26.

ANAXAGORAS, 27.

ANCHISES, 105.

ANDRÉ (Master), 320.

ANDREA (Cardinal), 288.

ANDREW (Saint), 186.

ANDROMACHE. Legendary Trojan princess, wife of Hector and mother of Astyanax. She was taken captive by Achilles'son Pyrrhus whom she married after the fall of Troy (Iliad, Greek tragedies). 16, 27, 99.

ANDROMEDA, 238, 239.

ANGEL, 11, 20, 28, 292, 319.

ANGELICA, 28, 269, 270.

ANNA SELBDRITT, 297.

ANNE (Saint), 260, 296.

ANNE Boleyn, 29.

ANSELM (Saint), 276.

ANTEROS, 322.

ANTIGONE, 223.

ANTIOPE, 163, 164, 330.

ANTONY (Saint), 210, 277, 278, 306.

ANTONY OF PADUA (Saint), 277.

APELLES, 22, 31, 101.

APOLLO or PHOEBUS. His name means "brilliant" or "shining." The son of Jupiter, he was god of the sun, fine arts and prophecy, as well as patron of the Muses, 31, 32.

APOSTLES. The twelve disciples closest to Jesus Christ, chosen to spread the gospel to all nations after his death. 34.

Arbela, 44.

Arcadia, 46.

ARGANTES, 137.

ARGUS, 193, 194.

ARIADNE. Daughter of King Minos of Crete and sister of Phaedra. She gave a ball of thread to Theseus to help him escape from the Labyrinth after he killed the Minotaur. Carried off and later abandoned by Theseus, she was found by Bacchus who married her and made her a goddess. 37.

ARION, 37.

ARIOSTO, Ludovicio. (1474-1533) Italian poet. Author of the romantic epic poem *Orlando Furioso*.

ARMIDA, 259, 260.

Ashdod, 239.

ASTASIUS, 285.

ATALA, 39.

ATALANTA, 58.

ATHALIAH. Biblical figure. She was the wife of the eighth king of Judah and ruled from 841 to 835 B.C.. She was hated by the priests and the Israelites for her worship of the Phoenician god Baal. Her name means "whom Jehovah has afflicted" (2 Kings, 2 Chronicles), 40.

Audenarde, 310, 311.

AUGERS (Knight of), 72.

AUGUSTINE (Saint), 20.

AUGUSTUS. Title of the first Roman emperor (ruled 27-14 A.D.) named Octavian, who granted Rome an era of peace, prosperity and unprecedented cultural development (Plutarch, *The Parallel Lives*), 40, 326.

AURORA, 56.

BABYLON, 110.

BACCHUS. Son of Jupiter and god of the vine, wine and revelry. Orgiastic feasts called *Bacchanalia* were celebrated in his honour (Greek equivalent: Dionysus). 105, 323.

BALTHAZAR, 176.

BARTHOLOMEW (Saint), 84, 245.

BASIL (Saint), 195, 278.

BATHSHEBA, 46.

BAYARD, 75.

BELISARIUS, 46.

BELSUNCE (Monseigneur de), 92.

BERNARD OF CLAIRVAUX (Saint), 278.

BERNARDINE OF SIENA (Saint), 245.

Bethany, 169.

Bethesda, 152.

BIRELLI (Father), 116.

BLIND (The), 230.

BOAZ, 272.

BOCCACCIO. (1313?-1375) Italian writer, author of numerous works, including the *Decameron*, a famous collection of tales.

BOISSY D'ANGLAS, 48.

BONAPARTE, NAPOLEON. *See* Napoleon.

BONAVENTURE (Saint), 115, 279, 280.

BOREAS, 50.

BRIOU, 303.

Brother Luce, 113.

Bruges, 86.

BRUNO (Saint), 211, 250, 281, 304-307, 337.

BRUTUS, 50, 172.

Burning-sickness, 200.

BYRON, LORD. (1788-1824) English Romantic poet and promoter of political liberalism, Byron was the author of *Childe Harold's Pilgrimage* and *Don Juan*.

CACUS, 132.

CAESAR (Julius Gaius). (101-44 B.C.) Roman general, statesman and writer, Caesar was famous for his military campaigns (Gallic Wars). He was assassinated by Marcus Junius Brutus and Gaius Cassius Longinus just as he was to attain to absolute power (Plutarch, *The Parallel Lives*).

CAIAPHAS, 63.

CAIN, 265.

Cairo, 258.

CALLIRRHOE, 76, 128.

CALLISTO, 165.

CALYPSO, 316.

CAMBYSES, 53.

CAMILLUS (General), 53.

CAMPASPE, 22.

Cana, 221.

CANDACE (Queen), 293.

CARACALLA, 103.

CARATELLO, Giovanni, 282.

CARLO, 53, 259.

CARLOMAN, 54.

CATHERINE DE SAINTE SUZANNE CHAMPAIGNE, 194.

CATHERINE OF ALEXANDRIA (Saint), 85, 178.

CATHERINE OF SIENA (Saint), 178.

CATHERINE-AGNES ARNAULD (Mother), 194.

CATO OF UTICA, 205.

CENTAURS. Creatures that were half man and half horse, produced by a union between Ixion and a cloud in the form of Juno. With the exception of Chiron and Pholos, of another ancestry, they were noted for their savagery and wickedness, 72, 86, 87, 102, 132.

CEPHALUS, 56.

CERES. Goddess of the harvest, wheat and fertile soil, she was the sister of Juno (Greek equivalent: Demeter), 26, 56.

Ceylon (The), 249.

CHARICLEIA, 103.

CHARLES I, 58.

CHARLES V. (1500-1558) Holy Roman Emperor. He inherited a vast empire that he was unable to defend and was frequently at war with France. He abdicated in 1556 and retired to a monastery in Spain, 58.

CHARLES VII, 149.

CHARLES VIII, 144.

CHARON, 54.

CHILDREN, 64.

Chillon, 251.

CHIRON (Centaur), 102.

CHLOE, 83.

CHRIST. His name, meaning "the anointed", i.e., chosen by God, refers to the Messiah or Savior who descended to earth. Hence Jesus of Nazareth is named Jesus Christ or Christ. 28, 41, 43, 53, 55, 59-66, 88, 100, 109, 111, 120, 121, 151, 152, 155, 157, 176, 201, 244, 265, 267, 317.

CHRISTOPHER COLUMBUS, 257.

CHRYSEIS, 327.

CIMBRIANS, 86.

CIMON, 57, 171, 331.

CIRCE, 67.

CLEOPATRA. Queen of Egypt (ruled 51-30 B.C.). She is famous for her irresistible powers of seduction and amorous adventures with Caesar and Marc Antony. She committed suicide after Marc Antony's defeat by the Romans, 69, 84, 205, 206.

Clichy (Gate at), 44.

CLIMENE, 140, 141.

CLOELIA, 69.

CLORINDA, 70, 136.

CLYTEMNESTRA. Wife of Agamemnon and sister of Helen. She murdered her husband after the Trojan War to avenge the sacrifice of her daughter Iphigenia. She in turn was killed by her children, Orestes and Electra (Greek tragedies), 71.

COMUS, 258.

CONSTANTINE, 336, 337.

Constantinople, 249.

CORESUS, 128.

CORIOLAN, 16, 339.

CORNELIA, 76.

COSMAS (Saint), 187, 281.

COUNCIL OF TRENT, 73.

CREUSA, 104.

Cross, 199, 244.

Croton, 341.

CUCHULAIN, 120.

CUPID. Son of Venus. God of love, he strikes the heart with arrows, and through the centuries has been considered either as the basis of the universe or as a small, mischievous god (Greek equivalent: Eros), 332.

CURIUS DENTATUS, 81.

CYCLOPS. The three sons of Uranus and Mother Earth, each with only one eye in the middle of the forehead.

CYRUS the GREAT. Founder of the Persian empire (ruled 550-530 B.C.), 81, 318.

CYRUS the YOUNGER. King of Persia (ruled 424-400 B.C.). He fought the Athenians by recruiting Greek mercenaries, one of whom, Xenophon, told the story of this war in *Anabasis*.

Cythera, 103, 236.

DAMIAN, 187, 281.

DANAË, 164.

DANIEL (Saint), 42.

DANIEL. Biblical figure. He was exiled to Babylon, where he became adviser to Nebuchadnezzar; he was noted for his miraculous escape from the lion's den. His name means "God's judge" (Book of Daniel).

DANTE. (1260-1321) Italian poet. Author of *La vita nuova* and the *Divine Comedy*, 82.

DAPHNE, 31.

DAPHNIS, 83.

Darha, 71.

DARIUS. The third Persian king of this name. He fought against Alexander the Great. He was defeated in 331 B.C., and was assassinated by his own men in 330 B.C., 117, 208.

DAVID. (10 th century B.C.) Biblical figure. A shepherd who became king of Israel, David was also a musician and poet, the author of many Psalms. He was the father of King Solomon (1 Samuel, 1 Kings, Psalms of David), 46, 83, 138.

DEIANIRA, 86, 87.

DELILAH, 301.

DEMOSTHENES, 206.

DENIS (Saint), 187, 281.

DENON, Vivant, 338.

DESDEMONA, 77, 91, 270.

DIANA. Daughter of Jupiter and twin sister of Apollo. She was the goddess of the moon and hunting. She was a fierce virgin who roamed the forests with her following of nymphs and satyrs (Greek equivalent: Artemis), 26, 92-95.

DIDO. Founder and queen of Carthage, where she welcomed Aeneas and his son Ascanius. She took her life when Aeneas departed (*Aeneid*), 95, 165, 264, 313.

Dinant, 312.

DIOCLETIAN. Roman emperor (ruled 284-305) when the vast empire was divided into four districts. He ruled in the East where, around 300, he started violent persecution of the Christians which lasted for a decade.

DIOCRÈS, Raymond, 304.

DIOGENES, 96.

DIOMEDES, 329.

DOCTORS, 153.

DOGE, 97.

DOMINIC (Saint), 80, 138

DOMITIAN. Roman emperor (ruled 81-96) and despot. He was famous for the cruelty of his repressions and his persecution of the Christians.

DON CARLOS, 129.

DON JUAN, 218.

DON PEDRO OF TOLEDO, 97.

DON QUIXOTE, 98.

DREUX-BRÉZÉ, 198.

DUCHESS OF ORLEANS (Helen of Mecklenburg), 110.

EBERHARD (Count of Württemberg), 100.

ECHO, 100.

EDWARD V, 101, 106.

Egypt, 124, 264.

EL CID, 338.

ELECTRA. Daughter of Agamemnon and Clytemnestra. She encouraged her brother to kill Clytemnestra who was responsible for their father's assassination (Greek tragedies).

ELI, 30.

ELIEZER, 102.

ELISHA, 128.

ELIZABETH I (Queen of England), 207.

ELOI (Saint), 199.

EMILY (Vestal virgin), 334.

EMMAUS, 236, 262.

ENDYMION, 104, 313.

Ephesus, 246, 293.

ERASMUS (Saint), 187.

ERIGONE, 112.

ERMINA, 136, 137.

EROS. *See* Cupid.

ESTHER. (5th century B.C.) Biblical heroine. She was the wife of King Ahasuerus (Book of Esther), 115, 262, 300, 320.

EUROPA, 107.

EURYDICE, 226.

EVANDER, 115.

EVANGELISTS, 121, 255.

EVE. The first woman, created by God as a companion for Adam. Her name means "life" (Genesis), 114.

Eylau, 217.

FATES, 179.

FAUSTULUS, 271.

FÉRAUD (Deputy), 48.

FINGAL, 120.

FLORA, 162, 163.

Florence, 172.

FRANCESCA DA RIMINI, 123.

FRANCIS I, 58.

FRANCIS OF ASSISI (Saint), 229, 280, 281.

FRANCIS OF PAOLA (Saint), 282.

FRANCIS XAVIER (Saint), 284.

Freiburg, 247.

344

GABRIEL (Saint). One of the seven arch-angels, the closest to man, he an-nounced the births of John and Jesus. He consoles the dying and is the angel of Grace.

GABRIELLE D'ESTRÉES, 126.
GALATEA, 14, 253.
GALILEE (Sea of), 155.
GALILEO, 126.
GANYMEDE, 126.
GEHAZI, 128.
GEORGE (Saint), 284, 303.
GÉRICAULT, Théodore, 207.
GERMAN CARTHUSIANS, 191.
GERVASE (Saint), 285, 322.
GERY (Saint), 246.
GIDEON, 127, 274.
GILLES, 80.
GLAUCUS, 157.
GOLIATH, 83.
GOOD SAMARITAN (The), 152.

GRACES. These three sisters, daughters of Jupiter, were the goddesses of beauty and grace (Greek equivalent: the Charities), 325, 331.

GRACHII, 76.
Granicus, 232.
GREAT DAUPHINE (Maria Anna of Ba-varia), 89.
GREGORY (Saint), 196, 251.
GUIGUES (Reverend), 278.

HAGAR, 11, 18.
HAMAN, 24, 74, 85.
HAMLET, 130.
HANNAH, 30.
HARPIES, 105.

HECTOR. Trojan prince, son of Priam and Hecuba. Leader of the Trojan army, he was killed by Achilles (Iliad, Greek tragedies), 13, 14, 117.

HECUBA. Wife of the Trojan king, Priam, to whom she bore nineteen children (Iliad, Greek tragedies).

HELEN. Daughter of Jupiter and Leda. She was a Greek princess and the wife of Menelaus. Reputed for her beauty, her abduction was the pre-text for the Trojan war (Iliad, Greek tragedies), 107, 231.

HELIODORUS, 131.

HENRY III. Son of Henry II. He was king of France from 1574 to 1589. He was assassinated by a monk. 131.

HENRY IV. (1553-1610) Prince of the house of Navarre, he succeeded Henry III who had no direct descen-dants. He became king of France in 1589 and married Marie de Médicis in 1600. Like his father Henry III, he was assassinated by a religious fanatic, 97, 132, 179, 182, 216, 247.

HERACLIUS, 103.
HERCK, Vincent, 191.

HERCULES. The most popular hero of mythology. As the son of Jupiter and a mortal, Alcmena, Hercules was en-dowed with prodigious strength. He was pursued by the wrath of Juno (Hera) who multiplied his challenges (including the Twelve Labors). His Greek name Heracles means "the glory of Hera." 132-135, 220.

HERMAPHRODITUS, 299.
HERMOGENES, 261.
HERO, 137.

HEROD, AGRIPPA. Grandson of Herod the Great, he ruled a reunited Gal-ilee, Judea and Samaria from 39-44. He was responsible for the death of St. James the Greater and the im-prisonment of St. Peter.

HEROD, ANTIPAS. Son of Herod the Great, from whom he inherited part of his kingdom (4-39 A.D.). He was re-sponsible for the beheading of John the Baptist and played a role in the crucifixion of Jesus, 42.

HEROD, THE GREAT. Recognized by the Romans as king of the Jews, he ruled in Jerusalem at the time of the birth of Christ (the Gospels).

HERODOTUS. (484-425 B.C.) Greek his-torian. He was the author of nine well-documented books, which at times combine history with legend.

HERSE, 193.
HERSILIA, 273.
HESIONE, 132.
HILARION (Saint), 317.

HIPPOLYTUS. Son of Theseus. He was persecuted by his stepmother Phaedra who fell in love with him and had him killed. He was brought back to life by Diana (Greek tragedies), 240.

HOLOPHERNES, 161.
HOLY FAMILY, 264, 297.

HOLY GHOST or HOLY SPIRIT. The third person of the Trinity, which includes God the Father and God the Son, Jesus. The Holy Ghost is God's word, the sanctifier of souls and the comforter. He descends from Heaven as a dove, 238.

HOLY WOMEN. The holy women followed Jesus in his preaching, served him and were present at the crucifixion; they were the three Maries (Mary, his mother; Mary Magdalene; Mary, mother of James and John), Salome, and several others including Saint Veronica (the Gospels), 299.

HOMER. Greek poet, presumed to be the author of the *Iliad* and the *Odyssey*. He is thought to have lived in the 9th century B.C.

HORATII, 310.

HORATIO, 129.

HUBERT (Saint), 337.

HUGH (Saint), 250, 305.

HYACINTH (Saint), 285.

HYANTHE, 140, 141.

ILDEFONSO (Saint), 142.

INNOCENTS, 191.

Invalides (Court of), 142.

IPHIGENIA, 331.

IPHIGENIA. Daughter of Agamemnon and Clytemnestra. She was sacrificed to Diana for the success of the Trojan War, but was saved and carried off by the goddess (Greek tragedies). 274.

IRENE, 296.

IRENE (Saint), 190.

IRIS, 144.

ISAAC. Biblical patriarch. Isaac was the miraculous son of Abraham and Sarah. He married Rebecca and had two children, Esau and Jacob. His name means "laughter" (Genesis), 144, 274.

ISABELLE OF ARAGON, 144.

ISHMAEL. Biblical figure. Son of Abraham and his handmaid Hagar, he was driven into the desert with his mother when Abraham's legitimate son, Isaac, was born. He was miraculously saved from death. His name means "whom God hears" (Genesis).

ISRAELITES, 145.

ISSUS, 45.

IXION, 145, 146.

JACOB. Son of Isaac and third patriarch in the Bible. Surnamed Israel ("soldier of God") after his conflict with the angel, he had twelve sons who sired the twelve tribes of Israel (Genesis), 147, 166.

JAIRUS, 265.

JAMES (Saint). Called St. James the Greater. James was the son of Zebedee. He and his brother John were called by Jesus as they were repairing their fishing nets. One of the twelve apostles, he was martyred by Herod Agrippa (the Gospels, The Acts of the Apostles), 188, 261, 286, 313.

JANUARIUS (Saint), 188.

JASON, 148.

JEPHTHAH, 275.

Jericho, 41.

JEROME (Saint). (342-420 A.D.) An ascetic and Doctor of the Church, he translated the Old and New Testaments into Latin. This version is known as the *Vulgate*, 36, 213, 287-289, 338.

Jerusalem, 91, 103, 111, 245.

JESUS or JESUS CHRIST. Christ, the Lord, the Savior, the Son of Man. Founder of Christianity. The Gospels describe his life, teachings, crucifixion and resurrection (the Gospels), 34, 37, 150-157, 237, 244, 248, 265.

JIMENA, 338.

JOAB, 12.

JOACHIM, 260.

JOAN OF ARC, 113, 149.

JOB, 158.

JOHN (Saint). One of the twelve apostles. It is not known whether John, son of Zebedee, John the Evangelist and John of Patmos, author of the Apocalypse, were in fact the same person (the Gospels, The Acts of the Apostles, the Apocalypse), 189, 286.

JOHN THE BAPTIST. The miraculous son of Zacharias and Saint Elizabeth. He was a cousin of Jesus and foretold his coming. Herod Antipas had him beheaded (the Gospels).

JOSEPH (Saint). Carpenter, husband of Mary and foster father of Jesus (the Gospels), 264, 290, 314.

JOSEPH OF ARIMATHAEA, 158.

JOSEPH. Biblical figure. The youngest of Jacob's sons, persecuted and sold to merchants by his brothers. Taken to Egypt, he became adviser to the Pharaoh and was noted for his interpretation of dreams (Genesis), 159.

JOSHUA, 160.
JUDAS, 321.
JUDITH, 161.
Juliers, 183.
JULIET, 270.
JUNIPERO (Brother), 123.
JUNO. Sister and wife of Jupiter, she was the most powerful goddess. Goddess of marriage and birth, her attribute is the peacock (Greek equivalent: Hera), 144-146, 163.
JUPITER. Ruler of the gods and men. Jupiter was enthroned on Mount Olympus, where he presided over Order and Justice, although he was himself subject to Fate. His attribute is thunder. Despite the jealousy of his wife, Juno, he had numerous affairs. Among his children were the gods Apollo, Diana, Minerva, Vulcan and the demigods Hercules and Perseus (Greek equivalent: Zeus), 148, 164, 165, 285, 330.

Kovno, 177.

LABAN, 147, 166.
LAPITHS, 145
LARA, 167.
La Rochelle, 174, 311.
LATONA, 168.
LAZARUS, 266.
LEA, 147, 148.
LEANDER, 137.
LEDA, 168.
LENS, 44.
LEODIEUX, John, 191.
LEONIDAS, 170.
LERNAEAN HYDRA, 135.
Limbo, 89.
LOT. Biblical figure; nephew of Abraham. He miraculously escaped the destruction of Sodom (Genesis), 124, 173.
LOUIS (Saint) or Louis IX. Son of Louis VIII and Blanche of Castile; king of France from 1226 to 1270, 290.
LOUIS XIII. Son of Henry IV and Marie de Médicis; king of France from 1610 to 1643, 174, 182, 183, 232.
LOUIS XIV, the Sun King. Son of Louis XIII and Anne of Austria; king of France from 1643 to 1715. 38, 233.

LOUIS XV. Great-grandson of Louis XIV and and Marie Thérèse of Austria, he was King of France from 1715 to 1774.
LOUIS XVI. Grandson of Louis XV and Marie Leszcynska; king of France from 1774 until 1792, when he was deposed. During the French Revolution, he was condemned to death and guillotined in 1793.
LOUIS-PHILIPPE, 174.
LOUISE OF SAVOY, 282.
LUCRETIA, 174.
LUKE (Saint). Author of the third Gospel. He is said to have been a doctor and is often represented as the painter of the Virgin (the Gospels, the Acts of the Apostles). 322.
LYCIA, 168.
LYCOMEDES, 327.
LYNCUS, 56.

Maastricht, 38.
MACARIUS OF GAND (Saint), 290.
MACBETH (Lady), 167.
MAGDALENE. See MARY MAGDALENE.
MAGI (The), 18.
Malta, 293.
MANOAH, 276.
MARC ANTONY. (83-30 B.C.) Roman politician and consul of Rome. After Caesar's assassination, he formed a triumvirate with Octavian (Augustus) and Lepidus. He ruled Egypt with Cleopatra. In 31 B.C., he was defeated by Octavian and later committed suicide (Plutarch, *The Parallel Lives*). 84.
MARCUS SEXTUS, 267.
MARIE DE MEDICIS, 179-184.
MARIES (The Three). Often together, probably Mary Magdalene, Mary, wife of Clopas and mother of James, and Salome (the Gospels). 34.
MARITORNES, 98.
MARIUS, 184.
MARK (Saint). One of Jesus' disciples and author of the second Gospel. He was an associate of St. Peter and St. Paul. His attribute is a winged lion (the Gospels, the Acts of the Apostles).
MARS. God of war and lover of Venus, (Greek equivalent: Ares).

Marseille, 92.

MARSYAS, 224.

MARTHA, 155.

MARTIN (Saint), 35, 197, 291, 292.

MARY (Saint). The Virgin Mary was the miraculous daughter of Saint Anne and Saint Joachim. She conceived a son, the Messiah, of the Holy Ghost and after her death ascended to heaven, crowned by angels. She intercedes on behalf of sinners who appeal to her. She is also known as the Virgin and Our Lady (the Gospels, the Acts of the Apostles, numerous apocryphal texts), 34, 35, 39, 66, 99, 102, 177, 209, 215, 249, 253, 273, 276, 285, 309, 334, 335.

MARY MAGDALENE (Saint). The most devout of the women who listened to Jesus and assisted him in his Passion. She is said to have been a repentant prostitute (the Gospels), 81, 150, 176, 298.

MARY OF BETHANY, 155.

MARY STUART, 268.

MATTHEW (Saint). A tax collector who was called by Jesus to become one of the twelve apostles. He was the author of the first Gospel (the Gospels, the Acts of the Apostles), 292, 339.

MAXIMILIAN (Emperor), 84.

MEDEA, 192.

MEDORO, 270.

Medusa (Raft of the), 256.

MEDUSA. One of the three monstrous Gorgons. She turned those who looked at her into stone and was eventually killed by Perseus, son of Jupiter and Danaë.

MEGARA, 241.

MELEAGER, 193, 209.

MENELAUS. Mythical king of Sparta. He was the brother of Agamemnon and husband of Helen (*Iliad*, Greek tragedies), 247.

MERCURY. Son of Jupiter. He was messenger to the gods. His attribute is a pair of winged sandals. He was also an industrious god, patron of travelers, merchants, thieves and doctors. He carries the Caduceus, a golden staff with entwined serpents at the top (Greek equivalent: Hermes), 193, 194.

MERLIN DE THIONVILLE, 75.

MESSIAH. In Judaism, the term applies to any person sent by God, particu-

larly to free Israel. In Christianity, it refers to Christ the redeemer, Jesus, who created a new world by sacrificing himself to atone for man's sins.

MICHAEL (Saint). One of the seven archangels and the guardian of the Hebrews. He defeated Satan and the rebel angels and sent them to Hell. He weighs souls in scales at the Last Judgment, 292.

MILTIADES, 125.

MINERVA. She was born fully armed out of the head of Jupiter, and was the goddess of warfare and also of wisdom. Her attribute is the owl (Greek equivalent: Pallas Athena), 71, 97, 197, 198, 216.

MINOTAUR. A monster, half man and half bull. To punish the Cretan King Minos, Neptune made his wife, Pasiphaë, fall in love with a bull and give birth to this monster. Confined to the Labyrinth, it devoured seven youths and seven girls every nine years.

MINTURNAE, 184.

MIRABEAU, 198.

MONEYLENDERS, 151, 152.

MORDECAI, 85, 323.

MOSES. (13th century B.C.) He created Hebraic law and united the tribes of Israel to form a single people; delivering them from the tyranny of the Egyptians (Exodus), 201-204.

MUSES. These nine divine sisters, daughters of Jupiter, presided over literature and fine arts. At first indistinguishable, they were later given specialities by legends: Calliope (epic poetry), Clio (history), Erato (lyric poetry), Euterpe (music), Melpomene (tragedy), Polyhymnia (sacred song), Terpsichore (dance), Thalia (comedy), Urania (astronomy), 198.

NAPOLEON BONAPARTE. (1769-1821) He was born in Corsica and became lieutenant and then general during the French Revolution, during which he demonstrated his military genius in brilliant victories. Elected consul then made emperor (1804) under the name of Napoleon I, he died in exile on the island of Saint Helena. 50, 124, 217, 273.

NAPOLEON III, 217.

NARCISSUS, 217.

NEBUCHADNEZZAR, 215.

NEOPTOLEMUS. *See* PYRRHUS.

NEPTUNE. Brother of Jupiter and Pluto, god of the sea and water. He was master of storms, sea monsters and earthquakes (Greek equivalent: Poseidon), 97, 220.

NERO. Roman emperor (54-68 A.D.), famous for his bloody despotism and extravagance. He held the Christians responsible for the great fire of Rome in 64 A.D. and persecuted them cruelly. After he was defeated by Galba, he committed suicide.

NESSUS (Centaur), 86, 87.

NESTOR. Legendary Greek king. An old man at the time of the Trojan War, he distinguished himself by giving wise advice (*Iliad, Odyssey*), 13.

NEY (Marshal), 177.

NICHOLAS (Saint), 292, 293.

NICHOLAS V, 229.

NICODEMUS, 158.

Noah's ark, 110.

NOAH. As the only righteous man, he was saved from the flood with his family to be the founder of a new mankind (Genesis).

NYMPHS. Lesser divinities personifying the elements of nature. The nymphs lived in the sea (Naiades, Nereides, Oceanides), the mountains (Oreades) and the woods (Hamadryads).

OEDIPUS. The main character in a cycle of myths. Oedipus unwittingly killed his father and married his mother, fulfilling the oracle of his birth. Upon discovering his crime, he put out his eyes and went into exile (Greek tragedies), 223.

OENONE, 231.

OINA-MORUL, 227.

OLINDO, 70.

OLYMPUS, 224.

OMPHALE, 134.

OPHELIA, 130, 209.

Order of the Trinitarians, 195.

ORESTES. Son of Agamemnon and Clytemnestra. A child at the time of his father's death, he was saved by his uncle and lived in exile. As an adult, he returned to Argos to avenge the murder of his father. With the help of Electra, he killed Clytemnestra and her lover Aegisthus (Greek tragedies), 258.

ORITHYIA, 50.

OEPHEUS. Musician and poet; son of the Muse Calliope. He charmed the entire world with his songs, including the monsters of the underworld where he descended to find his beloved Eurydice, 226, 227.

OSSIAN, 227.

OTHELLO, 228.

OTTO, 165.

OUR FATHER. *See* CHRIST, JESUS and MESSIAH.

OVID. (43 B.C. -17 A.D.) Latin poet. Author of *Metamorphoses*, which recounts the majority of the Greek myths.

PALLAS, 115.

PAN. God of shepherds and fertility, resembles the satyrs and their unbridled sexuality. The companion of Bacchus, he led dances by playing the syrinx, 229, 252.

PANDORA, 114.

PAOLO, 123.

PAPHNUTIUS, 229.

PARIS or ALEXANDER. Trojan prince and son of Priam and Hecuba. He abducted Helen, thus provoking the war between the Greeks and the Trojans (*Iliad*).

PATROCLUS. Companion of Achilles. He was older than Achilles and charged by the hero's father with moderating his ardor. Patroclus demonstrated his own bravery and died fighting Hector. Achilles avenged his death and prepared a magnificent funeral for him (*Iliad*), 91, 117, 161, 231, 247, 269.

Paul (Saint). A contemporary of Jesus, originally named Saul. He persecuted the Christians until his conversion on the road to Damascus. He was baptized Paul, preached the Gospels and was a martyr (the Acts of the Apostles, the Epistles), 75, 85, 246, 256, 293, 308.

PELEUS, 221.

PERICLES. (495-429 B.C.) Athenian statesman. As leader of the democratic party for 30 years, he contributed to Athenian greatness and received artists and men of letters, making Athens a cultural center (Plutarch, *The Parallel Lives*). 27.

PERO, 57.

PERSEUS, 238.

PETER (Saint). (Died in 64 A.D.) Leader of the twelve apostles. Jesus made him head of the Church. He was martyred under Nero (the Gospels, the Acts of the Apostles, the Epistles), 150, 155, 190, 261, 294, 295.

PHAEDRA. Daughter of Minos, King of Crete, and Pasiphaë. She married Theseus who abandoned her sister Ariadne, and later fell in love with her stepson, Hippolytus. She took her life and left a note which resulted in his death (Greek tragedies, Racine's *Phaedra*), 240.

PHAETON, 240.

PHARAOH, 203.

PHARISEES. Members of one of the main sects of ancient Judaism, criticized in the Bible for the sterile ritualism and rigidity. They were extremely attached to the law, but in fact did not hesitate to reinterpret and innovate it.

PHILIP (Brother), 224.

PHILIP (Saint), 293.

PHILIP II OF SPAIN, 97.

PHILIP OF ACARNANIA, 22.

PHILISTINES. People living on the coast of Canaan, who were constantly at war with the Israelites. Fought successively by Samson, Samuel, Saul and Jonathon, they were finally conquered by David.

PHILOCTETES, 220.

PHILOPOEMEN, 241.

PHLEGYAS, 82.

PIERIDES, 86.

PINDAR. (518-438 B.C.) Greek poet. He celebrated athletic champions by associating their genealogy with that of the gods.

PLATO. (428-348 B.C.) Greek philosopher. He was a disciple of Socrates whose dialogues he reworked and enriched with his own theories. Teacher of Aristotle.

PLUTARCH. (c. 46 — 120 A.D.) Greek biographer and moralist, author of *The Parallel Lives*.

PLUTO. Brother of Jupiter and Neptune. He ruled the underworld, Hades, with Proserpine, whom he abducted (Greek equivalent: Hades).

POITIERS, 44.

POLYPHEMUS, 14.

POLYXENA, 243.

POMONA, 333.

PONTIUS PILATE. (1st century A.D.) As Roman procurator of Judea, he participated in the trial of Jesus, whom he delivered to the Jews to be crucified, after having unsuccessfully attempted to save him (the Gospels), 100, 242.

PORUS, 23.

PRIAM. Trojan King; father of fifty sons and fifty daughters. He was already old at the time of the siege, and was killed when the city fell (*Iliad*, Greek tragedies), 117, 247.

PRODIGAL SON, 329.

PROMETHEUS, 133, 252.

PROSDOCIMUS OF PADUA (Saint), 42.

PROSERPINE. Daughter of Ceres. She was abducted by Pluto; her mother found her, but she was forced to spend six months of the year in the underworld where she was queen (Greek equivalent: Persephone), 108, 109.

PROTASE (Saint), 36, 285, 322.

PSAMMETICHUS, 53.

PSYCHE, 25.

PTOMELY II, 253.

PYGMALION, 253.

PYRAMUS, 254.

PYRRHUS or NEOPTOLEMUS. Son of Achilles. Pyrrhus was present at the pillage of Troy after the death of his father. He killed Priam, took Andromache, Hector's wife, captive and then married her. He was assassinated by rebellious Greeks (Greek tragedies; Plutarch, *The Parallel Lives*), 157, 220.

RACHEL. Biblical figure; the wife of Jacob and mother of Joseph. She died giving birth to her second son Benjamin. Her name means "ewe" (Genesis), 12, 147.

RACINE (Jean). (1639-1699) French playwright. His works include *Andromache*, *Iphigenia* and *Phaedra*. 256.

RANIERI RASINI, 48.

RAPHAEL (Saint). The third of the known archangels, he carries a pilgrim's staff and guides travelers.

REBECCA (character in the novel *Ivanhoe*), 109.

REBECCA. Biblical figure; wife of Isaac, mother of Esau and Jacob (Genesis). 102.

REGULUS, 88.

REMUS, 271.

Rhine, 232.

RINALDO, 259.

ROLAND, 210.

Rome, 239.

ROMEO, 270.

ROMULUS, 271.

RUGGERIO, 307.

Russia (Retreat from), 111, 112.

RUTH, 272.

SABINES, 109, 273.

Saint'Angelo (Castle of), 251.

Saint-Voult, 201.

SALMACIS, 299.

SALOME, 85.

Samothrace, 314.

SAMSON, 301.

SAMUEL. (11th century B.C.) Biblical figure; prophet and judge of Israel. He chose the shepherd David as successor to King Saul. His name means "heard of God" (Books of Samuel). 30, 35, 83, 225.

San Romano, 45.

SANCHO, 263.

SAPPHIRA, 211.

SARAH. Wife of Abraham. She gave birth to her first child, Isaac, at the age of ninety. Her name means "princess" (Genesis).

SARDANAPALUS, 204.

SATYRS, also known as Sileni (Fauns in Roman mythology). Sylvan divinities. Initially represented with the torso of a man, the lower body of a horse, a bock's beard and horns, they gradually lost their animal traits, but retained a tail and an oversized phallus. They played the flute, danced and pursued nymphs and mortals, 302, 332.

SAUL OF TARSUS. *See* PAUL (Saint).

SAUL. First king of the Israelites (1020-1000 B.C.). He suffered from melancholia and had David distract him with songs. Later he argued with him, displeased the Lord and lost his kingdom. His successor was David (1 Samuel), 225.

Scio, 308.

SCIPIO, 74.

SEBASTIAN (Saint), 190, 295, 296.

SENECA, 213.

SEVERUS (Emperor), 103.

SHAKESPEARE. (1564-1616) The greatest English dramatist and poet. Author of numerous plays including *Hamlet*, *Othello*, *Macbeth* and *Romeo and Juliet*, all of which have inspired painters.

SHEBA (Queen of), 300.

SHEPHERDS, 17, 28.

SIMON, 176.

SIMON PETER. *See* PETER (Saint).

SOCRATES. Greek philosopher. He introduced a new method of teaching, now known as the Socratic dialogue or dialectic (he encouraged his students to find truth in themselves). Socrates is known through the writings of one of his pupils (Plato). He was condemned to death by Athenian justice on the charge of corrupting youth (399 B.C.).

Sodom, 124.

SODOMA, 236.

Solferino, 217.

SOLOMON. Biblical figure; son of David and Bathsheba, king of Israel (972-932 B.C.). He was famous for his wisdom and the splendor of his reign. His name means "peaceable" (Chronicles, Kings), 85, 162, 226, 300, 310.

SOLON, 312.

SOPHRONIA, 70.

Souli, 119.

SPARTAN WOMEN, 77.

SPHINX, 223.

STEPHEN (Saint). First Christian martyr; he was stoned to death by the Jews (The Acts of the Apostles). 187, 245.

STOCK (Saint Simon), 335.

SUSANNA, 315.

Suse Pass, 232.

SYRINX, 229.

TABITHA, 295.

Taillebourg, 45.

TANCRED, 137.

351

TARQUIN, 174.

TASSO, Torquato. (1544-1595) Italian poet, author of the epic poem *Jerusalem Delivered*.

TATIUS, 273.

TELEMACHUS, 316.

THAIS, 229.

THEAGENES, 103.

THECLA (Saint), 35.

THEODOSIUS (Emperor), 104.

Thermoplyae, 170.

THESEUS. Son of Neptune and a demigod. He is the hero of Athens as Hercules is the hero of Thebes. Numerous exploits are attributed to him including the killing of the Minotaur.

THETIS. A sea goddess, the wife of a mortal, Peleus, and mother of Achilles, 77.

THISBE, 254.

THOMAS (Saint) 143, 256.

THOMAS AQUINAS (Saint), 324.

THOMAS OF VILLANUEVA (Saint), 296.

THORMOD, 227.

THREE WISE MEN. *See* MAGI.

Tiber, 69.

TIBURTINE SIBYL, 310.

TIMOCLEA, 23.

TITANS, 164.

TITIAN, 140.

TITUS, 319.

TOBIAS, 319.

TOBIT, 168, 320.

TOMYRIS, 318.

TRAJAN, 322.

TREVISANO Domenico, 258.

TRIPTOLEMUS, 56.

TRISSOTIN, 97.

TRIUMVIRATE, 192.

Troy,, 91, 95, 104.

TURNUS, 144, 326.

UBALDO, 53, 259.

ULYSSES. Hero of Homer's *Odyssey*. He combines courage, cunning and energy. He participated in the Trojan War and then returned to his kingdom, the island of Ithaca (*Iliad*, *Odyssey*). 220, 327.

Underworld, 90, 226.

URSULA (Saint), 170, 298.

VADIUS, 97.

VAFRINO, 137.

Vaucouleurs, 113.

Vénus (La), 249.

VENUS. Goddess of love and beauty, born of ocean foam. She experienced and inspired violent passions. Venus was the mother of Cupid (Greek equivalent: Aphrodite), 122, 185, 232, 324, 328-333.

VERONICA (Saint), 298.

VERTUMNUS, 333.

VESPASIAN, 324.

VETURIA, 339.

VICTOR (Saint), 296.

VICTOR III, 306.

Villefranche-sur-Mer, 250.

VIRGIL. (70-19 B.C.) Latin poet, author of the *Ecolgues*, the *Georgics* and the *Aeneid*, 82, 335.

VIRGIN MARY. *See* MARY.

VIRGINIA, 213.

VOLTAIRE, 269.

VOLUMNIA, 203.

VULCAN. Son of Jupiter and Juno. God of fire and metalworking. He was the husband of Venus (Greek equivalent: Hephaestus), 122, 185, 339.

WILD BOAR OF THE ARDENNES (Nickname of William de la Marck), 38.

WILLIAM DE LA MARCK, 38.

WOMAN OF CANAAN, 64.

WOMAN OF SAMARIA, 152.

WOMAN TAKEN IN ADULTERY, 64, 118.

YVES (Saint), 334.

ZEUXIS, 340.

Photographic credits

All of the photographs in this book come from the photographic services of the
Réunion des musées nationaux, with the exception of the illustrations on pages
139 and 245 which belong to the Agence Giraudon.

Translation : Susan Ashcroft
Cover design : Bernard Gaulin
Typeset : Traitext
Printed in France by Mame Imprimeurs